Simon Hughes won eight titles with Middlesex, including four county cricket championships, between 1980 and 1991 before finishing his playing career at Durham. He started writing for the *Independent* while still playing, and has written for the *Daily Telegraph* and broadcast for the BBC since his retirement in 1994. He is known to millions of cricket fans as 'The Analyst' for his role in Channel 4's cricket coverage, and is now part of Five's cricket commentary team as well as commentating for BBC radio. He is the author of five previous books including *A Lot of Hard Yakka*, winner of the William Hill Sports Book of the Year Award in 1997. He lives in Hammersmith with Tanya and their three children Callum, Nancy and Billy.

www.**rbooks**.co.uk

And God Created Cricket

Simon Hughes

BLACK SWAN

TRANSWORLD PUBLISHERS
61–63 Uxbridge Road, London W5 5SA
A Random House Group Company
www.rbooks.co.uk

AND GOD CREATED CRICKET
A BLACK SWAN BOOK: 9780552775069

First published in Great Britain
in 2009 by Doubleday
an imprint of Transworld Publishers
Corgi edition published 2010

A CIP catalogue record for this book
is available from the British Library.

Addresses for Random House Group Ltd companies outside the UK
can be found at: www.randomhouse.co.uk
The Random House Group Ltd Reg. No. 954009

The Random House Group Limited supports The Forest Stewardship
Council (FSC), the leading international forest certification organisation.
All our titles that are printed on Greenpeace approved FSC certified paper
carry the FSC logo. Our paper procurement policy can be found at
www.rbooks.co.uk/environment

Mixed Sources
Product group from well-managed
forests and other controlled sources
www.fsc.org Cert no. TT-COC-2139
© 1996 Forest Stewardship Council
FSC

Typeset in 11/14pt Giovanni Book by Falcon Oast Graphic Art Ltd.
Printed in the UK by CPI Cox & Wyman, Reading, RG1 8EX.

4 6 8 10 9 7 5 3

To M.S.B.F.P

Contents

What This is All About

Cricket is baseball on valium. Robin Williams, 1974.

There is a *lot* of literature on English cricket's history. There is so much, in fact, that as you scan the groaning shelves of the MCC Library at Lord's, looking at the anthologies and leather-bound manuals and cut-and-paste autobiographies chronicling how 'we somehow managed to get them out for 165 in 52.3 overs', you wonder what on earth persuaded you to want to add to it. I only have one explanation. That after a forty-year association with the game, I realize I actually know three eighths of two sixths of naff all about it. It's about time I found out a bit more. This is my 'journey' of discovery (permission to barf granted).

Don't expect a comprehensive account of every historical development and key match and notable patron as cricket evolves from a primitive seventeenth-century hitabout to a sophisticated – but still bewildering – business: one that can command billion-dollar rights from TV channels yet simultaneously remain a byword for manners and fair play. No. I want to retain an ounce of sanity and finish this book before I die and anyway an assortment of scholars and archivists and ex-prime ministers have already done the chronology job far better than I ever could.

What I'm doing here is imagining cricket as a sort of human settlement, and identifying the defining moments and people that transformed it from a collection of rustic dwellings to a throbbing metropolis. Well, a buzzing city anyway. I'll chat to old timers in the pubs and linger down a few back alleys to get under the skin and find the soul of the place and how it reflects society. It's what you might call 'selective excavation': and, as with any archaeological dig, there's an element of luck in what you find. Just as long as you get your hands dirty . . .

ONE

Stop Press: The French Invented Cricket!

In the beginning was the Word and the Word was *creag*. At least that was the word in the 1300 wardrobe accounts of Edward I referring to a ball game which may or may not have been an early version of cricket. Also there was *cryce* or *cric*, which was an Anglo-Saxon term for a stick or staff, and the Normans introduced the word *criquet* (a stick-and-ball game) into the English language after the Conquest. In the sixteenth century, immigrants from Flanders living in southern England are described playing *creckette* by the poet John Skelton. This morphed into *Crickett* (1598) in a coroner's account of schoolboy games in Guildford. All this sounds plausible to explain the origin of the word 'cricket'.

The game itself evolved from a variety of folk hitabouts played in villages on both sides of the Channel, each with its own local idiosyncrasies. The Almighty decreed that at some point one variety of this primitive cricket would usurp the others: *shock horror!* It could well have been the type the Frogs developed north of Paris. So we conclude that Brigitte Bardot's ancestors created cricket. As Norman French vocabulary also included *wiket* (a small gate) and *beil* (a crosspiece), it must be true. No one knows for sure, of course, because no one wrote it down. It's not really that surprising. In those Tudor times there were rather too many Armadas and plagues and beheadings going on for anyone to be overly concerned with silly ball games.

The early versions of cricket were undoubtedly confined to the forests and downlands of south-east England – particularly in west Sussex and the Weald of Kent (the first known match was at Coxheath near Maidstone in 1646). It was largely a game played by village peasants messing about with a ball near the stump of a tree (hence the target became known as the 'stumps'). On more open pastures shepherds used a 'wicket gate' – a small hurdle through which the sheep passed. The 'bat' vaguely resembled a hockey stick and the ball started off as a round piece of wood till seventeenth-century cobblers began stitching a leather cover round cork stuffing.

The bowling vaguely resembled Trevor Chappell's famous delivery in 1981 at the Melbourne Cricket Ground – namely underarm and skimmed along the ground. Perhaps in retrospect we underestimated Chappell, and he was really doffing his cap to cricket's early history rather than stopping New Zealand hit a six off the last ball to win a one-day international. Then again, knowing the Chappell family's bloody-mindedness and the Australians' intense rivalry with New Zealand, perhaps not.

'Club ball' seems to have been the generic title for this rural activity, with markedly reduced quantities of booze and worthless raffle prizes than you'd get at the modern equivalent. Initially it was seen as a sort of juvenile pastime, and regarded as a shade disreputable. In the early seventeenth century, a number of parishioners were fined for playing it in a churchyard near Goodwood on a Sunday, though it didn't help that the ball was often hit through the stained glass windows and the odd fielder hid behind a gravestone, rather contravening the so called 'spirit' of the game. More of that mythical concept later.

In fact, under Oliver Cromwell's leadership (1649–58) England became a rather joyless place ruled by Christian fascists determined to section anybody who was enjoying themselves. Music and gambling were banned, theatres closed, and penalties imposed on anyone found indulging in sporting endeavours, to satisfy the Puritans' religious zeal. So for a short time, God suspended cricket.

That's Not Cricket! . . . It is Now

The Restoration (1660) and the reign of Charles II liberated England from this absurd repression. In any case, there's nothing like official restrictions on an activity to encourage its proliferation, and impromptu cricket matches that had continued on farmland and common through the first half of the seventeenth century, each with its own local rules, now became more organized. It was a bit like those Sunday morning kick-abouts in the park that start off with a couple of fathers messing about with their kids and finish up as half an hour each way with team strips and a dad shouting, 'It's 4–2 for fuck's sake, that went in-off the rucksack!' Clubs began to be formed, some matches attracted a small crowd and pub landlords organized games on adjacent ground knowing they would draw punters. In that way cricket was the predecessor of the karaoke night.

At the time the game was a sort of cross between hockey and baseball with a curved bat and the wicket a foot high and two feet wide, so modern bowlers like Glenn McGrath and Curtly Ambrose would have been useless, bouncing every delivery way over the top. In the gap between the two upright stumps (which had a horizontal stick laid across them) was a hole. To complete a run (then known as a 'notch' because it was recorded by an incision on the scorer's stick – the origin of the phrase 'notched up'), the batsman had to 'pop' his bat into this hole before the fielder got the ball in it. An outbreak of battered fingers resulted in the more sensible requirement of them having to touch a stick held by the umpire to register a run instead. Eventually that was replaced by a line cut in the turf, still to this day referred to as the 'popping' crease.

Matches were often eleven-a-side, but sometimes five-a-side or single wicket. The season was short – from April to late June – structured round the farming community's calendar and their harvesting commitments. Members of the aristocracy who had been forced to their country seats by Cromwell's insurgency were intrigued to discover their labourers indulging in this quaint sport and they took it further afield, introducing it to London and beyond, bringing their servants and farmhands – the original players – with them. By 1700 there were regular matches on Clapham Common, and clubs all over London and the south-east and as far west as Gloucestershire. Gambling on games was rife and some were played for high stakes. Gaggles of men gathered near the pitch (there were no official boundaries) exchanging wagers. Stakes of 100 or 200 guineas (£210) were common.

Charles Lennox, the 2nd Duke of Richmond, who lived at Goodwood, was an enthusiastic early patron, kitting out his players in cricket's first-ever coloured strip (green waistcoats, breeches and yellow caps) and subsidizing the village team at nearby Slindon, at the time one of the best in England. Captained by England's first serious run-machine, Richard Newland, they were defeated only once in forty-three games in 1741. Lennox owed his interest to his father, the first Duke, who organized a game against the 'Arundel men' in 1702.

The only record of this match is the bar bill. The Duke, it was reported, 'spent 1s 6d on brandy during the game'. It is not known if this was to settle his own nerves or to incapacitate the opposition with alcohol as Ian Botham notoriously did to many opponents at his legendary all-night barbeques more than two and a half centuries later. If it was the latter it worked. The Arundel men were comfortably defeated. They would have had a chilly journey home too, as the match was played in mid-December.

It was at one of the 2nd Duke of Richmond's matches against Mr Alan Brodrick of Surrey in 1727 that some 'Articles of Agreement' were drawn up, laying down the rules for play. These were effectively the game's first set of laws. At that point the pitch was 23 yards long, the teams were twelve-a-side and the team 'owners' were permitted to contest decisions with the umpires.

These first laws were interpreted loosely for a while until officially laid down by the London Club in 1744. They were printed round the border of a white hand-kerchief (an original is on display in the Lord's museum) and are not unlike those 'Ins and Outs of cricket' tea towels designed to amuse/baffle American tourists (e.g. 'Each man that's in the side that's in goes out, and when he's out he comes in, and the next man goes in until he's out . . .' etc.).

These 1744 'handkerchief laws' begin: 'The pitching of ye first wicket is to be determined by ye cast of a piece of Money', and mention for the first time the concept of 'fair and unfair play', which the umpires were now sole arbiters of. They specify dimensions of the ball, stumps and pitch (22 yards long, the equivalent of a 'chain', which was a unit of land measurement standardized at 66 feet by a Mr Gunter in the previous century). There was at that point no restriction on the width of the bat.

Certainly batsmen had it all their own way in those early days (it was ever thus). The bowling was still exclusively underarm, and pretty tame, the wicket was low and looked like a croquet hoop, and you couldn't be out leg before wicket. At least these first laws penalize the 'striker' if 'he runs out of his Ground to hinder a Catch'. Before that it was not unknown for a batsman to literally assault a fielder as he was attempting to take the ball. Acknowledging that, it is astonishing how cricket inherited its 'gentlemanly' image.

These cricketing aristocrats were the first sporting entrepreneurs, laying on cricket matches mainly for gambling purposes. The main reason for the 'laws' was to limit the possibility of match fixing, all the more tempting with large stakes being wagered. That didn't always curtail it though. The scorers had a habit of 'losing' the notch stick after very close matches and umpires called 'time' suspiciously early in the 1731 match between the Duke of Richmond's team and a Mr Chambers' XI, with the Chambers side only requiring a few to win. This was one of the first instances of something being 'just not cricket', which is a strange paradox. The game had only been going two minutes and so far hadn't even reached base camp on the moral high ground.

County cricket had been established in 1709 when a 'Kentish' side took on London, and Kent also played matches against Surrey and Sussex. Usually this 'county' team was actually just a club or a peer's invitation XI masquerading as something more substantial to attract a crowd. The 'Kent' side for instance was frequently just an assemblage of players from the strong Dartford and Sevenoaks clubs and the local peer's sons. This only serves to illustrate that the concept of 'county' cricket was contrived from the start. And now, like London's South Circular Road, we are stuck with it (or on it) and incessant tinkering only emphasizes what a terrible idea it was in the first place.

As Sir Derek Birley points out in his comprehensive *A Social History of English Cricket*, the bizarre workings of the hereditary peerage system are magnified through the early days of county cricket. So the Duke of Richmond was bankrolling the Sussex team, while the Duke of Dorset lived in Sevenoaks and sponsored Kent for whom his son, the Earl of Middlesex, also played. Then there was the Duke of Devonshire's fabulous ground at, of all places, Chatsworth House in deepest Derbyshire. Confused? You should be. (In fact the latter was apparently due to a simple spelling mistake which wasn't corrected until it was too late. 'Apologies, my lord, there's been an error, and you have signed for the land rights to 1,500 acres in Derbyshyre.' 'Dash it, Spudkins! Oh well, the Duchess prefers hills to those blasted moors anyway.')

Surrey's early prominence owed much to the legacy of Frederick, Prince of Wales, who, just to complicate matters further, was three quarters German (his father King George II was 100 per cent Kraut). Cricket was the perfect vehicle for him to transmogrify himself into a true-blue Englishman, and he promoted many matches and often captained the county, though the newspapers drew a polite veil over his performances. He died relatively young after being hit by a ball in the field. (OK, he actually died from an abscess resulting from the injury.) Significantly there have been very few Schmidts, Kleins or Schwarzes who have shone at cricket in the intervening 300 years.

Possibly baffled by the nomenclature, writers were

slow to cotton on to the cricket craze, and the first proper account of a game wasn't until 1744, for a match between Kent and All England. Kent, the first unofficial county champions, won it by 1 wicket, the match being decided when a fielder, Thomas Waymark, dropped a simple catch. A young poet, James Dance, relayed the incident thus:

> The erring ball amazing to be told!
> Slipped thro his outstretched hand and mocked his
> hold.

At least he was spared eighteen slow-mo replays from seven different angles and having a turnip superimposed on his head in the *Sun*.

The London Club was the dominant force, and its home, the Artillery Ground, was cricket's Mecca. It still exists, wedged between Sir Fred Goodwin's piggy bank and the Whitbread Brewery, just off City Road in the Square Mile. Along with Hong Kong Cricket Club, it must be the most expensive location for a sports ground anywhere in the world. Consulting my property-expert friend Alastair reveals that you could create four office buildings on the site with a net useable area of 2.765m sq ft (allowing for lifts, stairs and toilets etc., according to Alastair – property developers are a bit anal about these things – see appendix 1). At current rates that would give the site a value of about £1.2 billion. It's going to take quite a few £12.50 players' match fees (lunch and tea) to recoup that.

By the 1730s the Artillery Ground was the main venue for commercial matches in London; it was there where the 1744 revision of the game's laws took place and it was one of the first grounds to have a boundary rope (before that batsmen had to run for everything, so the most productive shots were obviously those that ended up in thorn bushes or stuck high up in trees). An individual score of 40 was regarded as 'top notch'.

Though the aristocracy promoted and gambled extensively on matches in London, the best players were of quite diverse origins: the aforementioned Waymark was a groom, others were tailors and shoemakers and gardeners, some strappingly strong. One Surrey farm-hand hit a ball clean out of the Artillery Ground, a distance of at least 100 yards. It was the only way to register a six. Women's matches were also staged at the ground, often between Sussex villages, and, if the mothers' races at school sports days are anything to go by, they were taken very seriously.

Still, it remained mainly a game for the common, sometimes unsavoury, man. There was an incident when a magistrate complained about 'swarms of loose and disorderly people' who assembled to play cricket in the fields around London. These I suppose were the gaggles of youths you now find being a nuisance hanging about round McDonald's.

Somewhere in the early 1750s, probably coinciding with the formation of the Jockey Club, the dosh-wielding bourgeoisie turned their attentions to horse racing and cricket in the capital slightly lost its allure for a while. The people who picked up the primitive bat and ball and ran with them to new levels of sophistication and renown were the men of Hambledon.

A Small World

We are now at 1759, the year Great Britain was voted world's MVP (Most Valuable Player). They wouldn't have imagined then that there was to be only one other time in the whole Millennium (World Cup 1966). Still, two major trophies in 1,000 years for an island the size of Oregon ain't so bad! Actually, that's bending the truth a bit. Britain had been declared 'Most Powerful Country' after its successes in the Seven Years War and there was a new optimism in England as George III became king. (He was in fact the grandson of George II, but inherited the throne because of the part-German heir Frederick's tragic encounter with a cricket ball. At least the new king, born in Britain, was likely to be a better fielder.)

Robert Clive was on every chat show going after his military successes in India and science was all the rage as a result of Sir Isaac Newton's earlier discoveries about gravity ($F = F^2 = G \times m_1 \times m_2/r^2$ in case you'd forgotten, which is an incredible thing to dream up after being hit on the head by an apple). And it was now, thanks mainly to a village in Hampshire, that cricket evolved new dimensions of skills and strategies. It was a good deal more than Dr Samuel Johnson's 1755 definition of cricket as 'a sport at which contenders drive a ball with sticks or bats in opposition to each other'.

One popular image of eighteenth-century Hambledon is of a chocolate-box-perfect cricket ground in a bucolic tree-lined valley, with men in whites and top hats – smug in the knowledge that they had initiated the game – clapping visiting batsmen to the manicured wicket as their female escorts looked on winsomely (they hadn't yet been lured inside to make the tea). In fact, as with most sentimentally infused beliefs, such as the assertion that if England found the right football manager they'd win the World Cup again, it's a myth.

Broadhalfpenny Down is actually a bleak, windswept field on a hill two miles from the village of Hambledon, the pitch and outfield were rough as befitted a sheep paddock, the men wore waistcoats and breeches that had gone blue-grey from filthy laundry water and the (very) close fielders, sometimes wigged but unhelmeted of course, stared gimlet-eyed at the new batsman (must have been quite disconcerting if a sudden gust blew the wig off). And, as has now been realized, none could claim to have invented cricket. It had filtered across into Hampshire from its origins in Kent and Sussex at least a hundred years before.

What Hambledon does deserve recognition for is giving the game new shape and style. Records are sketchy, but there is some evidence that the Hambledon club was a going concern well before the 1760s. However, it was only after this point that it really gained any prominence. The motivating force was Richard Nyren, nephew of Slindon's batting ace, Richard Newland, who captained the side and converted the rundown pub The Hut into the reputable Bat and Ball inn.

Nyren senior started a 'gentlemen's' social club at the inn, and they funded the team, recruiting the notable players from around the region. In old records Hambledon is often miswritten as 'Hampshire' and it wasn't far from the truth. At first the players were largely from within a ten-mile radius, but as the club's prominence grew they travelled from north, south and east of the county, and from west Sussex too, to be regulars at Broadhalfpenny Down. Bowling became more artful, instead of just the straightforward skim along the (bumpy) ground, with spin and trajectory. As has always been the way, batsmen countered such innovations with new techniques of their own.

John Small, from Empshott, a few miles north of Petersfield, pioneered the 'straight' bat method of play, working out that you had more chance of making contact with a bouncing ball if you kept the blade vertical rather than horizontal. This was in about 1765. He would be amazed to know that this still takes an age to dawn on schoolkids, village players, wholehearted clubmen, even international tailenders. In fact, virtually anyone who has ever played the sport. Apart from Geoff Boycott, who realized it aged 4½ months and has been reminding everyone ever since.

The fact is, though, it really would be a boring old game if everyone adhered to these percentage principles and no one ever attempted a good hearty swipe across the line, only to miss and see their stumps splattered everywhere. It adds to everyone's enjoyment, particularly those in earshot of the dressing room while the coach is giving the culprit a rollicking.

Small was, however, a phenomenon who once, when playing for Hambledon against 'England', couldn't be dismissed for three days. He was an expert judge of a quick single but was renowned more as a 'blocker', generally making slow progress to some of the first hundreds recorded in the history of the game. He was hugely influential though, nudging Hambledon to consistent success and national prominence. His method encouraged a swathe of imitators and the carving of straight blades like his to replace the old curved hockey stick type, a trend he capitalized on by converting his shoemaking business into cricket bat manufacture. His stoic obduracy was, however, also an early indicator to commercially obsessed terrestrial TV bosses that given the choice of buying live England cricket matches or *The Simpsons*, they'd plump for *The Simpsons* every time.

Small was a pillar of society in every way: not only did he play 'straight', but he was also a 'capital' shot, sang bass in the Petersfield choir, played the violin, and repaired them in his workshop, and once calmed a loose bull down by serenading it, and excelled at 'skating' on Petersfield Heath pond. This tells you something about global warming if nothing else. They haven't had serious ice on that bit of water for half a century. Small lived till he was eighty-nine so all this activity must have done him good.

His prowess with the bat also brought about another major change in the game. Despite the presence of a couple of deceptive underarm bowlers – if that's not an oxymoron – he was consistently hard to dismiss. The two stumps were so thin that on the rare occasion that he missed the ball it went straight between them and his wicket remained intact. This happened three times in succession in a match in 1775 against the legendary Kent bowler Edward 'Lumpy' Stevens – rightfully renamed 'Grumpy' after that. It'd be a bit like knocking over Mr Boycott's wicket three times in succession only for it to spring back into position with the bails somehow still in place, while he smirked down the pitch and exclaimed, 'My moom could bool quicker than that!' From that point it was decreed a third stump would be placed in the gap (though some self-aggrandizing dukes elected to do without it when it was their turn for a bat).

So now we have three stumps, a roughly scythed (or sheep-chewed) pitch, creases cut into the turf, underarm bowling and straight bats that had been restricted to 4¼ inches in width after Thomas 'Shock' White of Reigate attempted to use one about two feet wide. It was shaved down to half its size on the day, and the Hambledon committee, who ran the game at the time, had an iron frame made which, from then on, all bats had to conform to (and which they could whack non-compliers over the head with).

Harris Tweak

Hambledon in the 1770s was a sort of Chelsea of today. It attracted the best players, who were on a massive win bonus of five guineas (£5.25) a match, and they spent their money reshoeing and resaddling their horses, the eighteenth-century equivalent of getting customized suspension and Dolby surroundsound for your

Hummer. The Hambledon team was superior to 'England' (an amalgam of Kent and Surrey), beating them twenty-nine times out of fifty-one over a fifteen-year period, and often had crowds of 20,000 turning out to watch them, and afterwards buy a tacky Polyester replica shirt made in Taiwan. They were also notorious entertainers famous for their after-match singing and revelry, the forerunners of today's top footballers getting smashed on Cristal champagne and organizing spit roasts.

You'd never know it looking at the rather dingy nature of the Bat and Ball pub now. The lunchtime I went with a friend it was practically deserted, and hung with a haphazard assortment of 'memorabilia' (a euphemism for old junk), including someone's rather smelly 1960s-style cricket boots in the dusty fireplace. There is an early bat – which looks more like an oar – on the wall, but no reference to whose it was or when it was used, and framed drawings of some of Hambledon's famous players jostle for wall space with cheap ornamental plates, an incongruous caricature of Imran Khan (who had no connection with the place) and the barman's signed bat.

An opportunity has been missed to create a complete cricket-themed experience, using equipment – stumps, bats – as furniture (boxes as sugar bowls?) and having stunning pictures of the great players dotted around and spicing up the menu perhaps with a Warne-burger (he did play for Hampshire and famously said that his idea of a balanced diet was a cheeseburger in each hand) and a Gower banoffee-pie (he lives nearby). The apology of a monument – an ugly lump of stone, like part of a meteorite – dumped in a corner of the exposed ground across the road sadly sums up the total lack of artistic vision at one of the most significant sporting sites in the world.

On that draughty field 250 years ago, bowling was evolving from the primitive underarm skidders which Richie Benaud, if he had been on commentary, would have described as 'mullygrubbers'. The prime mover in this was the anonymous-sounding David Harris, who in the twenty-first century you'd assume would be an accountant or a central-heating rep or something even more boring like a property developer. (Have you ever met anyone duller than a commercial property bloke with his pallid, greasy face and his grey-suited paunch and his intimate knowledge of office rents in Basingstoke?)

Harris was a potter by trade, but in cricket just as much a pioneer with the ball as John Small had been with the bat. In many ways he was like an eighteenth-century Warne – well, one without the earring or the predilection for texting buxom blondes anyway. With an idiosyncratic way of releasing the ball – still under-arm – Harris managed to get it to bounce and deviate off the pitch, posing a constant threat within a suffocating blanket of accuracy. He practised assiduously both outdoors and in a specially adapted barn (so not only did he perfect 'length' bowling, but also invented indoor schools). He kept a metro-nomic length, landing the ball some way short of the half-volley the batsmen preferred, and often got it to lift up and bruise their unprotected fingers.

John Nyren, son of the Hambledon captain (and barman) and cricket's first great chronicler, wrote an account of Harris's unique bowling action. 'First he stood erect like a soldier, upright. Then, with a graceful and elegant curve, he raised the fatal ball to his forehead and, drawing back his right foot, set off on his left.' His delivery was mercurial: 'he would bring it from under his arm by a twist and, nearly as high his armpit, and with this action *push* it, as it were, from him.' Lord Frederick Beauclerk, one of the best amateur batsmen of the day, called Harris's bowling 'one of the grandest sights in the universe'. Clearly he needed to get out more.

There was no denying Harris's prowess though. He had an uncanny eye for the roughest patch of grass to bowl on (the visiting team were allowed to choose where the stumps should be pitched and Harris had a particular penchant for mole hills) and he made the ball fizz and spit off the surface. This demanded a whole new approach to batting, forcing batsmen to step forward to smother the movement and attempt to play it with a perpendicular bat rather than try and swipe it into the heather. Nimble footwork was required, otherwise batsmen became virtually scoreless.

Still he outwitted them, removing numerous batsmen caught, a mode of dismissal which in those days wasn't credited to the bowler. He knew how to exploit a pitch and in one match in the mid-1780s took 3 wickets in 3 balls. He was presented with a gold-laced hat for his achievement. By the 1800s it was the norm to give a bowler a similar gift for such a feat. It is the origin of the term 'hat-trick', now common parlance in most sports for an individual getting three of a kind whether it be wickets, goals or wins.

Harris was so good that even when in later years his body was ravaged with gout he was allowed to walk to the middle on crutches, bowl his deliveries and then recline in an armchair for the rest of the game. Now that's the way to play cricket.

Get Your Legs Out of the Way, Man!

The advent of Harris and other devious bowlers brought about a more cautious approach from batsmen. This was the age of the 'block'. Tom Walker, a celebrated opening batsman, took this to considerable extremes in one match, scoring only 1 run off 170 deliveries he received from Harris. He would have made Geoff Boycott look like Kevin Pietersen.

Runs were accumulated, 403 of them in one Hambledon innings in 1777, then a record, as was James Aylward's individual contribution of 167. In another match Noah Mann scored an all-run 10 when he hit one behind the wicket and miles down the hill at Broadhalfpenny, though you do wonder what the hell the fielders could have been doing. Accidentally on purpose treading it into the ground and declaring a lost ball would have been more sensible (costing them only 6). The *Wisden Cricketers' Almanack* doesn't record the most runs ever achieved off one ball, but I once saw a

12 registered during an indoor international at the Millennium Stadium in Cardiff when the Pakistani Shahid 'Boom Boom' Afridi managed to launch a ball into the roof, a height of nearly 300ft.

But despite the generally slow scoring, cricket as a sport was progressing rather well. In schools and universities it was thriving, and it had penetrated the Midlands and as far north as Durham (where the first recorded match was in 1751 at Raby Castle). Decent crowds attended major club matches. Professional players earnt quite handy money and the big landowners took their turns at one-upmanship and creaming a bit off the top. The game remained relatively simple, with no limit to the amount of time a batsman could stay in or how long a bowler could bowl for. There were, realistically, only three ways of being out – bowled, caught and run out – all fairly easy for the umpire to adjudicate. And there were no stump mikes to pick up new batsmen saying, 'Who the fuck has thrown a jelly bean on the pitch?', thus causing an international incident.

It was all rather lovely and idyllic and mercenary. And then someone threw a spanner in the works. They invented leg before wicket. This aspect of cricket has probably aroused more dispute and death threats than any other rule in sport, and definitely more confusion. The cockier someone sounds about the lbw law the greater the likelihood that they are absolutely clueless. It has spawned a sort of unofficial private sect – the LBW Society – containing a select band of individuals who properly understand its intricacies and have honey and Marmite finger sandwiches religiously at 4.10pm every day and make the legs of their children's beds from old wickets. Yes, Dad, *you*!

The Star and Garter in Pall Mall was the place the posh sporting set liked to meet, and it was here in 1774 that an assortment of dukes and squires and clergy met to revise the Laws of Cricket. The principal change reflected the new style of batting. The striker with the upright bat – standing closer to the line of the stumps than his hockey-stick-wielding predecessor – would sometimes deviously use his legs as a second line of defence, risking bruised shins in the process (pads were not worn in those days). The London committee, anxious to keep the game 'fair' – mainly for the sake of gambling on it – agreed that a batsman be given out if 'he puts his leg before the wicket with a design to stop the ball and actually prevents the ball from hitting the wicket'. In essence, getting your leg deliberately in the way was regarded as not in 'the spirit' of the game.

The new law immediately vested responsibility on the umpire to be (a) eagle-eyed, (b) able to remain standing up and alert for hours on end despite a scoring rate of half a run an over, and (c) a sort of Mystic Meg and predict the future. It is, of course, impossible to be *sure* the ball was going to hit the wicket if the batsman's leg hadn't been in the way, just as it's impossible to be sure that driving a gas-guzzling Range Rover in Chelsea is going to ultimately bring about the flooding of Holland.

And that's the perennial problem with lbw: no one really knows. The umpire can't say to the bowler, 'Hey, bowl that one again without the batsman in the way and we'll see if it hits the stumps or not.' Occasionally, when the batsman is standing right in front of his wicket with a stump visible either side of his leg and the ball cannons into his shin, you can be pretty certain of the outcome. Usually, though, it's total guesswork, and as time has gone on more complexities have been added to the lbw law – 'Was the batsman struck outside the line of the stumps?', 'Was he attempting to play the ball?', 'Did he buy me a beer last night?' – to make the umpire's job even harder.

Lbw should stand for a Lot of Bloody Worry, and the problems of applying the new law were underlined by the fact that twenty years elapsed before anyone was officially given out in this way. In 1795 the Hon. John Tufton of Surrey became the first of a zillion batsmen who mutter as they're walking off, 'Where's your white stick, ump? Couldn't you see that ball was missing leg stump?' Hearing the litany of aggrieved complaints about lbw decisions from batsmen (or bowlers) is one of the sadistic joys of dressing room life ('It was too high', 'That was going down . . .', or 'It wasn't fast enough to knock the bails off' – 'Why d'you miss it then?'). The old whingers didn't shut up even in 2001, when Channel 4 introduced the predictive tool Hawkeye to project the exact path of the ball using modern missile guidance technology. 'How can you trust that?' they said. 'Well, the RAF do, and it's a lot better than guessing,' I'd reply but they wouldn't have it. Some people, you see, are just never satisfied.

TWO

Life of Britain

Some very important things were happening in Britain in the 1780s. Firstly curry powder was invented. This immediately enlivened egg salads, camouflaged the stale flavour of old mutton, gave everyone diarrhoea and ultimately made chicken tikka masala a more popular British meal than fish and chips, though that happened more than 200 years later. It also eventually made Glasgow the spice capital of the world, with more than 5,000 curry houses (1990 census). It is where the umbilical link between curry and cricket began. More of that anon.

A few slightly less significant things occurred in that decade. James Watt perfected the steam engine (1780), the United States of America was established (1783) and a penal colony was created in a vast useless desert full of spiders (Australia). That was in 1788, the year *after* the Marylebone Cricket Club (MCC) was formed. In a cricketing sense it's about the only time England has been ahead in its perennial tussle with the dastardly Aussies.

Watt's invention was the catalyst for the Industrial Revolution to go into overdrive. Factories and mills were being built everywhere, and with transport rapidly improving and all the best-paid labour in urban areas, there was mass migration to the cities. That applied to cricket too.

The ringmaster was George Finch, Earl of Winchilsea. An old Etonian, he was extremely rich, raising his own regiment to fight the American revolutionaries, and an inveterate gambler. He was a prominent Hambledon member and, as an influential part of the 'Committee of Noblemen and Gentlemen', a London mover and shaker. It was this committee of landowners who in 1784, again at their Star and Garter watering hole in Pall Mall, revised the Laws of Cricket once more, chiefly to reassure the betting fraternity (i.e. themselves). Sometimes more than £20,000 was staked on a match, with numerous side bets.

The Earl also had the title Lord of the Bedchamber, though he was a 'confirmed bachelor', which is another way of saying he was so ugly no woman would sleep with him. He had a Machiavellian streak too. Despite his Hambledon connections he had obviously got fed up playing with the rural riff-raff, preferring to mingle with the upper-crust set in London and play cricket at White Conduit Fields, a popular ground in Islington which eventually made way for the eyesore which is King's Cross railway station. Seeing the potential profits to be made in London the Earl was systematically siphoning off some of the best Hambledon club talent to play at the White Conduit/Star and Garter club.

He was a sort of forerunner of Roman Abramovich.

One of his chief targets was Billy Beldham, a pugnacious all-rounder he had spotted playing for Farnham and whom he first lured to Hambledon and then to London. 'Silver' Billy (so known for his fair hair) became famous for his agile footwork and buccaneering style, being the first to advance up the pitch to play his shots. 'You do frighten me there, jumping out of your ground,' said Squire Paulet, of Hambledon, obviously a bit of a wimp. Beldham made the ball 'rise up' when he bowled and was a brilliant fielder. 'Men's hearts throbbed within them, their cheeks turned pale and red', apparently. That was the case with women too, since he was alleged to have fathered thirty-nine children. *He* should have been the Lord of the Bedchamber. As he was also outspoken and partial to the punch served at the ground, he was the nearest thing at the time to Ian Botham. He just lacked the ten-year contract to do Sky's pitch report and the swanky golf villa in Spain.

Of farming stock, Beldham might have looked like Catweazle but he had, according to the celebrated twentieth-century cricket writer E. V. Lucas, 'a genius for cricket . . . the grandeur of the attitude, the piercing lightning of the eye, the rapid glance of the bat, were electrical.' For thirteen years Beldham averaged 43 with the bat at a time when 20 was a 'long hand'. This probably translates as an average of 60-plus today, which puts him up there with the Sobers and Pollocks and Sutcliffes of the game. Then again, he was only facing underarmers.

Essentially Beldham was cricket's first great all-rounder and was much sought after to play for Surrey, Hampshire and Kent – the arrangements were pretty loose between counties, adding further evidence that it was a spurious concept – as well as all the gentleman's clubs. His career spanned thirty-seven years. He was one of the only constant features of a game, and a country, that was going through radical change.

It was the government that caused the upheaval (isn't it always?). A succession of acts through the eighteenth century ensured that by the end of it half the farmland in England became enclosed. Rich landowners assumed control of their property and suddenly the countryside, which had been open to everyone, became out of bounds. It's still the same today. I mean, there you are, staying in a nice 'country' hotel for the weekend looking out across the vast swathes of green and imagining a nice walk over the hill with your partner and can you find a public footpath? Can you hell. The English countryside is cordoned off by barbed wire. It's not to keep the sheep in. It's to keep the people out.

Back then the small-holding farmers and cottage industries were eased out, and so were rural cricketers. The people's rights to play on the local land had been taken away. Now they had to ask permission. The change at Hambledon was symbolic. Matches were transferred from Broadhalfpenny Down which belonged to the community, to Windmill Down on the other side of the hill, which may have had better facilities, but it belonged to 'The Club'.

Everyone had to abide by 'rules', cash was king and

the aristocrats bought up the best players for their 'entertainment'. Cricket, in all its delicious variety and self-expression, was being straitjacketed into rich urban society. Or as the historian David Underdown put it in *Start of Play*, the village game was on 'a path of rural innocence into the maelstrom of gambling and corruption that was soon to engulf cricket' . . . Oh yes, that was the other notable thing that happened in the 1780s. The phrase 'fings ain't wot they used to be' was heard for the first time.

The Dark Side

The White Conduit Club's teams were initially made up exclusively of toffs: in fact an early rule was 'None but gentlemen ever to play.' There were the Earl of Winchilsea, various dukes and viscounts, and their privileged friends. But they were obviously pretty rubbish because, as time went on, the team began to include the old Hambledon contingent – Beldham, Small and the Walker brothers (I know, you thought they were a sixties pop band famous for 'The Sun Ain't Gonna Shine Any More', but the fact is none of them were actually related or had the surname Walker). The Earl, it is recorded, rarely troubled the scorers or the opposition with his bat.

He was probably one of those annoying types with the flashiest gear and the biggest swagger who is absolutely useless and misses the first straight one that comes along and then blames the distraction of a woodlouse on the sightscreen 100 yards away for his mistake. Clearly Winchilsea was disconcerted by some of the unruly passers-by at White Conduit Fields in Islington because he and the Duke-of-Richmond-to-be asked one of their professionals, Thomas Lord, to find them a private ground instead.

They pledged financial backing and Lord, a Yorkshireman, didn't need to be asked twice. In May 1787 he leased some land in Dorset Square, off Marylebone Road about two blocks from Madame Tussauds. Good thinking: on Saturday mornings he could guarantee a decent crowd from the tail end of the queue for the waxworks, and, having erected a high fence, could charge them 6d admission. The first match at the original Lord's, between White Conduit and Middlesex, was played on 21 May 1787. Ten days later, Middlesex played Essex there. In that bustling location, Henry Blofeld would have had a field day on commentary:

'Oh I say, there goes the Oxford flying coach, and just behind it the Liverpool stagecoach, packed with people and their belongings, and I say, isn't that the Whitbread brewery wagon crammed with beer barrels? My dear old thing, the poor old carthorses are really heaving that one along . . . now . . . Beauclerk polishes the ball on his cream breeches, adjusts his cuff, moves in and bowls another one to Walker, a loopy delivery, and he pats it gently to the short cover point fielder and there's no run . . .'

The White Conduit Club was soon renamed the Mary-le-bone Cricket Club (the Dorset Square field actually encroached on to what is now platform 6 of Marylebone station). And so began two centuries of confusion about MCC that most people think stands for Moneybags CC or Massive Conservative Clique or something equally exclusive. Of course, the Aussies try to claim MCC (the Melbourne Cricket Club) as theirs, but that was formed later, in 1838, so they're just plagiarists.

It's amazing to think that from these fairly in-auspicious beginnings was formed an institution with thousands of members all over the world which governed the game for nearly 200 years and toured as England right up to the mid-1970s and still they hold up play by moving about behind the bowler's arm. This despite large signs in the pavilion saying: 'DO NOT MOVE ABOUT BEHIND THE BOWLER'S ARM'. (There was a popular theory in the 1980s that some used to do this deliberately around 1pm because the total was nearing the pre-lunch score that they had laid £50 on with Ladbrokes. You see, everything can be traced back to gambling in the end. I mean, let's face it, God put Adam and Eve on the earth. That was the biggest gamble of the lot. And look what it's led to: global warming and internet dating agencies.)

The MCC soon began arbitrating on disputes in the game (one of the first was in a match between Leicester and Coventry in 1788 featuring biased, not to say bent, umpires and a batsman who had been given out on the first day resuming his innings on the second). Lord could squeeze 5,000 paying spectators into his little ground, at which he put on a veritable smorgasbord of cricket matches from serious encounters like MCC v Middlesex and Eton v Harrow to more contrived games such as left-handers v right-handers. He also staged running races, pigeon shooting (again right down Blowers' alley), hopping matches and other events. In fact Lord was a right old mercenary and when the rent of Dorset Fields was raised in 1810 he moved his ground, turf and all, to a cheaper plot a mile up the road in Lisson Grove. The construction of the Regent's Canal forced him to move again, but the landowners offered him the present Lord's site instead for a bargain £100 a year, and the current ground opened for business in 1814.

Lord's is, of course, world-famous (and distinguished from the House of Lords by that all-important apostrophe) and a large portrait of Thomas Lord hangs in pride of place over the committee room mantelpiece in the pavilion. He looks a bit like the comedian Mel Smith (well, with their chubby faces, bulbous noses and bushy side hair, most of them did, to be honest). It is a moot point, however, whether he really deserves such prominence.

True enough he was the founder of Lord's, but he was almost its bulldozer too. Ten years after it opened he had hatched a plan to make his fortune by converting the site into housing. It was only the last-ditch intervention of William Ward, a prolific batsman of the time and also a director of the Bank of England, that rescued the ground from the developers. In 1825 he paid Lord £5,000 for his share of the land, ending the originator's association with the place, though he continued to live locally.

But the real saviour of Lord's was James H. Dark. In the 1830s the MCC's interest in cricket had waned, and Ward was looking to sell his portion of the lease. Dark, a saddler's son, was a former professional whose first connection with the MCC had been as a ballboy at Dorset Fields in the early nineteenth century, receiving sixpence a day for his trouble. He not only bought William Ward's share but totally rejuvenated the ground, upgrading the pavilion and other facilities, adding a real tennis court, planting 400 trees and ensuring the outfield was properly drained and cropped (by sheep), though the pitch was decidedly ropey.

Dark's brothers made equipment at Lord's – bats, balls and pads – and took money at the gate. His sister-in-law did the catering. J. H. Dark supervised all this activity for twenty-five years until he retired in 1860. It was quite a dynasty, and as recently as 1980 there was still a sweet shop under the Mound stand carrying the family name. Now, apart from one inconsequential little drawing of him hidden away in an anonymous corridor, there is nothing. There is strong belief that the name of J. H. Dark should have a greater legacy at the ground that he shaped. Then again, boasting possession of tickets for the second Test between England and Australia at 'Dark's' just doesn't have the same ring about it.

Double Standards

We've jumped forward in the story quite a bit. Time to rewind. As Lord's and the MCC developed, so

Hambledon faded. Well, it's pretty hard to keep a club going if people keep nicking your best players. A match between White Conduit and All England at Lord's (Dorset Fields) in 1787, for instance, featured the Walker brothers, Harris, Beldham, Small senior and junior, Aylward, Purchase, Mann, Bullen and Taylor – all Hambledon professionals (all with 'Mr' in front of their name, incidentally, while the amateurs had the more privileged title 'Esq.' unless they were an earl or a knight).

The urban professionalization of the game, the war with France and a sequence of terrible harvests drastically curtailed village cricket in the late eighteenth century. Hambledon's last recorded match of this early period was in 1793, after which it metamorphosed into Hampshire for a time. In the cities cricket was flourishing, and, having been regarded as a sort of aristocratic eccentricity in the early part of the eighteenth century, it was now seen as decent and virtuous. It was a vigorous pursuit that still embodied a spirit of 'fairness' (you had to appeal to the umpires to give a man out, for chrissake!). A lot of early cricket literature describes it as a game of 'manly toil', which is quite at odds with William Temple, Archbishop of Canterbury, declaring it was just 'organised loafing' in the 1940s. Cricket in the late eighteenth century was regarded as synonymous with 'Englishness'. *The Times*, reporting an exhibition cricket match in Paris in 1786, declared, 'The French cannot imitate us in such vigorous exertions of the body.'

Matches were covered actively by the press, even the

more bizarre encounters. There was the 1793 game between the Married Women and the Maidens at Bury Common (won by the Smug Marrieds), and in 1796 at Montpelier Gardens eleven one-armed Greenwich Pensioners took on eleven of their peers each with a wooden leg. *The Times* reported that '5000 people were highly entertained by the veterans of the ocean' and that when darkness fell 'the contest was so much in favour of the Timber-toes as never to be recovered by the dint of Arms'. Well, they couldn't bat or field, poor hand-less bastards!

If there was an imbalance in the teams, one side just fielded extra players. It didn't necessarily help. In July 1793 at Swaffham, an England XI took on XXXIII (that's 33 to you Roman numeral ignoramuses) of Norfolk. For England the ubiquitous Tom Walker, nicknamed 'Old Everlasting', scored 5 more on his own than all XXXIII of Norfolk managed to put together. But the match took three days, so it's fair to assume that by the time Norfolk went in they were all suffering from rigor mortis after watching him bat.

Portraying cricket as decent and proper was already proving myopic. That, in itself, is very 'English' – the sentimental view of something through those oh-so-English 'rose-tinted spectacles'. In fact gambling on the game was rife and the whiff of corruption was tangible. Bookies would approach lowly paid professionals in pubs, play on their dissatisfaction and offer them inducements to play badly. 'Oi, Jim, you up for batting like a halfwit today?' – 'But he always bats like that!'

Added to that, bowling at players like Walker drove

opponents to new levels of verbal abuse, and one man in particular. The Revd Lord Frederick Beauclerk, son of a duke, entered higher cricket echelons as a (very) slow underarm bowler in the 1790s, but he soon revealed a vicious temper and a devious greed. He would hurl his 'white beaver hat' to the ground in a rage if things didn't go his way, or stand and glare. He was the sportsman who invented the 1,000-yard stare.

During one encounter with the obdurate, rake-thin Walker, with his 'wilted, apple-john face' (Nyren), Beauclerk became increasingly apoplectic, threw his hat to the ground ostentatiously and declared, 'You confounded old beast!' Michael Atherton-like, Walker remained unperturbed and did not respond. He just carried on batting. He was 'a devilish troublesome customer to get out', observed Nyren.

Despite being a man of the cloth (vicar of St Albans), Beauclerk was notorious for his deceit. He tried to distract the batsmen with coloured sashes round his waist or by stuffing cloth inside his shirt, or he feigned a limp, and he employed unconventional fielding positions to further confuse. At the crease – where he was prolific, scoring some of the first centuries at Lord's – he would occasionally dangle an expensive watch on one of the stumps to provoke the bowlers into trying to hit it. There was a famous verse written about him.

My Lord comes in next and will make you all stare
With his little tricks, a long way from fair.

He was an avid gambler, who claimed he made 600

guineas (£630) a year from cricket, which was a good deal more than any of the pros. Clearly not all of his activity was above board. There are numerous stories of collusion between players in single-wicket matches that he organized – chiefly to allow the one they had all backed to win – and there was a match in Kent in 1807 when Beauclerk was easing 'All England' to victory in partnership with Billy Beldham. Suddenly 6 wickets fell for 11 runs and 'England' lost. *Plus ça change*, eh? Except in this case it was admitted some time later that the rest of the team had been bribed to get out. The captain was Beauclerk. Two words immediately spring to mind. Hansie and Cronje. Like Beauclerk, the famous match-fixing captain was (supposedly) an intensely religious character. Clearly both had taken the Hypocritic Oath.

Basically Beauclerk was a good old-fashioned swindler. The problem was he was also extremely influential. He had an intimate knowledge of the game's laws and as a regular, and successful, MCC captain (and later president of the club) he was frequently consulted on issues or disputes, adjudicating with less than total integrity. He had a personal dislike of the leading professional of the time, William Lambert, who like most of the pros in the early 1800s received hefty back-handers for manipulating results. Beauclerk conducted a smear campaign against him and succeeded in getting him ostracized. He was happy to accommodate an unorthodox round-arm bowler in his team. But this bowling style (i.e. the ball released in a sweeping movement from shoulder level) gained impetus and Beauclerk had difficulty playing it. So he had it banned.

Well, most would agree that the aristocracy have always been a law unto themselves . . .

Throwing the Book at It

The *Ladybird* books of sport were the 1960s version of the Nintendo Wii: birthday presents that shut kids up for a while, until they discover that the real-life versions of the games portrayed are not remotely as glamorous or as easy as they seem. My *Ladybird* book of cricket made the sport appear beautiful, refined, elegant. And then, on my first day as a county player, I encountered Mike Gatting demolishing a plate of lamb chops. My one abiding memory of that book is the picture on page 17 of the ninetenth-century Jane Austen figure in a voluminous, hooped purple skirt tossing a slow over-arm delivery to a teenage boy. The accompanying text explains that women invented modern bowling. I always assumed this to be an old wives' tale similar to the assertion that eating carrots improves your eyesight and masturbation makes you go blind (both erroneous, though I have had problems deciphering street names in A–Zs lately).

In fact there seems to be a grain of truth in it. There were one or two isolated bowling 'transgressions' at Hambledon in the late eighteenth century, notably when the arch blocker Tom Walker tried his hand at round-arm bowling. He was swiftly rebuffed by his club masters and never did it again. But it had set a precedent and all the literature agrees that it was in 1806 that a

Kent player, John Willes, first bowled 'round arm' at Lord's, using a sort of low slinging motion. He had supposedly learnt this method from batting against his sister Christina, whose full skirt inhibited a traditional underarm delivery.

Hooped skirts weren't in fact fashionable until the 1850s, so Christina was either ahead of her time, or the *Ladybird* illustrator was using a bit of creative licence. Probably she had been wearing a cumbersome layered gown more typical of the time, but this would have looked drab in the drawing. At least it adheres to the number one rule of reportage: never let the truth get in the way of a good picture.

Though Willes's action aroused the kind of dark mutterings from the old brigade that accompanies boys with long hair, the trend caught on and everyone was soon trying it. The authorities (MCC) declared it was 'throwing' and tried to ban it (1816: 'the ball must be delivered underhand . . . with the hand below the elbow') and, in 1822, Willes, back at Lord's again, was pointedly no-balled by an umpire obviously primed by Lord Beauclerk. He reportedly hurled the ball to the turf (for which he was presumably no-balled again), stormed off the ground and rode away. Symbolically the horse had bolted too: in 1835 round-arm bowling was legalized.

The change spawned the first cricketing dynasty. The rotund William Lillywhite – who with his portly figure, top hat and braces resembled a circus ringmaster – had made no impression in his early years, probably because he couldn't get his underarm past his belly.

Using the new style he winkled out more than a thousand batsmen with his probing round-arms, and once took 18 wickets in a two-innings match, though this was against a team of 16. He was not a pioneer of smart fielding off your own bowling, once explaining a missed caught and bowled by saying, 'Look here, sir, when I've bowled the ball I've done with her.' But he played till he was sixty, fathered three sons who all played for Sussex, and his nephew James (junior) captained England in their first-ever Test match, against Australia in 1877 (which England lost).

William and his offspring ran sports outfitters, amalgamating in the famous Lillywhite's store, established in the Haymarket in 1863. Now occupying the only section of Piccadilly Circus not dominated by neon adverts for Samsung computers, Lillywhite's was for many years a prestigious vendor of sporting goods who also supplied my first sporting hero, the Kent and England opener Brian Luckhurst, with his bats. (My obsession was so great I even removed the Gray-Nicholls sticker from my own bat and coloured on a Lillywhite's emblem, which attracted some caustic observations from thirteen-year-old opponents like 'Wonder if he gets teddy bears for his birthday as well as crayons.')

Lillywhite's bats disappeared without trace and the shop's grand exterior belies an emporium stuffed with cheap replica football shirts, fashion-trainers and other tat, and populated by tubs of lard riffling through racks of shellsuits trying to find XXXL sizes. Is this what is known as the 'fat of the land'? At least their physiques are in keeping with the shop's founding father.

Back to round-arm bowling. The purists took a dim view of the development. Run scoring was initially harder with the ball bouncing up more, and the celebrated writer John Nyren lamented that 'the elegant and scientific game of Cricket' would be reduced to 'a mere exhibition of rough, coarse horseplay'. You wonder how he would have reacted a century and a half later to four bouncers an over from the West Indies quicks to the England no.11 Devon Malcolm (probably in similar panic to Malcolm's).

The Luddites were defeated and batsmen gradually got the gist of this new bowling and found it presented fresh scoring opportunities with balls landing wider of the stumps. But the law (to ensure the ball was released from below shoulder height) was difficult to enforce without third umpires looking at super-slo-mo replays. In fact it's difficult to enforce even *with* third umpires looking at super-slo-mo replays. Bowlers' arms crept higher and full overarm bowling was prevalent by the 1840s.

Still there were misgivings, including, pointedly, the first printed exclamation of something (dangerous fast bowling) being 'not cricket'. This was from the Revd James Pycroft in *The Cricket Field*. Aha, so *he's* the culprit. In the book he also wrote, 'a cricket field is a sphere of wholesome discipline and good order.' Already seriously deluded, he went on: 'The game of cricket, philosophically considered, is a standing panegyric [high estimation] of the English character: none but an orderly and sensible race of people would so amuse themselves.' Clearly he invented jingoism too.

As the book had nine editions and sold for forty years, he had a lot to answer for.

All this was brought about by the apparent triviality of the bowler raising his arm a few degrees. Yet the dispute reflects one of the perennial essences of cricket: for batsman against bowler read landowner v labourer or gent v rogue. It's a metaphor for the class war. Batsmen are the privileged ones with their belongings (the stumps) and are born to prosper. Bowlers are at best trespassers, at worst light-fingered lowlifes trying to con their superiors. Throughout cricket history, whenever batsmen are dominant (as they were around 1800) the ruling class are content in their clubs on St James's. As soon as the 'subversive' bowlers come up with a cunning new strategy, they are slapped down by a restrictive law. It's a never-ending cycle of wealth and subterfuge that has culminated in the orgy of muscle-flexing which is Twenty20 cricket. This is an exhibition of total batting power to which the poor humiliated bowler has no real answer, and which offers a cheap thrill to the masses. It's like a squire putting a miscreant gardener in the stocks. And inviting the rest of the village to come and pelt him with bad eggs.

THREE

American Psyche

In the first decade of the nineteenth century the Napoleonic wars were in full swing, and Admiral Lord Nelson was managing to entice Bonaparte's forces from land (where they were mighty) to sea (where they were cannon fodder). The only relevance this has to cricket is that the score 111 is referred to as 'Nelson' (and 222 as 'double Nelson') on the basis that, during the course of his noble efforts, the Admiral lost an eye, an arm and a leg (therefore had one of each). Except that he didn't. He had one eye and one arm, but two legs as anyone who has scaled the 50-metre column in Trafalgar Square would know. So actually the score of 'Nelson' should be 112.

It is regarded as a bogey number, and traditionally a batting team on the score of 111 all raise their feet off the ground as the ball is delivered; fine if you're reclining on the dressing room balcony, but rather more tricky if you're the batsman facing someone wanging them down at 90mph. There's certainly a stronger inclination to dive than jump in that situation, and, as the whole Nelson thing is all based on an erroneous fact, it's all superstitious nonsense if you ask me.

King George III reigned until 1811, when he was declared insane, presumably on account of having fifteen children. To make matters worse (for their carers), the United Kingdom had just abolished the slave trade. Nigerian nannies were suddenly in short supply. On the games field cricket was the dominant mass-participation sport, way ahead of football, which in the early 1800s hadn't significantly evolved from a lawless free-for-all. Maybe someone will let me know when it does . . .

The British Empire remained pre-eminent in the world, despite various losses – the thirteen colonies of North America which had become the USA, as well as Minorca, allowing it to send home all the package holiday makers from Wolverhampton. After 1815, Britain controlled a quarter of the world population and a third of the land area. This is even more remarkable when you consider the typically constrained male of the time as portrayed in Jane Austen's novels. They seemed incapable of securing themselves a woman let alone a country. On the other hand, maybe understanding what a country wants is easier.

Cricket spread along the tentacles of the empire, largely via the military. The first mention of a match in South Africa was in 1806, ditto West Indies, Canada's first cricket club (Toronto) was founded in 1827 and Sri Lanka's in 1832. There was also Australia, of course, where the first recorded match was in 1830. But as the first Western arrivals in 1788 were all convicts escorted by the cricket-loving British army, it is fair to assume they would have nicked some of the soldiers' bats and balls for their own games before that.

The most interesting early cricketing nation was the United States. There was a match in 1751 in New York between New York and London which the New Yorkers actually won (before you conclude that English cricket was obviously destined to go down the pan from that point, I should tell you that both teams were made up of Americans). There were various pockets of cricketing activity – Maryland, Connecticut, Philadelphia – which became dissipated after the American Revolution of the 1770s.

But interest lingered on, and in 1844 the world's first cricket international was staged at St George's Cricket Club in New York, when the USA invited Canada down for a challenge match. The game was attended by more than 10,000 people, many of whom felt inclined to shout, 'You're the man!' and 'Get in the hole!' at every opportunity. The United States lost the match by 23 runs.

Baseball, which wasn't suffering the same bickering about the laws as cricket and didn't have the same elitist tag, slowly took hold of the American populace after that, though the real highlight of United States cricket was still to come. In 1878 a team from Philadelphia actually beat the full Australian XI on first innings and eventually held them to a draw. They toured England too, holding their own against several first-class counties. But once the simplicity and individualism of tennis and golf grabbed the American psyche after the First World War, cricket faded from the picture.

It was locally re-energized by the Hollywood Cricket Club in the 1930s and there are clubs still dotted about America, chiefly sustained by expat Indians and Pakistanis (it is they who are the cricket colonists now). Believe it or not there is a third MCC – Microsoft Cricket Club – patronized by Indian software engineers based in Silicon Valley. There was a mad idea to stage some of the 2007 cricket World Cup in Florida, till the authorities came to their senses. The fact is white Americans don't get cricket. 'There's a limit to what Americans understand. The limit is cricket,' says a character in Joseph O'Neill's Booker-nominated novel *Netherland*. It's one of those things, like irony and taste, that has just passed them by.

The evolution of cricket in India is the ultimate contrast. There are mentions of the game there in the 1720s, and the first proper association – the Calcutta Cricket Club – was formed in 1792. It was then exclusively an English game played by soldiers in their English-style clubs where the Indians served them lunch and tea and mainly looked on in total bewilderment at their antics on the field.

There is a relic of those times still active in Mumbai today. The Cricket Club of India has a grand entrance decorated with honours boards and portraits and the various public rooms are named after famous ex-players. In the panelled-wood dining room you can order fish and chips and pots of tea served in porcelain cups and look across to the veranda where jacketed (now Indian) members sit in wicker chairs sipping gin and tonics and playing bridge. It's more English than England. Only the loud honking buses, the dodgy wine and the odd scurrying cockroach give the game away.

The Parsi community, a unique sect who put their dead on the roof to decompose, engaged with the game by the 1830s and it was soon flourishing on Bombay's Maidan, a swathe of common land framed by grand gothic buildings (which is still a popular venue for organized and impromptu games). The Parsees formed their own Bombay clubs – named after either planets or British prime ministers (Jupiter, Mars, Gladstone . . .) – and began to produce excellent players and later toured England with some success.

There were other catalysts, such as the influence of the great Sussex and England batsman K. S. Ranjitsinhji, whom we'll come to later. But undoubtedly the tempo and ethos of cricket synchronized with the Indians' slow-moving life and never-ending curiosity. They cannot help lingering by the roadside after a minor accident watching the situation unfold, offering their opinions and waving their arms a lot. And in cricket there is a minor accident – a fumbled stop, a lousy delivery, a mishit – virtually every over. To an Indian whose job is to laboriously mend sandals or fill in cash ledger books or operate a lift, cricket is positively racy. Americans haven't got the patience to wait two minutes for a burger never mind half an hour for a boundary.

Box-ercising

Like the country itself, the game in England was changing in the first half of the nineteenth century. Transportation was developing rapidly with the invention of Stephenson's *Rocket*, which Richard Branson's great-great-great-grandfather immediately tried to buy and equip with fully reclining seats and a travelling masseuse, and the burgeoning textile industry was making the 1820 equivalent of Philip Green very rich indeed. This had a relevance to cricket because (a) the advent of the railways helped the game to spread further and (b) the new faster bowling meant you needed extra padding down your trousers.

The first pads were boards strapped to the leg, soon overtaken by lumps of sacking or rubber sewn into trouser legs, with a handkerchief packed round your genitals. ('Is that a pocket 'kerchief or you just pleased to see me?' . . . etc.) Batsmen tried to hide this protection for fear of being labelled a nonce by old cads such as Beauclerk who believed it was OK for practice but not in a match. He decreed that 'leggings' must not be worn. (In this sense he was a sort of early version of Trinny and Susannah.) A serious injury to a star player – the gargantuan Alfred Mynn, whose leg was so badly bruised by the round-armers of William Lillywhite during a North v South match in 1836 that he only narrowly avoided amputation – presumably made old Beauky think again. By the 1840s cork pads were in circulation and Robert Dark, the brother of the saviour of Lord's, had established a business selling balls, pads and batting gloves.

The 'box' (or abdominal protector, to give it its official title) was a later development. Not till the 1850s was such an accessory mentioned, described as 'a cross-bar India rubber guard' and superseded eventually by 'Palmer's Patent Groin Protector', a sort of padded codpiece. Later still, in the 1930s, you could get a tin version, and if, as sometimes happens, the batsman was hit 'amidships', he often removed it and knocked the dints out with his bat handle. And its successor, the pink plastic triangle, had a habit of splitting in the most inconvenient and painful locations. That is if it was in the right position in the first place. I remember the horror of realizing my box had slipped down my trouser leg just as a strapping West Indian fast bowler was approaching the wicket. Luckily the ball merely uprooted my off stump as I made a timid attempt to hit it and I shuffled off with what looked like a large callus on the inside of my knee. 'I fink his arsehole fell out!' said a colleague when I got back to the dressing room.

The thought of that made me squirm in my MCC Library seat as I was researching this section. Ken, the spindly librarian, sensed my discomfort and brought me a cup of tea. He showed me a whole shelf of books on bat-making and equipment and dress from the mid-nineteenth century. 'We've got even older stuff in the archive room,' he said. The archive room? Now Lord's has been a workplace for me for almost thirty years, and I thought I knew every nook and cranny and secret entrance, like the staff one that gets you into the pavilion in jeans and T-shirt avoiding the Gestapo on the door checking your attire. Yet I'd never heard of the existence of an archive room. It's down a back corridor behind the pavilion decorated with line drawings of old players and a terrible oil painting of Ian Botham on the floor awaiting hanging space. You go through a door and there is a room stashed with boxes and bookcases and large rolling cabinets full of priceless stuff. Well, priceless if you're into cricket history anyway. Probably not if you collect Chagalls.

There are lines of boxes full of old photos, old score-books and original insomnia cures, like the minutes of every MCC committee meeting since about 1814. There are cabinets full of the first cricket books and manuals, published from the 1830s onwards, each leather-bound and immaculately kept by Glenys, the archivist. It was there that I found the early-cricket bible – John Nyren's *The Young Cricketer's Tutor*, published in 1833.

John Nyren was the son of Richard Nyren, the man who facilitated Hambledon's development and ran the Bat and Ball pub. John was a left-handed batsman who played a few times for the fading Hambledon and later for 'England', though his selection has to be considered dubious since his first-class batting average was 8.36. This is on a par with modern rabbits like Glenn McGrath and Devon Malcolm. Run scoring was a bit harder in those days – especially in matches where there were twenty fielders – but still. His prominence rose, however, on publication of his book, which, written with the help of sport's first ghost, contains evocative portraits of the players of the time.

The Young Cricketer's Tutor is only small – the size of one of those pocket travel guides to Ibiza – and describes itself inside as providing 'full directions for playing the elegant and manly game of cricket'. It's pretty comprehensive though, going through all the rudiments of batting and bowling and explaining all the fielding positions. These included 'long mid-off' and 'Point, 5–7 yards from the bat, requiring a man of sharp reactions to watch the ball with great minuteness.' It just happened that Nyren himself was a specialist point. No ego apparent there then.

The Laws of Cricket (early 1800 version) are reprinted in the book. 'The wicketkeeper,' they state, 'must remain quietly at a reasonable space behind the wicket and not stir till the bowler has delivered the ball. The wicket-keeper is not allowed to annoy the striker, either by noise, uncalled for remarks or unnecessary action.' Some contrast with the keepers of today like Matt Prior – fond of calling bespectacled batsmen 'Harry Potter' – who've caused stump microphone operators to go half deaf with their inane banter.

Boom and Bust

English cricket was still a haphazard affair in the early nineteenth century. If you look at the fixture list for a random year – say 1817 – you see a strange assortment of first-class matches, including Sussex v Epsom, W. Ward's XI v F. Beauclerk's XI, and England v The Bs – a team of players whose surnames all began with B. I'm not making this up. The Bs won, and in fact an all-time England Bs XI, featuring Boycott, Botham, Bedser,

Bailey, Barnes (S.F.), Barrington, Bosanquet, Beldham and bloody Beauclerk, captained of course by Brearley, would take some beating.

The numerous professional players advertised themselves in *Bell's Life*, a forerunner of *Sporting Life*. There were one-day, two-day and three-day matches, single-wicket exhibitions, teams of twenty or twenty-two against eleven, and a bizarre array of one-offs. In May 1827, *The Times* reported a 'novel game on Harefield common between two gentlemen of Middlesex, and Mr Francis Trumper with the help of a thorough-bred sheepdog. In the first innings the two gentlemen got three runs, and Mr Trumper three for himself and two for his dog.' Sounds riveting. When the ball was hit 'the dog started off after it with speed and would carry the ball in his mouth and put it in his master's hand with such wonderful quickness that the gentlemen found it very difficult to get a run.' The trouble is the master couldn't bowl with it because it was covered in spittle.

The above match attracted 'a great number of gentlemen from Uxbridge and neighbouring villages to see so extraordinary a game' (there really wasn't a lot going on in those days, was there?) and 'the money lost and won on it was considerable.' Gambling was still a major focus of cricket matches. There was even a separate section on betting in the Laws of Cricket. But at Lord's, where the MCC stipulated the rules, bookies were finally banned.

Pitches were invariably terrible, even at Lord's. The improbably named Sir Spencer Ponsonby-Fane, long-time treasurer of the MCC, describes it thus:

> No scythe was allowed and the grass was never mowed. It was usually kept down by a flock of 400 sheep, penned up on match days in the north-east corner, which, on Saturdays were driven on to the ground on their way to the Monday Smithfield Market. From the pitch itself half a dozen boys picked out the rough stalks of grass. The wickets were sometimes difficult – in a dry north-east wind for instance.

He doesn't specify why, though perhaps it was because of the pong from the sheep pen. I can promise you, however, that if the West Indian Malcolm Marshall was bowling with a nor'easter at his back even the flattest Lord's 'wicket' seemed like it was littered with landmines.

Kent was the place to play in the 1830s, not least because the further south you went the better you could see the ball. Such was the density of smoke-belching mills oop north, the teams were permanently off the field for bad light. Well, they would have been if Dickie Bird had been umpiring. Kent were the pre-eminent team, stashed with outstanding players. The most notable of these was Alfred Mynn, the man who had nearly had his leg amputated. Mynn, weighing in at 20 stone, was cricket's first colossus. 'He hit hard and he hit often,' said the distinguished cricket writer E. V. Lucas. He could bowl too, round-armers as fast as anyone in England, 'except perhaps,' Lucas continues, 'for Brown of Brighton who once bowled a ball right through a coat which longstop was holding, and killed a dog on the other side.' In spite of the textile revolution, the standard of workmanship (and the hardiness of dogs) clearly left something to be desired. And what was longstop doing holding a coat anyway?

With luxuriant Harry Secombe-like sideburns, and a similar waistline, Mynn had a huge appetite for food and life and his power was immense: 'he lifted two balls into some adjoining county,' a contemporary, Frederick Gale, remembered, which, while sounding unlikely, is physically possible at Tunbridge Wells, where the boundary between Kent and Sussex runs just behind the scorebox. Mynn's enthusiasm for bowling was obvious when he was asked what he thought of increasing the number of balls in an over from four to six. 'Myself, I should like a hundred,' he said. He was one of those bowlers whom you could never get the ball off. You probably know the type:

'OK, thanks, Reg.'

'Just one more, skip!'

'But you've had 16 overs!'

'So what difference does it make if I have one more?!'

Ten overs later:

'OK, great, time for a little rest.'

'Hang on, I think I've got him now.'

'But he's got 124!'

'Well, get some fielders instead of cardboard cut-outs.'

The mainstay of the Kent team and unbeaten for eight years in single-wicket tournaments, Mynn was a national institution, but he struggled to make a living as a professional player – they earnt about £4 a match out of which they had to pay for travel, food and accommodation – and was twice briefly imprisoned for going bankrupt. The magistrate must have been a brave man though, because by that time Mynn was a 24-stone giant. His name is forever coupled with Fuller Pilch, a prolific batsman born in Norfolk but who also played for Kent and complemented Mynn's brawn with elegance and style. He was Gower to Mynn's Botham.

Deemed to be the best batsman in England, Pilch was tall and stylish and resourceful too, travelling with his own scythe to give the lush, mottled pitches an extra trim. His batting average, however, in a thirty-four-year career, was a modest 18.61, perhaps indicative of how tricky the surfaces were in general. A good score was 30 and run-rates were barely 1 per (four-ball) over. Later Pilch turned to umpiring and, seeing matters from the batsman's perspective, would remonstrate with bowlers who too often appealed for lbw. 'None o' that,' he barked. *'Bowl 'em out!'*

Because of these two and the dexterity of the left-handed batsman and artist Nicholas Felix (real name Wanostrocht, who used to scribble his score on his shirt front), Kent were all-powerful – too good even for the Rest of England teams. But without an official county championship, there was no real barometer of success. As ultimate arbiters of the game, the MCC could have arranged the end-of-season play-offs, with bunting and cheerleaders and *Super Boundaries!* newspaper pullouts. But their politburo of earls, viscounts, barons and marquesses were more interested in buggering off to Scotland for the start of the grouse-shooting season.

Class Distractions

In amongst the various county, inter-schools, Marrieds v Singles and Amputees v Dwarfs matches, the big games of the English season were Gentlemen v Players and North v South. The Gentlemen v Players contests had begun with a whimper in 1806, with the Gentlemen 'given' two of the best pros. They still got beaten and were continually hammered by the Players even when they were allowed to field a team of eighteen and insist upon the Players defending a double-sized wicket. It didn't prevent the pious Revd James Pycroft from declaring: 'The Players, though superior on the whole, are not as superior to the Gentlemen in real cricket as the score would represent . . . there is more invention in their play and while it lasts it is infinitely better worth seeing.'

It is this kind of attitude that has held English cricket back for generations. It's a stance rooted in *Upstairs, Downstairs* class distinctions, the implication being that the gentlemen (amateurs) played elegantly and properly, while the players (the pros) were calculating and undesirable and employed ugly methods. He was basically accusing them of being pikeys. Their preference for scoring runs on the legside was derided as if it undermined the refined purity of the game (what purity?). The West Indian Viv Richards blew that assertion out of the water 125 years later by demolishing Test match attacks with legside play of incredible elegance and power, but even he wouldn't have prevailed if he'd listened to English coaches imploring him not to hit 'across the line, son'.

Yet in spite of Richards, and others, there is still a misguided assumption that shots to leg are somehow distasteful and that the offside is the 'posh' side. Still much emphasis in the English game is placed on correctness and refinement, as if a batsman is dining with the Queen rather than repelling a hard piece of leather. I bet she licks her knife anyway. It's almost as if a batsman isn't worthy unless his innings are studded with elegant strokes, and someone like Mark Ramprakash was too concerned, early in his career, with how his batting looked. He continually played aesthetically pleasing offside shots . . . straight to the fielder. On this issue the Aussies, of course, are utterly pragmatic. 'It's not how, it's how many,' they'll say, and, given that they produced the undisputed champion of batting, Don Bradman, score at 4 an over without breaking sweat and have beaten us a good many more times than we've beaten them (131 against 97 as at the start of the Ashes 2009), it brooks little argument.

With the growing prosperity of the Lancashire cotton mills, the Yorkshire coalfields and the Eccles cake, the annual match between the North and South had a needle essence. It was Raw against Respectable, the Proles against the Plums, the Labourers against the Landowners (augmented by a couple of pros). Cricket was burgeoning in the north, with clubs playing all-day matches, usually on Fridays or Mondays. Pitches were dodgy and scores were low (50 all out was an average total in Durham in the 1830s), but they played with great determination. (I mean, where would we be without true northern grit? . . . Probably Germany.)

There was much northern rejoicing – well, pints of Theakston's anyway – when the North won the first encounter with the South in 1836, though they soon remembered their manners and lost the rematch.

The growth of newspapers was helping the game to spread. *Bell's Life* printed scorecards, and local papers followed suit, though there were the inevitable letters from Outraged of Oswestry claiming not enough coverage of much more important issues like the lazy pronunciation of vowels these days. Gradually reports became more analytical, with classic comments like 'We advise Mr Wetherell not to jerk his balls so much', though that pales by comparison with Harry Carpenter on BBC TV saying, at the end of the 1977 Boat Race, 'Ahhh, there's Princess Michael kissing the Cambridge cox . . .'

The press, mainly full of announcements and reports of meetings, lapped up any cricket match, no matter how quirky. It seemed to inspire an even greater, and more unlikely, participation. Like the single-wicket game between two octogenarian Cambridge blues. One man, known only as 'B' in the story, batted first and made 12. But 'A' was so exhausted from his bowling and fielding he was unable to bat (there was method in the madness of that Middlesex man's sheepdog). Therefore, to win, 'B' merely had to go out and bowl down his absent friend's wicket. Lying on the sofa indoors bemoaning his lost youth, 'A' was startled by the return of his friends. 'Bravo, you've won the match!' they cried. 'He's bowled 13 wides!'

The One-Eyed Visionary

Princess Victoria, eighteen-year-old niece of William IV, acceded to the throne in 1837. Britain was experiencing rapid industrialization, and exports of cotton, linen and woollen garments were booming. London and Manchester were the sweatshops of the world, churning out cheap kids' T-shirts by the million. Charles Dickens, who once ceremonially opened the bowling on the ground outside his Rochester home, painted a vivid picture of London life that year with his monthly serialization of *Oliver Twist*, and had everyone humming, 'You gotta pick a pocket or two-ooooo . . .' Into this smoky, exploitative world of opportunism stepped a man who might have had only one eye but his two entrepreneurial antennae were buzzing.

This was William Clarke. Born in 1798 in Nottingham, Clarke was a bricklayer by trade who'd lost the sight of an eye as a child, but his slow underarm bowling soon got the attention of the Nottingham Club, for whom he played as a teenager. In his twenties he gave up his trade to run a pub, the Bell, which also became the headquarters of local cricket. Although he occasionally hired himself out as a professional player, his cricket took a backseat for a while, particularly after his first wife died, leaving an absence of help and exposed cleavage behind the bar.

Clarke was clearly a late developer. Despite the advent of round-arm bowling, he was chosen in 1836, at the age of thirty-seven, for the first North v South match, and underarmed the North to victory, luring numerous batsmen to mishit catches into the outfield – regarded as a rather antiquated form of dismissal. A year later he captured the key wicket of the landlady of the Trent Bridge Inn, and set to work to enclose the field behind and convert it into a cricket ground. The first match at Trent Bridge, between Forest Club and South of the Trent, was played on 1 June 1838.

Clarke ran a programme of inter-county and other matches and charged 6d for admittance. Through his occasional representative appearances he got to know the southern stars like Pilch and Mynn, and in 1846, after the rather apathetic MCC had completed their season, he assembled an All England XI to play three matches in the north. This was Proper England, not some assortment of motley pros and amateurs who happened to be acquainted with an influential toff. Clarke's star-studded team lost their first match to XX of Sheffield – well England always have been slow starters – but he expanded his programme in 1847.

'We're going to play Liverpool, Leeds, York, Stockton, Sheffield, Birmingham and Newcastle,' he told James Dark, saviour and proprietor of Lord's.

'Newcastle?' Dark replied. 'They have no players fit to stand against the All England team . . . even with Kevin Keegan as manager.'

'*Especially* with Kevin Keegan as manager,' Clarke replied. 'Never mind,' he went on undeterred. 'I shall play sides strong or weak, with numbers or bowlers given, and all over the country too – and it will be good for cricket.'

He was right. Wherever they went, special trains and

feasts were laid on, the best local players paid to play against them and large crowds flocked to see them including 'four or five hundred ladies in their gayest attire'. They were like the Harlem Globetrotters, putting on a fabulous exhibition of their skills during the day and then chasing skirt in the evening, while Clarke himself ate a whole goose (he had usually only had a bottle of soda water and a cigar for lunch) and counted his money.

Because, if Clarke's England XI was good for cricket, it was even better for William Clarke PLC. He charged each venue £70 for the match plus a percentage of the gate receipts, and paid his players between £4 and £6 each. This was verging on tight, but, over a summer of twenty matches, better wages than his talented assortment of carpenters, printers, tailors and shoemakers would make from their original trades. And Clarke could go off and buy himself a barge on the Grand Union Canal (or whatever was the nautical equivalent of today's super-yachts).

In many ways Clarke himself was the star attraction. The spit of Michael Caine in *Get Carter*, he had an idiosyncratic delivery style – releasing the ball with a bent elbow from under his right armpit – enabling him to impart spin on the ball. He had devious changes of pace – his faster ball was apparently lethal – and he set crafty fields. He accompanied his deliveries with sarky asides – 'We shall have a haccident in a minute!' or 'He's as good as ready money to me – if he doesn't hit, he can't score; if he does I shall have him!' This was 160 years before the advent of the Australian captain Steve Waugh's 'mental disintegration' – a euphemism for spouting blatant insults – and it had the same effect.

Batsmen succumbed by the hundred. Literally. Between 1846 and 1853 Clarke took 2,385 wickets, averaging an amazing 340 a season. In 1853, when he was fifty-four, he took 476. Few manage that in an entire career. His achievements dwarf the mercurial feats of Kent's diminutive spin wizard of the 1930s, A. P. 'Tich' Freeman, if you'll pardon the pun. Not bad for a one-eyed bricklayer.

A visit of the top-hatted All England XI became the social highlight of the year up and down the country and even the cynics were converted by Clarke's entre-preneurial zeal. One historian called him 'a missionary for cricket' and the arch-Luddite Reverend James Pycroft con-ceded, in his over-written prose, that it 'draws the labourer from the dark haunts of vice and misery to the open common' and 'the squire or parson o' th' parish or the attorney may raise him without lowering themselves by taking an interest if not a part in his sport.' Loosely trans-lated, he was saying cricket was a sport for all. Consider yourself lucky you never had to endure his sermons.

MCC, still cricket's official body, looked on with a mixture of bewilderment and disdain as Clarke made cricket England's national sport: the first football club (Sheffield) wasn't formed until 1857. It's funny how in England it always seems to take a visionary individual to jolt a corporation out of its lethargy. Clarke had created a blueprint for inter-city cricket which, if it had survived, might have held football at bay for ever. But then, as is the British wont, someone doused the spirit of free enterprise with anti-growth hormone.

FOUR

Boys on Tour

London, with 2.3 million people, was the most populous city in the world in 1851, twice the size of the next biggest, Paris. It was a nineteenth-century Tokyo – buzzing with activity, trains and hookers: an estimated 80,000 ladies of the night were in gainful employment. About one for every ten men. Appropriately, it was the year of the Great Exhibition, celebrating the best of British industry, manufacturing, art and science (Ann Summers wasn't born yet) in the grand glass edifice of the Crystal Palace. Lacking our usual self-deprecation ('Gee, that's an amazing weaving machine with flying shuttle operation!!' – 'Oh, it's nothing, just a few bits of scrap metal . . .'), it was really quite un-British. Then again, it was conceived by Queen Victoria's husband, Prince Albert, who was German.

Duke and Sons, the Kent firm who were the first manufacturers of the cricket ball and were developing the first sprung bats, won a major design award at the Exhibition, camouflaging the discontent simmering below the game's surface. The players were becoming irked by William Clarke's parsimony (he was still only paying £4 a game), and the establishment by his refusal to let players off for traditional fixtures such as Gents v Players. Meanwhile the southern cliques thought the northerners were getting too big for their boots. It was ever thus.

What happened? Some players, like John Wisden – eventual founder of *Wisden's Almanack* – formed a breakaway touring England team – the United England XI. The MCC remained in its ivory tower. And various social commentators like Pycroft wrote idiotic stuff about the 'free trade in cricket' diminishing the power of the landed elite. County cricket – that structureless body of amateurs and pros that played each other in random fashion – was being marginalized, they said. This was classic 'Englishness': looking backwards into the future, apprehensive of 'ruining what we have', neatly ignoring the fact that they didn't have very much in the first place.

Clarke's parting shot was to present his book *Practical Hints on Cricket* to a Mrs Martha Grace and her son, who had an unusually luxuriant beard for a seven-year-old kid. Clarke died in 1856, having taken a wicket with the last ball he bowled, though the two events were not connected. England XIs spread like bacteria, as various wannabe proprietors eyed the good times. Some didn't last long, but the two originals – the All England XI and the United England XI – played each other once a season at Lord's in mid-summer. They also collaborated on England's first overseas tour – to Canada and the United States in 1859.

Playing XXII of Canada in the first match in Montreal, which must constitute the longest scorecard in international cricket history, they rolled them out for 85 in the first innings, but managed only 117 all out themselves (well, there were nine fielders in the covers and eight in a ring on the legside, the kind of field setting you dream of having to Viv Richards, Kevin Pietersen or, in fact, anyone). Canada were reduced to 43 for 16 second time around before rallying to 63 all out, leaving England 32 to win their first-ever international match, which they did for the loss of 2 wickets. A crowd of 6,000 apparently watched the match.

Canadian cricket never got out of first gear, but a man who played in that first England international and Great Britain's most famous novelist are the culprits who enabled Australia to get quickly into overdrive from a standing start. The former was the Surrey professional William Caffyn, who, with a certain Julius Caesar, was the fulcrum of the successful Surrey side of the 1850s. A punchy, fluent batsman and an effective round-arm medium-pacer, Caffyn was a regular in the United England XI and, after the tour of America, was selected in 1861 for the first 'England' team to tour Australia.

Again this trip was initiated by private enterprise, in this case two owners of a Melbourne café, which is where the famous novelist comes in. The café owners, Messrs Spiers and Pond, had attempted to land Charles Dickens for a lecture tour around Australia, but Dicko wasn't happy unless they paid for his entourage of quill sharpeners and moustache trimmers, so he turned them down. An English cricket team was drafted in as a replacement, an eventuality from which the phrase 'What the Dickens are you doing?' clearly originated. Under the captaincy of Surrey's Heathfield Harman Stephenson, England set off on 21 October from Liverpool on the steamship *Great Britain*.

After more than two months of playing deck quoits, their underarm shies at the stumps were sharp when they arrived, and they needed to be as they were often playing against twenty-two opponents – the Aussies were trying it on from the start. The English were astonished by the enthusiasm for cricket Down Under – 15,000 turned up for the first match in Melbourne – and their raw team's ability. They even inflicted a couple of defeats on the tourists.

Caffyn, who was highly successful on the first tour, returned for a second two years later with George Parr of Nottinghamshire in charge of a team that also included a Grace (Edward not Gilbert). A former coach of Eton College, Caffyn liked Australia so much he stayed on afterwards and set up home there. He combined his family hairdressing business with a job as Australia's first cricket coach. So, when you think of the greats of Australian cricket – notably Bradman, Miller, Lindwall, Lillee, Thomson and latterly Warne – you ought to know that an Englishman was ultimately to blame for their awesome menace. And their awful mullets.

Caffyn stayed for eight years, first in Melbourne then in Sydney, and in collaboration with Charles Laurence, also a Surrey player, enhanced the Aussies' batting repertoires and their fielding, soon had them bowling overarm (a trait that was becoming the vogue in

England) and improved their pitches. Caffyn returned to England in the early 1870s. Soon afterwards Australia were defeating England in the first-ever Test match – and with an equal number of players. It has got to the stage now where it's England that need to field the twenty-two men.

Back home, a power struggle ensued between Surrey – then the best county team and the first to restrict themselves to players born within its boundaries – and MCC. Surrey had more members, a superior side and a better ground (The Oval) than MCC, who, as supposed rulers of the game, were also dithering over everything. It all came to a head in August 1862, when Kent's Edgar Willsher, a fast left-arm bowler who had been pushing the boundaries of legality for years with his high, jerky action, was suddenly no-balled playing for All England against Surrey. 'It had,' *The Times* noted, 'become a growing fashion to get high . . . and with Willsher particularly so.' But his action had never been 'interfered with' before. He, like the round-armer Willes forty years earlier, went off in a huff (as did the rest of his team), but the umpire who had called him, John Lillywhite, was replaced and no further action was taken.

The chaos in the game – the various 'England' elevens, northern counties taking umbrage against southern ones and refusing to play them, the dispute about bowling actions – led to calls for a Cricket Parliament, but no one could agree on that either. Finally in June 1864, nearly two years after the Willsher incident, the MCC committee agreed to alter Law X (what constituted a fair delivery). It now read: 'The ball must be bowled; if thrown or jerked, the umpire shall call "no-ball". Overarm bowling had been legalized. The MCC committee congratulated each other and supped on their pink gins, fondly believing that a thorny issue had at last been sorted out once and for all.

In fact, of course, throwing and other deviations of the bowling action have continued to cause more controversy than just about anything else in the game. Bowlers, you see, are naughty boys who will forever try to see what they can get away with. What they need to keep them in check is not a vague and bendable law or a 'working party' to look into it, but a strict mother figure to police them. 'Right! That's it!' she'd say. 'You're always trying to push it and this time you've gone too far, bending your arm 25 degrees like that. No Nintendo Wii for a week. Go to your room this minute!'

Yes, Your Grace

The year 1864 was a defining one for a number of reasons. Apart from the bowling law, there was the publication of the first *Wisden*, which, in addition to the cricket scores, included 100 pages of racing and the rules of quoiting, and the opening of Charing Cross station, allowing city commuters from Kent vital access to Soho's teeming red-light district. It was also the year a certain Mr W. G. Grace (he had not yet earnt his doctorship) emerged on to the scene.

His mother, Martha, had initiated matters, with a letter to George Parr, captain of the All England XI in

1859, which said: 'I am writing to ask you to consider the inclusion of my son, E. M. Grace – a splendid hitter and most excellent catch – in your England XI. I am sure he would play very well and do the team much credit. It may interest you to learn that I have a younger son, now twelve years of age, who will in time be a much better player than his brother because his back stroke is sounder, and he always plays with a straight bat. His name is W. G. Grace.' Clearly WG's first advantage, then, was having a pushy mother.

He also had a very technically minded uncle, Alfred Pocock, who, like many of the best coaches, wasn't much cop at cricket himself, but was fascinated by the game. Pocock's enthusiasm and attention to detail – advising his protégé to adopt different stances for different bowlers, for example – introduced a level of sophistication into batting for the first time.

One of five brothers, WG – 'Gilly' to his siblings – learnt his game in the family orchard near Bristol, where he sometimes batted with a broomstick. His insatiable desire for runs evolved out of long days fielding and trying to bowl out his obdurate elders. He and his brothers played at any time of day throughout the year, and from their fast 'daisy cutters' that jumped up from treacherous ground, evolved his rapid eye and his resourceful technique. He also played fives, which was good for reflexes. The benefits were immediately evident when, aged just fifteen, he went on tour with the wandering South Wales Cricket Club. On 14 July 1864, WG made 170 (out of 356 all out) in the first innings of the three-day match against Gentlemen of Sussex at Hove.

It was his first century, and he added an undefeated 56 in the second innings to see South Wales to victory, after they'd made Sussex follow on. It's a more than useful double for a teenager unknown to everyone (except his relatives). And that is not all. In the same match he also opened the South Wales bowling and sent down 33 overs in the first innings (2-57) and 32 in the second. God knows what Martha Grace fed him on, but he would have been an automatic choice to advertise Shredded Wheat.

A week later and three days after his sixteenth birthday he played at Lord's for the first time, making 50 for South Wales against the MCC, 'a fine innings' according to *The Times*. It earnt him an appearance in the Big Match – Gentlemen v Players (a euphemism for Amateurs versus Professionals) – the following year, in which he opened the batting and the bowling, and made an undefeated 34 to hustle the Gentlemen to a rare victory. Previously they had won only seven matches in thirty-five years of the contest. In the WG era of fifty such encounters, the Gentlemen won thirty-one and lost only seven. In the course of them WG made fifteen centuries, took 271 wickets and ate 113 steak and kidney puddings. (OK, I lied about the puddings.)

The country was in a right tizzy at that point, not through war or pestilence but because a burgeoning middle class had clouded the meaning of the term 'Gentleman'. The Victorians spent inordinate amounts of time trying to define it, about as useful a task as the modern studies to ascertain what size of (female) breasts men prefer (22 per cent said they wouldn't date anyone above a D cup, as a matter of fact). They eventually decided that the word meant 'persons generally received in society as gentlemen', which has to be one of the biggest cop-outs of all time.

WG embodied the hypocrisy of the period by playing for the 'Gentlemen' (i.e. amateurs) while actually being paid a good deal more than the Players. It is estimated that he earnt £120,000 through cricket during his lengthy career (over £1m in today's money). He demanded a minimum of £20 a game to play for Gloucestershire, plus considerable expenses (which his brother EM controlled as club secretary) and on a United England tour of Australia commanded a fee of £1,500, whereas the professionals received only £170. On a subsequent tour his fee doubled. There were numerous testimonials. In cricket, his only qualification for the term 'Gentleman' was that he had an alternative profession. He was accorded the title 'Doctor' but even that was a sham. He took a decade to qualify as a GP and then his rich benefactors paid for a locum to run his practice. He had no more idea about bronchitis than Dr Who.

(The story goes that when he was about to go off to play for Gloucestershire, a lady knocked on the door and declared, 'Can you come quickly, Doctor, I think my twins have measles!' 'Sorry ma'am,' Grace replied, 'I can't stop. I'm just off to play cricket. Contact me at the ground if their temperatures reach 210 for 2.')

The fact is he was big enough to get away with it. The bald statistics back that up. Aged 18 he was already a prodigious talent, scoring 224 not out for England off the much-vaunted Surrey attack at the Oval, completing a remarkable performance by being spared fielding on the last day to go off to Crystal Palace and win the 440-yard hurdles championship. In 1868 he scored two centuries in a match, a feat that had only been achieved once before, fifty years earlier. In 1871, when he was in his early twenties, he scored ten centuries in a season, finishing with the unprecedented figure of 2,739 runs, with an average of 78. No one had ever passed 2,000 runs before and the next-best batting average in the country that year was 37. And this was on an assortment of dodgy pitches – either puddings or dust heaps – that bore no resemblance to the manicured batting paradises you see today. He quickly eclipsed the not inconsiderable feats of his elder brother, EM, also known as 'The Coroner', who once had a corpse put on ice until he could examine it after a day's play.

WG had transformed the art of batting by being the first player to be able to play forward *and* back and have an appropriate method for any pitch. Coupled with his huge physique (6ft 4in and 18 stone), his overpowering aura, his inexhaustible supplies of energy and his reputation for bending the laws, his fame was soon immense. No one gave a jot about his position in society or his bogus title or his gamesmanship. People just flocked to watch him bat (the admission charge of threepence was doubled if he was playing). He once got a standing ovation at Lord's for stopping four shooters in a row. You can hear Richie Benaud's exclamations now: 'Another mullygrubber . . . and Grace has kept it out! Mervellous badding . . . One of the best innings you'll ever see. Now, let's go downstairs and see what the Analyst makes of it.'

'Thanks, Richie. Fascinating defensive play by W. G. Grace. If you just look at these slightly fuzzy black and white clips you can see a wristy backlift, quite an upright, well-balanced stance, but he moves quickly when he sees the ball and gets in a perfect position, left elbow up, head right behind the line. You certainly wouldn't call it Gracefull, but it's mighty effective . . . Notice with this one how he's using his pads as a second line of defence. He knows he's never going to be given out lbw . . .' (and he never was in his entire twenty-two-Test career).

Grace's presence was the main reason a rudimentary county championship was formed in 1873. There had been an unofficial competition from 1864, with counties playing different numbers of games and one being declared the champions in the press. But for the first time in 1873, various stipulations were introduced including that no one could play for more than one county in a season and two years' local residency was required for anybody to change their allegiance. Nine teams took part and predictably WG's Gloucestershire won the 1873 competition and dominated it for the next half-dozen years. They were the Man U of the 1870s. But the county championship wasn't properly organized until 1890 and nothing is regarded as official before that date. Therefore none of Gloucestershire's pre-1890 titles count, and, remarkably, they have never won it since.

The Bearded Boundah

The concept of 'it's not cricket' was hardening in people's minds around this mid-Victorian era. As the industrialization of Britain gathered pace, so its inhabitants were searching for a code of behaviour, and cricket, with its laws and moral 'code', provided one. *Lillywhite's Cricketer's Guide* outlined the 'morality of appealing' saying, 'Do not ask the umpire unless you think the batsman is out: it is not cricket to keep asking the umpire questions.'

WG rode roughshod over it. He soon earnt a reputation for excessive appealing when he was bowling his round-arm leg breaks, and he exploited the laws – which he had a forensic knowledge of – to the full. He was prone to moving fielders behind the batsman's back as the bowler was delivering, and running out men he didn't like when they left their crease to repair the pitch. Neither was regarded as in the spirit of the game. Although when the batsman in question was an Australian there was a standing ovation. He is known to have indicated an imaginary flock of geese to a batsman who could see nothing. 'No? Pity. They've gone behind the trees,' Grace said before hissing at the bowler, 'Sharp, Fred, a quick one on leg stump!' knowing the batsman was still squinting from looking into the sun. He hoodwinked a young Notts batsman into lobbing the ball back to the bowler, then appealed to the umpire for 'handled ball' and got him out. He was, as the accomplished Caribbean historian C. L. R. James so aptly described him in *Beyond a Boundary*, the type of man 'whom you can trust with your life, your fortune and your sacred honour, but will peep at your cards when playing bridge at a penny a hundred'.

His gamesmanship when batting is legendary. Against Surrey he ran 3, and, after the return throw lodged in his shirt, ran 3 more, reluctant to give the ball back for fear of being given out 'handled ball'. An opponent who'd been given permission by Grace to leave a match early to get back to Yorkshire was ordered to drop a chance, WG hissing, 'Take the catch and you miss the train!' The fielder did as he was told. There are numerous tales of him in minor matches replacing the bails after he'd been bowled, declaring that the crowd had come to see him bat not some lackey bowl, and many umpires were in awe of him. Playing in a benefit match in the West Country in front of a large crowd, for instance, he had made 20 when he stepped out to a ball and missed it. The local wicketkeeper whipped off the bails and screamed 'Howzaaaat!' 'Not out,' retorted the umpire, 'and look 'ere young fellow, the crowd has come to see Doctor Grace bat and not any of your monkey tricks!'

The odd official stood up to him. Batting on a very blustery day, WG missed the ball which just flicked the bails off. Replacing them, the Doctor said, 'Windy day today, umpire!' Whereupon the umpire replied, 'Very windy indeed, Doctor. Mind it doesn't blow your cap off on the way back to the pavilion!'

The awe in which he was held is reflected in the story of the Australian pace bowler Ernest Jones, who, getting one to lift sharply at WG, sent the ball through his beard on the way to the keeper. C. B. Fry, about whom more later, was playing in the match and confirms that WG then exclaimed, in his strange falsetto, 'What? . . . What? . . . What!' and the bowler, reprimanded by his captain with a 'Steady, Jonah!', then stammered, 'Sorry, Doctor, she slipped . . .'

His performance at Leyton in 1896 encapsulates his attitude. He took seven wickets in one Essex innings, including a hotly disputed caught and bowled, the umpire undoubtedly having been swayed by Grace exclaiming 'Not bad for an old 'un!' when he 'caught' it. Having made 100 in Gloucester's first innings, he was then caught and bowled for 6 in their second, but refused to go. Finally, on the third morning he came up against a reinvigorated Charles Kortright, the fastest bowler of the time. The first ball pinned him on the pads in front of the stumps. Not out, said the umpire. Grace snicked the second to the keeper, but again the umpire voted in his favour. The third missile uprooted his middle and leg stumps. As Grace stood there, somewhat stunned, Kortright remarked, 'Surely you're not going, Doctor, there's one stump still standing.'

The stories are legion and one cannot always vouch for their veracity, but one thing is certain: he had the most incredible zest for cricket. Invariably he began his outdoor practice in the chilly frosts of March and was rarely injured or unavailable for any match, friendly or serious. His commitment was total, and his mantra simple: 'There is no such thing as a crisis in cricket,' he once said, 'only the next ball.'

In 1876, his *annus mirabilis*, he finished the season in a blur of run-making. On 11 and 12 August he made

344 against Kent at Canterbury (the first-ever triple hundred recorded in first-class cricket). He took a train to the West Country and on 14 August made 177 versus Notts. Two days later he travelled to Sheffield and made 318 not out against Yorkshire. That's 839 runs in three innings (one undefeated) while going up and down the country on rolling stock that makes a journey on Virgin trains seem like flying on a magic carpet. To cap it all he then made 400 not out against XXII of Grimsby, with all twenty-two players fielding and on a damp and sluggish outfield (although a timid umpire failed to give him out plumb lbw when on 6). The innings took 13½ hours. Afterwards he treated bystanders to his traditional party piece, swigging a bottle of champagne and then balancing the empty vessel on his head.

Amidst his colossal run-making, his bowling is often overlooked, but he was an ingenious wicket-taker. He bustled up to the wicket, ball held in both hands – often concealed under his great beard – his MCC cap dazzling the batsman. He would release a slow, round-arm leg break, often from round the wicket, aiming at leg stump, with legside-orientated field settings cannily adjusted for different batsmen. He subtly varied his pace and trajectory, maintained excellent control, and in both thinking and execution was like an embryonic Shane Warne, brilliant at using temptation and provocation to con batsmen out of their wickets. Often with the umpire's help. Grace frequently jumped across to the offside after releasing the ball. This was chiefly to seek catches from straight drives, but had the bonus of completely blocking the umpire's view, after which only the hardiest could resist his stampeding lbw appeal. He took 2,876 first-class wickets in his career (average 17.92), the tenth most in the history of the game. Ball in hand, he was a master kidologist.

With his gargantuan physique, and insatiable appetite, he continued to break records. He was the first to do the double of 1,000 runs and 100 wickets in a season. On his Test début on Australia's first visit to England in 1880, he made 152, bowled 28 overs in one innings and was not out at the end as the Aussies were humbled by 5 wickets. In a match for MCC in 1886 he scored a century and took all 10 wickets in one innings. He passed 1,000 runs in a season twenty-eight times.

When he notched his hundredth first-class hundred at the age of forty-seven everyone assumed that would be it. But he went on that year, 1895, to become the first man to pass 1,000 runs in a season *before the end of May*, added a further twenty-four hundreds in the next few years and was even still opening the batting for England aged fifty. As the legendary Indian-born batsman K. S. Ranjitsinhji put it, 'WG discovered batting: he turned its many narrow straight channels into one great winding river.' The small matter of 54,896 runs (and those 2,876 wickets) was the final product. Pretty useful for a bloke who, from childhood, had only had one lung (aged thirteen he had contracted serious pneumonia, which, he was informed, had cost the use of one lung).

Fuelled by a hearty lunch, which included religiously sinking a large Irish whiskey with Angostura bitters and soda, Grace's incredible stamina was only surpassed by his smelliness – one keeper said he had the dirtiest neck he had ever seen – and his extraordinary self-belief. He professed to prefer quick bowling – 'the faster they bowl, the better I like them' – and practically single-handedly he destroyed the intent of a new breed of fast bowler that had arrived since the legalizing of overarm; this in spite of the majority of pitches being more suitable for potato cultivation than batting. When told that a demon bowler he hadn't seen before 'mixes 'em up', he took careful stock of the new man before hitting him into the distance and loudly declaring to his partner, 'We'll mix 'em up for him, we'll mix 'em up!' as they ran between the wickets. Towards the end of his career, he was on 93 not out when he suddenly declared. Asked why, he replied that it had dawned on him that it was the one score between 0 and 100 he had never made.

Looking at some old Pathé film of him knocking up before a match, stepping back jerkily to poke the ball about like someone sweeping up leaves, you do wonder about the standard of his contemporaries' bowling. He looks ungainly and eccentric. But in his era no one else was even half as prolific, and he was fifty-four years old at the time the film was shot. Despite appearing rather comical with a little striped cap perched on top of his huge bearded frame, and a sur-prisingly high-pitched voice, he had a colossal presence. He was as instantly recognizable as Queen Vic herself, and became the first sportsman to be identified with a product, appearing in large full-colour adverts for Colman's Mustard.

William Gilbert Grace was Britain's first sporting hero and with his exceptional ability, outrageous personality and good-natured affiliation with the masses he appealed to a broad spectrum of the population, his fame elevating cricket above all other forms of entertainment. He was a sort of nineteenth-century David Beckham, though with more talent and less manners and without the tattoos or the *Hello!* wedding or the artificially enhanced wife. In fact, thinking about it, he wasn't much like David Beckham at all.

WG's career straddled, as he put it, the shift 'from open commons with rude tents as dressing rooms' to 'the vast enclosure and palatial pavilion', from 'the bumpy pitches to the smooth turf and billiard table wickets'. His success was unprecedented and he became a national treasure, though not amongst the establishment, who were less than enamoured of his sharp tactics and his shamateurism, and his generally disreputable appearance. It wasn't until his tenth Test that he was invited to captain England (captaincy was exclusively the domain of amateurs until Len Hutton became England's first professional captain in 1953) and he was generally shunned by the elite.

But if you can imagine a sportsman with the overpowering dominance of Tiger Woods, the outright effrontery of Kevin Pietersen and the nationwide popularity of Jamie Oliver, you get some idea of his extraordinary impact in what became known as cricket's Golden Age. Possessing the artful deviousness of the pre-Victorians and the ambitious sophistication of the industrial age, he bestrode two eras. He died in 1915, aged sixty-eight, of a heart attack after an air raid. War was suspended for a day, and it was symbolic that his passing coincided with England's loss of global influence. The large bronze statue of him in the Coronation Garden at Lord's looms over the Test match picnickers, gigantic, immoveable, inimitable but even that doesn't do him justice. He wasn't a man, he was a monolith.

FIVE

Demon Bowling

The last quarter of the nineteenth century was boom time. Well, for some anyway. Britain commandeered nearly a third of Africa, partly as a consequence of the discovery of gold near Johannesburg in 1886. The automobile, the telephone and the wireless were all invented – paving the way, some hundred years later, for a vital source of government revenue from drivers caught participating in radio phone-ins on their Nokias. Football, rugby and 'lawn' tennis were codified, and it was the one and only time that Britain led the world in these three sports.

Things were definitely looking up for the man in the street. Bank holidays were introduced, as were domestic toilets, manufactured by the redoubtable Thomas Crapper, usually built outside and often shared between houses. A massive outbreak of silly facial hair resulted in King Camp Gillette introducing the disposable razor. This was the great ancestor of the twenty-first century Mach III Turbo triple-blade – supposed to 'shave you closer than ever before' but which generally just cuts you deeper than ever before.

Cricket cantered ahead in harness. Nine counties took part in the embryonic County Championship, though Derbyshire were excluded for a time for being rubbish. Given that they have produced very few cricketers of note since and for most of their existence forced visiting players to change in a damp, unfumigated hovel at a draughty, converted racecourse, it's probably a shame it didn't stay that way. A proper points system was introduced in 1895 (by which time there were fourteen teams), though cricket's perennial lament that 'the game is not what it was' means this system has been reviewed more than thirty times. Since records were officially collated in the 1890s, Yorkshire have won the County Championship more often than anyone else (thirty titles), Surrey are next with eighteen, and Middlesex third with ten.

The first Test match was played in 1877. It came about during a tour of Australia led by James Lillywhite (nephew of the infamous round-arm bowler William who founded the famous sports store). Lillywhite's team was a fully professional XI, minus WG as well as other notable 'amateurs' left behind after ructions between the gents and the players on a previous tour. They hauled themselves around Australia and New Zealand for several weeks, playing local XVIIIs and XVs, before Lillywhite was talked into playing a Combined Victoria and New South Wales XI at the Melbourne Club.

The match, played at the Richmond Police Paddock (now the MCG) and staged over four days in March, was won by the Australians by 45 runs, though they were hugely indebted to Charles Bannerman, born in Kent, for his 165 in the first innings and Tom Kendall, also English, for his 7-55 in bowling out a semi-inebriated 'England' for 108 after a beery lunch. Although it was an English team's first defeat abroad, the match, enthusiastically attended, was hailed in *The Times* as a financial success. So that's all right then.

A return match was arranged for a fortnight later at the same venue, which this time the Englishmen won by four wickets, chasing 122 for victory. These two encounters are regarded as the first Test matches, so called because they were reckoned a proper and fair 'test' of the relative strength of the two sides, although the term wasn't in fact coined until some years later. Also those first two matches didn't feature England's best side. Their number one wicketkeeper, Ted Pooley, had been jailed in New Zealand for fighting a renowned gambler when he didn't settle a wager they'd had on a match in Christchurch.

Australia were invited to England the following year (1878). Lillywhite organized the itinerary. The Aussies made an inauspicious beginning, losing heavily to Notts, but then came an extraordinary performance against a strong MCC side containing WG at Lord's. The pitch was damp and MCC's first innings declined from 27-2 to 33 all out, in the face of devastating bowling from the remarkable Frederick Spofforth, known as 'The Demon' and, since he took 6 wickets for 4 runs, with good reason. A tall, lean figure, described as 'all arms, legs and nose', he was obviously fast, clean bowling three batsmen, though not *that* fast, as examination of the scorecard reveals two others were stumped. He was more a devilish bowler, mixing speed with cut and curve and a meticulous appreciation of batsmen's weaknesses.

After Australia had themselves been dismissed for 41 for a lead of 8, Spofforth's 4-16 in MCC's second innings – including WG bowled for nought – helped rout them for a pathetic 19 all out. This left Australia to make just 12 for victory, which they did for the loss of 1 wicket. The entire match lasted less than six hours. That's a wicket falling every eleven minutes. It was the original Kwik Cricket, and 'the Colonials were loudly cheered by the assembled multitude for their achievement' (*The Times*). It did not count as a 'Test' match.

'The Demon' habitually tormented England for a decade. In the next official 'Test', in January 1879 and again in Melbourne, he recorded the first Test hat-trick and took 13 wickets in the match to hustle England to a 10-wicket defeat. He took literally hundreds of wickets on England tours (an astonishing 216 in eleven-a-side matches on Australia's 1884 visit was his record) and was the first to make serious eye contact with his opponent. As a relative unknown, he once took the rise out of WG in the Melbourne nets, lobbing down a few friendly deliveries to him, then slipping him a surprise quick one which removed his off stump. 'Where did that come from? Who bowled that?' an inflamed Grace exclaimed. But Spofforth had slipped away into the crowd. His duels with Grace were described as 'like forked lightning threatening the great oak'.

'The Demon' was injured for the first Test in England at the Oval in September 1880 ('after some questionable bowling at Scarborough', *The Times* reports), and his absence was sorely felt. England, captained by the esteemed Lord Harris, constructed a formidable first-innings total of 420 around WG's flawless 152. Australia, having capitulated for 149 in their first innings, did well to force England to eventually bat again, but left them requiring only 57 and they won the fourth Test of all time by 5 wickets. At that point it was two Tests all between the countries.

By the time of the Oval Test of August 1882, it was England 2, Australia 4, draws 2, with all but one of those Tests played Down Under. It was then that Spofforth really earnt his moniker. The match was rain-affected, and the bowlers dominated, despite being hampered by saturated run-ups. Spofforth took 7 wickets in England's first innings, including WG bowled for 4, but his *tour de force* was in their second innings, when they sought just 85 for victory.

At 51-2, with WG 32 not out, an English win seemed assured. But Spofforth was riled. A couple of hours earlier, during Australia's second innings, the no.8, Sammy Jones, assuming the ball was 'dead' after completing a run, had left his crease to repair the pitch. Ever the opportunist, WG removed the bails with the ball in his hand and appealed. The umpire had no option but to give Jones out. A man in the crowd observed that 'Jones ought to thank the champion for teaching him something' but Spofforth was furious and stormed into the English dressing room between innings to call Grace a cheat. So began 125 years (and counting) of verbal spattery between the sides.

Now, switching to the pavilion end on the drying pitch, the Demon was unplayable. He had Ulyett caught behind, and Grace ladled a catch to mid-off. Cutting the ball back dramatically, Spofforth then bowled Lucas and Lyttelton and caught and bowled Steel. It was 75-8. Lyttelton described facing the Demon as like 'standing on the edge of the tomb'. England still needed 10 to win. One spectator had already died of a burst blood vessel during this gripping encounter and now another chewed through the handle of his umbrella. The nagging Harry Boyle finished England's innings off. Australia had won by 7 runs. Spofforth, who had taken 7-44 from 28 (four-ball) overs, giving him 14 wickets in the match, was chaired from the field by his triumphant team.

England's loss gave rise to a raft of scathing articles bemoaning England's lack of resolve. *Plus ça change*, eh? The most famous of these was penned by Reginald Shirley Brooks, a jobbing journalist on the *Sporting Times* who, after his usual liquid lunch, wrote a mock obituary on 2 September 1882:

In Affectionate Remembrance

of

ENGLISH CRICKET

WHICH DIED AT THE OVAL

on

29th August 1882.

Deeply lamented by a large circle of sorrowing friends and acquaintances.

RIP

N.B. – The body will be cremated and the ashes taken to Australia.

Thus was born the concept of the Ashes. It's hard to think of a more powerful or durable sporting emblem, or, especially given the author's predeliction for drinking on the job, one created so unconsciously.

A Parting Gift

The origin of the famous Ashes urn and its contents is so clouded in mystery even Inspector Morse might struggle to unravel it. The problem, of course, is that the urn itself is sealed and has never been opened since the day it was presented to the England captain, the Hon. Ivo Bligh, at the Victorian home of a wealthy Australian after a friendly match in December 1882.

Bligh, an Etonian and a Cambridge blue who played for Kent, was the archetypal amateur captain, batting at no.9 and not bowling. Essentially he was a specialist fielder. He was obviously a confident chap though, and had started the ball rolling on arrival in Australia, declaring jovially at a welcome dinner that 'we have come to beard the kangaroo in his den and try to recover those ashes.' Partly in jest, a group of society ladies – one of whom, Florence Murphy, he later married – presented him with a small gift – a miniature terracotta urn containing some ashes after Bligh's team had won the country house match against Sir William

Clarke's XI at Rupertswood on Christmas Eve. It was a glorified eggcup with a lid.

Initially the ashes inside were thought to be those of the match ball, which had been so savagely assaulted the leather casing had been knocked off. Later it was conceded that they were actually of one of the bails that had been burnt after the match. But quite recently Bligh's daughter in law, the Dowager Countess of Darnley, confused the picture by saying the ashes were of a veil Florence Murphy used to wear. Best, it seems, to draw a veil over the whole issue.

What does seem likely is that the simple trophy assumed much greater importance when Bligh's team subsequently beat the Australians at Melbourne and Sydney the following month to take the three-match Test series 2–1. The urn was a token of that success. The teams played a further one-off Test as an afterthought, with, as an experiment, a separate pitch being used for each of the four innings. Australia won that match, but Bligh's team sailed back to England with their spoils, on which was inscribed (with apologies to the Poet Laureate):

> When Ivo goes back with the urn, the urn;
> Studds, Steel, Read and Tylecote return, return;
> The Welkin will ring loud,
> The great crowd will feel proud,
> Seeing Barlow and Bates with the urn, the urn;
> And the rest coming home with the urn.

There was no open-top bus celebration or the

handing out of OBEs when the victorious team returned, nor an invitation to tea with the prime minister (Gladstone) during which the leading all-rounder urinated in his flower bed. Everything was a bit more restrained in those days. Indeed, far from the ashes being put on public display so that everyone could pay homage, Bligh squirrelled them home, and they remained on his Kent mantelpiece until presented by his widow to the MCC in 1927. They are on permanent display in the Lord's museum – looking rather small and insignificant given all the fuss – and have only ever been let out once for a visit to Australia (when they had their own business class airline seat) before the 2006 series. Those who turned up for the 'Little Urn tour' expecting an appearance by the surviving half of the Morecambe and Wise comedy duo were sorely disappointed.

The pursuit of the Ashes adds an absorbing extra dimension to contests between England and Australia, because the holders must be actually defeated in a Test series for them to 'change' hands (a replica urn is presented to the victorious captain). Being in possession of the Ashes is a bit like the security of scoring an away goal in the Champions League. It is why the 2005 Ashes tussle was so tantalizing, because, after twenty-four days of knuckle-chewing tension, Australia, the holders, only had to sneak a win on the last day of the final Test to level the series and therefore keep the blasted eggcup for another eighteen months. They didn't, of course. So ensued the bus tour, the OBEs and the pissing in Blair's garden.

Amateur Dramatics

England v Australia contests, then as now, elevated English cricket from the shambles of the County Championship. Games in big cities were reasonably well attended, but the competition itself had vague qualification criteria and rules. There was no guidance about what constituted a county team, nor about how many matches each had to play. It was left to the press to decide which team were the champions, usually based on fewest defeats rather than most wins. On that basis, the fewer games you played the better, as Notts (P12 W4 L1) calculated when they were declared the winners ahead of Yorkshire (P16 W9 L2) in 1883.

This was consistent with the Victorian ethos of the time, which elevated participation above success. It is where the cloying adage 'It's not the winning but the taking part' emanated from, shaping the country into a nation of good losers, to the delight of the tabloid press, who positively revel in sporting disaster. The public lap it up, intimating that they sadistically enjoy other people's misfortunes too; the more famous the better. Why else would programmes featuring celebrities eating witchetty grubs while imprisoned in an artifical jungle get ten million viewers? The truly driven British sportsmen, of whom W. G. Grace was probably the first and Steve Redgrave and Chris Hoy the most recent, are in a tiny minority. Where they got their win-at-all-costs mentality from is still a state secret.

In fact the Victorians saw sport more as a preparation for the much more grown-up business of war and expansion. Experiencing sporting failure was regarded as character-building (the same as eating witchetty grubs). 'Playing the game', abiding by the laws, obeying officials – in other words, not stepping out of line – were of paramount importance. It made the English excellent at square-bashing and lousy at winning big games.

Cricket embodied this virtuous approach – and largely still does. In modern sport, the behaviour of cricketers – clapping opponents' achievements, respecting officials and the laws – is still second to none. Even Geoffrey Boycott – Mr Verbose himself – never answered back to an umpire. There is a story of him staring in disbelief at the official's raised finger giving him out lbw, after which he muttered, 'What happened to your guide dog, ump?' to which the umpire retorted, 'I got rid of it for yapping, same as I'm doing to you, now piss off!' – but it is apocryphal.

Sir Henry Newbolt's famous verse 'Vitaï Lampada', the theme of which, 'Play up and play the game', was muttered by committee types when some West Indian 'boundah' bowled a succession of bouncers at some unsuspecting Englishman, hails from this period. It tells the story of how a future soldier learnt stoicism from cricket matches at Clifton College:

> There's a breathless hush in the Close to-night –
> Ten to make and the match to win –
> A bumping pitch and a blinding light,
> An hour to play, and the last man in.
> And it's not for the sake of a ribboned coat,

Or the selfish hope of a season's fame,
But his Captain's hand on his shoulder smote
'Play up! Play up! And play the game!'

The sand of the desert is sodden red –
Red with the wreck of the square that broke –
The Gatling's jammed and the colonel dead,
And the regiment blind with dust and smoke.
The river of death has brimmed its banks,
And England's far, and Honour a name,
But the voice of a schoolboy rallies the ranks,
'Play up! Play up! And play the game!'

This is the word that year by year
While in her place the school is set
Every one of her sons must hear,
And none that hears it dare forget.
This they all with a joyful mind
Bear through life like a torch in flame,
And falling fling to the host behind –
'Play up! Play up! And play the game!'

It's a powerful bit of rhetoric. Bloody infuriating that it doesn't tell you if they got those ten to win though.

In the cricket of the 1880s, hard-nosed attitudes and sharp tactics were derided as 'professional'. The amateurs would not stoop to such depths – in theory anyway. That was the main reason both county and England Test captaincies were exclusively the preserve of amateurs. The autocratic Lord Hawke, captain of Yorkshire and England, once declared, 'Pray God no professional may captain England.' They were regarded as a sort of servant class, and not thought capable of leadership or making decisions or upholding the spirit of 'fair play'. The amateurs were always addressed as 'Sir' or 'Mr' by the professionals, who could be punished if they forgot. The pros were addressed solely by their surnames. It is a legacy of public school, and lasts to the present day. During a match for Middlesex some years ago, for instance, I was standing next to a Bentley parked by the boundary. It was owned – and occupied – by the *éminence grise* Gubby Allen, the Etonian who captained England in the 1930s and was later chairman of selectors. There was a small whirring noise and the driver's window slid down. 'Hughes! Too many no balls!!' the voice said, before the window purred closed again.

Usually the amateurs had different dressing rooms from the professionals, and often came out of different gates. The Lancashire opening pair of Hornby (amateur) and Barlow generally met in the middle of the pitch. This class rift continued right through the first half of the twentieth century. At the Oval it was truly *Upstairs, Downstairs*. Alec Bedser, the Surrey and England wicket-taking machine, recounts that even in the 1950s you only entered the amateurs' room if you were specially invited. 'We won the County Championship seven years in a row,' he said, 'and not once did we ever have a team meeting.' He winces now when he sees the ubiquitous team huddle interrupting play, usually to ascertain whose turn it is to nip off for a pee.

The two camps even had different dress codes. The

amateurs emerged clad in brightly coloured blazers, ties and boaters. Meanwhile the professionals, who had once taken the field in harlequin stripes and spots, had a more regimented uniform of cream or white shirts and pressed flannels, with the only splash of colour on the county cap. It was in this period that cricket whites really came into being, leading to a sudden increase in marital problems ('If you just want a wife to scrub out your grass stains you better marry someone else!') until the invention of Persil in 1907.

The pros were expected to do menial tasks too, like whiten the pads and boots of the amateurs and help with the preparation of the pitch. Again these distinctions lingered. Sitting down to lunch at a Middlesex 2nd XI match in 1980, I was summoned on to the field to help with the covers during a short, sharp rain shower. When I got back to the pavilion I found a former amateur player turned committee man had eaten his lunch and was now polishing off mine.

Maintaining these social divisions suited the amateurs, since they could protect their status in the game. They didn't want to see cricket turning into a meritocracy. 'I mean dammit, Perkins, letting the professionals run the game would be allowing the country to go to the dogs!' Not only was this snobbery with bells on, but the whole distinction was utterly hypocritical. The definition of an amateur was someone who didn't make a profit from the game. But as with W. G. Grace, their expenses for first-class hotels and travel far exceeded match fees paid out to the professionals. It was a point England's best professional batsman, Arthur

Shrewsbury, raised during England's tour of Australia in 1887–8. Not surprisingly, it fell on deaf ears.

Striding into this divided world came the Hon. George Robert Canning, better known in cricket circles as Lord Harris. Canning, the son of the 3rd Baron, was born into privilege. His grandfather was a Lieutenant General in the battle of Waterloo, and his father was governor of Trinidad and later Madras. Born in Trinidad in 1851, Harris spent his childhood in India, learnt the game at Eton and Oxford, and is regarded by many as the most influential cricket administrator who ever lived. Looking the spit of Michael Gambon in *Gosford Park*, his portrait stares down from the walls of the MCC committee room at Lord's, where he watched his first match aged eleven, played regularly for Gents v Players, chaired a thousand meetings, and later became president and honorary treasurer.

Certainly Harris's commitment to cricket cannot be questioned, even if he didn't always get his own way. He had already had a significant impact as batsman and leader in his twenties, reviving Kent's fortunes and assembling and captaining the England side in that first home Test in 1878. In the mid-1880s his administrative juices began to flow, first to insist on stricter interpretation of the throwing law. His opinion and influence managed to get a number of chuckers marginalized. Michael Parkinson, a prime campaigner seeking the banning of the Sri Lankan spinner he referred to as 'Muchachuckalot', undoubtedly wishes Harris had been born a century later.

A stickler for playing the game the right way, he

insisted that cricket's guidelines should be referred to as laws not rules. 'Rules are made to be broken,' he argued, 'laws are made to be kept.' He was keen to popularize cricket – by changing the hours of play, or adapting the lbw law to stop batsmen blocking for hours, though neither of his initiatives was adopted – and he helped establish the (tax-free) benefit system. The professionals were generally lowly paid and exploited. Benefits guaranteed them a fund towards the end of their careers, though it also effectively tied them to their county because it was the county that had the power to grant them.

Harris cobbled together the first County Cricket Council – the ancient ancestor of the ECB – to govern the game. One of the body's first actions was – yes, you've guessed it – to set up a working party to assess the validity of a County Championship with three divisions, promotion and relegation. It was all a bit too radical, and after the inevitable round of monthly meet-ings, each one largely ratifying the minutes of the previous one while drinking house claret, the working party announced their recommendations, which were promptly rubbished, as usual. About 110 years later the same proposal was put through the same process, with the same result. I suppose we should have realized by now that the phrase 'working party' actually means 'successful piss-up'.

A big opportunity was missed here. With football still struggling to make an impact, cricket could have secured itself the beginnings of a dynamic infra-structure, creating a ladder involving everyone from the biggest county to the smallest town. But oh no, cricket is not given to taking progressive, all-embracing steps like that. Instead cricket remained wedded to the arbitrary anachronism of the county unit, and it still is. In 1890 the existing eight first-class counties (Gloucestershire, Notts, Surrey, Middlesex, Kent, Sussex, Lancashire and Yorkshire) maintained their cartel, the CCC was abolished and Harris buggered off to India to become governor of Bombay.

He spent five years there, after which Indian cricket really began to take off, and he was christened in some circles 'the Father of Indian cricket'. Closer analysis suggests he was nothing of the sort. He did invite some prestigious touring teams from England who impressed the Indians with their classic skills, but he didn't utilize his power to stop polo from ruining an important municipal cricket park, even after much pleading from the cricket fraternity, and he seemed reluctant to get involved in matches with the native population. Cricket, anyway, preceded him in India by over a hundred years. His drinks bill at Government House – including annual consumption of 2,414 bottles of champagne, 1,323 of claret and 545 of whisky – reads like the expense account of the disgraced peer Conrad Black – and perhaps gives more of a clue to how he spent his time. It is therefore appropriate that the place named after him at Lord's – the Harris Garden – is converted to a champagne bar during international matches.

Death and the Maiden

Harris arrived back home in 1894. What sort of England did he find? Certainly one still in thrall to W. G. Grace, whose testimonial the following year raised £8,500 (the average national annual wage at the time was £200). London was teeming with businessmen and horse-drawn cabs and had the first underground railway – known as the 'twopenny tube' for its flat fares – and suburban development along the tentacles of the Underground was displacing large herds of cows like the 800 that were grazing in Willesden.

Healthcare had improved vastly, but still life expectancy for the burgeoning working classes was only forty-five. Organized sport at least gave them something to get their teeth into – if they'd had any. Judging from old Pathé newsreel footage of the gap-mouthed masses, the best business to have been in was soup manufacture.

Football, galvanized by the creation of a professional league in 1888, had taken off. The Oval had staged the first FA Cup final in 1872, attended by about 2,000 spectators. Twenty years later, when 32,810 jammed the arena, the event had outgrown its Kennington origins. Many football teams originated out of cricket clubs (Spurs, Wolves, Blackburn, Manchester City, Ipswich, Middlesbrough and Newcastle to name but a few, also the two 'counties', Notts and Derby) and by the 1895 season two million people were being lured through the turnstiles.

County cricket, partly inspired by the about-turn of England's fortunes – trouncing the Aussies fourteen times between 1885 and 1894 – was also flourishing. Crowds of 10,000-plus were the norm, and up to 30,000 for popular fixtures such as Notts v Surrey. (This was especially surprising since Notts' leading bowler was the niggardly Alfred Shaw, who, in his entire career, bowled more overs than he conceded runs. Two thirds of his overs were maidens. Not a particularly demanding public, were they? I suppose the chance to escape the humdrum of life and stare at white figures strolling about on a green sward while discussing your lumbago with mates was as attractive then as it is now.) So finally the administrators got their act together, and the County Championship, which had lurched along spluttering for nearly two decades, finally found some momentum.

It is typical of cricket's procrastinating inclinations that arguments still continue about the first official year of the championship. Proper records were kept from 1890, but only the original eight teams contested that competition. With the addition of Somerset, Essex, Leicestershire, Hampshire, Warwickshire and Derbyshire, that had swelled to fourteen by 1895, when there was also the first approved points system. This was 1 point for a win, and 1 point deducted for a defeat. Ill-conceived from the start, as logic decreed that if you couldn't win you sure as hell made sure you didn't lose, it promoted a sequence of boring draws. It also led to the first realization that, after the three certainties in life – death, taxes and nurses – there was a fourth: people will forever proclaim that cricket needs something to 'spice it up'.

Such a lament has never deterred spectators from watching the game, however, almost as if its *raison d'être* is to give people something to moan about. Enduring a mind-numbingly interminable draw, like the Lord's Test of 2008, when England managed to take only 3 South African wickets in two and a bit days on a pitch as flat as Nasser Hussain's vowels, is a sort of rite of passage. After that, anything – ironing, clipping your toenails, reading a Salman Rushdie novel – is a blessed relief.

The deadlock between teams wasn't helped by the advent of the roller and the lawn mower, ensuring better preparation of pitches. The potholed, undulating dung heaps of cricket's early history had all but disappeared. At Lord's, the MCC dispensed with the grazing sheep and bought the field at the back of the ground – known as Henderson's Nursery and famous for producing the best pineapples in England – and converted it into a practice area, retaining the Nursery name.

The batting-friendlier conditions paved the way for some astronomical scoring. In July 1895, Archie MacLaren, an old Harrovian, eclipsed W. G. Grace's highest first-class score of 344, making 424 for Lancashire against Somerset. Lancashire's eventual total of 801 all out had only been exceeded twice, once by the Aussies (843) against Oxford and Cambridge Past and Present in 1893, and once by the Non-Smokers (803) against the Smokers in 1887. *The Times* does not report what the Smokers coughed up in reply. A lot of phlegm most probably. A year later, in May 1896, Yorkshire trumped them all with 887 against Warwicks.

Surrey were again the superior team, spearheaded by

the extraordinary George Lohmann, a master of nip and cut, and also a brilliant slip fielder. Not quick but phenomenally accurate with subtle variations of pace, he sliced batting orders apart, once taking 8 wickets for 7 runs for an England team against South Africa (whose early matches – on matting pitches – were retrospectively given Test status). Lohmann is still the proud possessor of the best strike-rate in Test history. He took a wicket every 34 balls, a rate of which modern assassins like Glenn McGrath (52 balls per wicket) and Wasim Akram (55) can only dream. It took it out of him though. He died of tuberculosis aged thirty-six.

Lohmann apart, batsmen dominated. Prominent among them, apart from WG and MacLaren, was Arthur Shrewsbury, who, by coincidence, had made a double century in that colossal Non-Smokers total. Shrewsbury, a small man, prematurely bald, was a prolific run-maker who was as obstinate with the bat as he was in seeking proper renumeration for the pros (see pages 103–4). Accumulating runs with a solid, resourceful method, he scored runs by the bucketload for Notts and England, often saying to the Trent Bridge gateman in the morning, 'Bring me a cup of tea at four o'clock' and frequently being still at the wicket at that point to receive it (the tea interval was introduced in 1892).

He captained England in seven Tests, winning five, and his 164 on a dodgy Lord's track to defeat the Australians in 1886 ranks as one of the great Test match innings. WG rated him higher than any man alive. But Shrewsbury's prodigious talent concealed a dark side. A confirmed bachelor, he was embarrassed about his baldness and was never without headgear, even in bed. In this, as in his batting style, there are strong parallels with Geoff Boycott (though Boycs doesn't actually wear his personalized titfers to bed), and Shrewsbury was also something of a social misfit, making a beeline for his personal lodgings (a Nottingham hotel) from wherever he was playing, regardless of the distance.

There are shades of Marcus Trescothick in the way he worried about life and gradually withdrew from everything. Trescothick's revealing autobiography seemed to act as therapy. Shrewsbury didn't have that outlet. His stress culminated in kidney pain and he was bowled for a duck in the final match of 1902 during what was otherwise a good season. Somehow in the subsequent months he convinced himself he would never be able to play again. In May 1903 he bought a revolver and a few days later shot himself in his bedroom. He was forty-six. It was the original definition of a dead bat. Nottinghamshire's match with Sussex was abandoned when news of his death filtered through.

Some years later Shrewsbury's England opening partner Andrew Stoddart killed himself in similar fashion, as did the dashing Middlesex all-rounder of the time, Albert Trott, a Botham-type character famous for being the only man to hit a six that actually bounced *over* the pavilion at Lord's (for MCC v Australia in 1899). It was a feat that had extra piquancy for Trott since he was an Australian who had emigrated to England in a fit of pique because he wasn't picked for their Test team.

If this all sounds pretty macabre, they are just three of

an astonishing twenty Test cricketers who have taken their own life. Newspaper reporters often describe a batsman's dismissal to a wild slog as 'committing suicide', but this is no laughing matter. Real suicide is so frequent in cricket that the cricket historian David Frith has written two books about it (*Silence of the Heart* and *By His Own Hand*). Through his research he has unearthed more than 150 cases of cricketers doing themselves in, some English, some foreign, some unknown, some famous, such as the ebullient Yorkshire and England wicketkeeper David 'Bluey' Bairstow, who hanged himself at home in 1998. He was also forty-six.

This is not a scenario consistent with other sports, whose suicide rates are negligible. (Apart from amongst England football fans. Well, the desire is frequently there, anyway.) So is it cricket's all-encompassing, character-scrutinizing, often brutal nature that pushes some over the edge, or is it just that the game attracts individuals of a particularly sensitive disposition?

It's probably a bit of both. There are a considerable amount of deathly metaphors in cricket – not only 'dead bat' and 'dead ball', but also 'death rattle' (the stumps being hit) and 'bowling at the death' (at the end of the innings), and batsmen, when reprieved with a dropped catch, are said to have been given a 'life'. There is nothing quite so terminal in sport as being out in cricket – your first mistake could be your last – consigning the victim to the pavilion for eternity. Well, until the next innings anyway.

So cricketers should be attuned to the prospect of finality. The fate of a batsman being out in a match is, however, only temporary, and in many ways preferable to a bowler being 'murdered' by a Viv Richards or a Kevin Pietersen, which is just prolonged humiliation. But being dismissed from the game for good (i.e. dropped or sacked) has a permanence that some have found impossible to overcome. Many of the suicides – all the above, for instance – occurred when the individual had been cast out of the family, rejected from cricket's bosom. It's a lonely, helpless feeling that I can vividly recall when I was ejected from Middlesex in my early thirties. They couch it in the politest possible terms, saying you've been 'released', as if they're doing you a favour. In reality, having given your all to this endlessly fluctuating, captivating, frustrating game for nearly two decades, you suddenly feel spent and worthless, like an old washing machine thrown on the tip. Cricket sucks the spirit out of you. It isn't a sport, it's an addiction. Denied it, you need serious rehab. Tragically, a few didn't sign up fast enough.

SIX

Hypocrites United

The period between 1895 and 1914 is referred to as cricket's Golden Age. It alludes to a time when the game not only settled down into something stable and coherent, allowing a throng of stylish batsmen to express themselves, but also spread outwards along the tentacles of the Empire. Or maybe it was so called because Great Britain won gold in cricket at the 1900 Olympic Games. Staged in Paris, the Games included a cricket tournament supposed to be contested between four countries. Belgium and Holland withdrew, leaving a GB team that was actually Devon and Somerset Wanderers CC to fight it out with a French one largely made up of staff from the British Embassy in Paris. 'France', set 185 to win in the second innings, were routed for 26, giving 'Britain' victory and the gold medal. Cricket has never been part of the Olympics since, and after that apology of a competition you can see why.

This was undoubtedly an age of superlative batting,

notably by Ranjitsinhji, Fry, Jessop, the Australian Trumper and the charismatic Woolley. There's also my favourite, A. E. J. Collins, whose phenomenal 628 not out in a house match at Clifton College in 1899 is imprinted on every cricket anorak's mind as the highest individual score ever made. (No, sorry, Tony, the 853 you made in the back garden against your four-year-old son doesn't count. You were caught off the trellis on 574 anyway.) The scorecard of Collins's epic innings – which was spread over four afternoons – is still on the wall inside the Bristol pavilion. The scoring shots, written rather illegibly in pencil, obliterate the page. It's a wonder anyone was able to keep count. (Collins must have used up all his luck in that innings. He was killed in World War 1.)

It was certainly a run-laden period. But golden? Well, as with any sweeping generalization of an era, there were blots and complications. They began when the 24-year-old Prince Kumar Shri Ranjitsinhji, who was born and schooled in India but had been making piles of runs for Cambridge University and Sussex, was blocked from playing for England by our old friend Lord Harris, now president of the MCC.

Ranji learnt to bat at the Rajkumar College, Rajkot, then at Harrow School, but having gone up to Jesus College, Cambridge, in 1891 he was prevented from trialling for the university side because of his colour. Instead he filled his boots on Parker's Piece, the sprawl of communal cricket pitches in the city, once scoring three centuries in separate matches on the same day. He finally got into the team for the Varsity match in

1893 and went on to play for Sussex, with prodigious success. The groundswell of opinion clamoured for his inclusion in the England side to play Australia in the first Test at Lord's in 1896. But England selection at that point had always been at the whim of the individual ground authority, and on behalf of MCC Harris decreed that only 'native-born' players be chosen. He was conveniently forgetting that he himself had been born in Trinidad, but a prerequisite of people in power is that they never look in the mirror.

The Lancashire committee, who historically despised Harris for sidelining one of their bowlers for a dodgy action, took great delight in calling up Ranji for the second Test at Old Trafford, and seeing him make 62 and 154 not out. It remains one of the great Test débuts. After this, England Test teams were always selected by a specially appointed panel.

Ranji exhibited a style of batting new to English eyes. Black hair slicked down, silk shirt sleeves tightly buttoned to his wrist, he exuded feline stealth at the wicket, stealing runs with deft leg glances or wristy late cuts, angling balls in directions they'd never been before. 'His bat was a scimitar,' wrote the cricket historian H. S. Altham, and his great friend C. B. Fry said, 'he moves as if he has no bones.'

Deflecting the Australian fast bowlers dextrously off his hip, he eased them about for 175 in the first Test at Sydney in 1897 and reeled off centuries for Sussex, becoming the first man to pass 3,000 runs in a season in 1900. The next year he made his highest score, 285 not out against Somerset at Taunton, despite having been up the entire night, fishing. That's the way to live, eh?

He captained Sussex for five years, continued to break records and cut a dash, and still turned out for them after the First World War, despite returning to India in 1907 to inherit the title of Maharajah Jam Sahib of Nawanagar (the main qualification being an ability to pronounce it). Having learnt about his amazing feats at Hove, which included two centuries in a day against Yorkshire, I now understand why Sussex officials were so protective of a dilapidated wicker armchair I attempted to sit in as a guest in the committee room. It was the day Sussex had finished bottom of the championship in 1990.

'Sign of the times, I suppose,' I said, indicating that the seat's ropy condition symbolized the state of Sussex cricket.

'You leave that be,' the official said. 'It's Ranji's and it'll still be here a long time after you've been gone and forgotten.'

Ranjitsinhji wore a cravat, spoke with a posh public school accent and regarded himself as an English gentleman. He left a considerable legacy. Not only did he create a new art form with the bat, but he compiled a definitive work on the game, *The Jubilee Book of Cricket*, dedicated to Queen Victoria after sixty years on the throne. Essentially it was a modern textbook on cricket, covering all disciplines and containing rich appreciation of the greats of the game, though it barely mentioned Indian cricket. 'W. G. Grace,' he wrote modestly, 'is the maker of modern batting. He turned the old one-stringed instrument into a many-chorded lyre.'

Queen Victoria, of course, read it from cover to cover.

Even more significantly, Ranji's return to India in the 1900s was the catalyst for cricket to properly flourish there. His exploits in England had stimulated huge interest, particularly amongst the upper echelons of Indian society, and numerous princes and maharajahs fostered cricket in their states, sponsored teams and brought in English professionals to coach. To them, possession of a cricket team, with all its upstanding British connotations, was as much a status symbol then as Western oligarchs owning premiership football teams is now. Tours were arranged and a campaign begun to seek Test status. Ranji himself hardly played in India, but a new competition contested by the five major Indian zones was named after him. The Ranji Trophy became the bedrock of Indian cricket and, in spite of the precocious child that is the new Indian Premier League, still remains so.

Superman

Cricket has unearthed a multitude of strange characters, from the loners like Shrewsbury and Boycott to the extroverts like Beauclerk and Botham. Gilbert Jessop was certainly the latter. The son of a clergyman, he made his début for Gloucestershire as a fast bowler, and came in for his first bat with the bowler on a hat-trick. There was no pussyfooting about here though. Nervelessly, he hammered the hat-trick ball to the boundary, and hit another four in the same over.

This set the tone for two decades of Botham-like assaults. Strong and compact, Jessop wielded a railway-sleeper of a bat and would gaily waltz down the wicket to flay the fastest bowlers to all parts. 'The Croucher', as he was known for his wide, hunched stance, blitzed his way to two of the fastest centuries in cricket history, one against Yorkshire at Harrogate taking only forty minutes (only feasible in those days of 20-plus overs an hour) and including six blows out of the ground. If his twelve additional shots clearing the boundary had counted as six (rather than four as was the rule in those days) it would have been even faster.

Described as 'a human catapult who wrecks the roofs of distant towns when set in his assault', he is most famous for the dramatic about-turn of the 1902 Test match against Australia at the Oval. England, chasing 263 to win, were 48-5 when Jessop came to the crease. Undaunted by the situation, he blazed the bowling over or through the legside, and in partnership with some stoic Yorkshiremen, got England to within sniffing distance of their target. Every boundary was greeted with a confetti of straw-boaters being flung into the air. When Jessop was caught on the boundary he had scored 104 in seventy-seven minutes, still the fastest century in Ashes history, and England squeezed home by one wicket. Appropriately that Test is always known as 'Jessop's match', and although England had already lost the Ashes for the fourth consecutive time, it revived their spirit – just as Botham himself did eighty years later – and the urn was soon regained.

Not content with big-hitting records, Jessop also

played rugby for Gloucester and football for the Casuals and was handy at golf. He probably downed a pint of stout in 3.6 seconds too. He didn't walk the trail of Hannibal's elephants through the Alps though and wasn't banned for smoking dope. You see, in the whole rich history of cricket, one personality stands head and shoulders above the rest, certainly in terms of range of talent and exploit.

No, it's not Ian Terence Botham, but Charles Burgess Fry. It would be a lot easier to tell you what he didn't do. He didn't invent the domestic gas stove or the oven-ready chip. He did just about everything else. Born with unimaginable gifts in head and body, he was beyond the realms of even *Boy's Own* fantasy. Educated at Repton, he won a Classics scholarship to Oxford, scored runs in torrents for Sussex and England, including ninety-four hundreds, played football for Southampton and England, rugby for Blackheath and the Barbarians, broke the world record for the long jump with a leap of 7.17 metres, was outstanding at boxing, golf and tennis, and swam the Channel in a mind-blowing seven hours. Actually he didn't, but clearly he could have done if he'd wanted to. Or walked across it, for that matter. Seeking an alternative sporting challenge in his early seventies, he announced to a friend that he was thinking of getting into horse racing. 'What as,' asked the friend, 'trainer, jockey or horse?'

Quite apart from his athletic prowess, he was also a prolific writer, compiling and editing *Fry's Magazine* and producing a novel and several other books, including co-authoring Ranji's *Jubilee Book of Cricket*; served on the

League of Nations; and stood as a Liberal candidate for Parliament. Just reading the list of his achievements brings on premature exhaustion.

As a batsman Fry was an innovator. With a rebellious streak he confounded current custom to play forward and to the offside, and stood back and cuffed the ball through mid-wicket (it had been the norm, if a batsman hit the ball in an unconventional direction, to apologize to the bowler). His and Ranji's prowess influenced a new batting method to 'play back or drive'. Although unorthodox, he still managed to make batting look stylish, and was, according to the great cricket writer Neville Cardus, 'the handsomest sight seen on a cricket field by anybody'. A large white sun hat added to the cavalier effect.

The summer of 1901 was the apex of Fry's career. He scored centuries in six successive innings, a feat which had never been achieved before and has only been equalled in first-class cricket twice since, by Don Bradman and Mike Procter. Neither of them, however, went on to appear in the FA Cup final a few months later (though Fry's Southampton lost to Sheffield United in the replay).

The charismatic batting of Fry and Ranji has come to embody the Golden Age. It had elegance and élan and *joie de vivre*. It was probably a bit pretentious. It also concealed Fry's dark side. Possessing a superiority complex – and who can blame him? – he was actually prone to depression, and perhaps because he wasn't good at personal relations dressed more and more quirkily. What is it about Frys and eccentricity? (During the Ashes of 2005, Stephen Fry requested a defibrillator to be provided at his seat in case the excitement got too much.) Later C. B. Fry also developed a fascination with the Nazis and once spent an hour chatting to Hitler, trying, and failing, to persuade him to form a cricket team. He spent so long explaining the lbw law it drove Germany into invading Poland. The Second World War was all C. B. Fry's fault!

Plum in Front

All in all, the turn of the century was an eventful period. Three weeks into it Queen Victoria died, aged eighty-one (probably of boredom from reading Ranji's book), the whole nation was in mourning after her sixty-three years' sitting on the throne (she must have had terrible constipation), and a BBC newscaster announcing her passing was vilified for not changing his paisley tie for a black one. He would have needed it regularly too, because the ongoing Boer War (1899–1902) in South Africa cost the British (and Empire) army 20,000 lives. It was, in every way, a very expensive defeat.

In early 1900 the Labour Party came into being, to flex the growing muscle of the unions, women were becoming liberated from household routine to meet at Starbucks for a skinny latte, and the *Daily Telegraph* printed an editorial declaring that the British, far from being the 'athletic country' so proclaimed, had developed instead into a 'raucous, grasping multitude, good enough at pushing through the turnstiles or bellowing at a player, but who have no notion of taking any decent exercise for themselves at any time'. The advent of the couch potato was fast approaching.

On the cricketing front, the West Indies had now joined Australia and South Africa on the touring map. The initial harmony between white and black players in South Africa was weakening as racial discrimination took hold – a talented black fast bowler, Krom Hendricks, was excluded from the squad for a first tour of England in 1894, and Ranji was omitted from an England tour there, at the request of white South Africans.

But in the West Indies the rudimentary inter-island tournament featured a number of black players – usually fast bowlers. Three English amateur sides visited the Caribbean before 1900, assembled by Lord Harris and his indomitable sidekick, Lord Hawke of Yorkshire. Their tour parties were not supported by perspiring hordes of Midlanders dressed in Homer Simpson T-shirts and garish shorts, but Thompson Holidays have a lot to thank them for.

Hawke's team included Pelham 'Plum' Warner, the Middlesex and England batsman, after whom the Warner Stand at Lord's is named. Like Lord Harris, Warner was the son of a diplomat and also born in the Caribbean. He recognized the importance of the 'natives' in the opposition, condemned some islands for their whites-only selection policies and declared that any West Indies side visiting England would need at least four or five black players to challenge the county teams.

A tour was arranged in 1900, and Warner, also a part-time journalist, wrote:

The fielding will certainly be of high class. The black men will, I fear, suffer from the weather if the summer turns out cold and damp, as their strength lies in the fact that their muscles are extremely loose. Woods [a paceman who preferred bowling in bare feet] takes only two steps and bowls as fast as Mold [a Lancashire fast bowler with a suspect action]! Englishmen will be very much struck with the throwing powers of these black men, nearly all of them being able to throw well over a hundred yards.

His warnings proved prescient, because the tourists were a handful, beating Surrey by an innings.

A slight, nimble batsman, Warner was a cricketing evangelist, spreading the game's gospel as he toured the world. He contributed to the *Sportsman*, and wrote a book, *Cricket in Many Climes*, in which he proclaimed cricket's ability to forge international relations or soothe disputes: 'its friendly intercourse does much to strengthen the amity of nations, and to make for international understanding.' They could have done with him to get a game going on the banks of Natal's Tugela River to stop the British army and the Boers blowing pieces out of each other in the Battle of Spion Kop.

He captained the first England team to tour Australia under the official banner of the MCC in 1903–4, reclaiming the Ashes, and also led Middlesex to the County Championship in 1920. He was still playing for the MCC in his mid-fifties, by which time he had founded *The Cricketer* magazine. An inveterate traveller, he was an automatic choice for tour manager once he'd retired, doing the job on England's infamous 'Bodyline' tour in 1932–3. He distanced himself from England's tactics in that series, but made no attempt to stop them. Four years later he was knighted for his services to the game. The Aussies would have preferred to have had him castrated.

Back-handers

Batsmen and bowlers have the same sort of relationship as burglars and security services. Bowlers are cricket's thieves, forever striving for new ways to steal the batsmen's jewels. The law-makers (security staff) constantly seek to protect them. It's a century-old duel that keeps the umpires on their toes and the committees in nights on the claret.

In the bat-dominated first decade of the twentieth century, it was inevitable that the bowlers would fight back. It's like the interplay between supermarkets and shoppers. The stores get irritated when shoppers just whip in for the same things all the time. It's a flat track and they just run in and blithely fill their trolleys and run out again. So they change all the aisles round and you can't find what you want any more. It's called retail bafflement. It's bloody infuriating. That's what the batsmen thought of a young upstart's innovation in 1900. The batsmen were wandering out and filling their boots, until he invented a new way of bowling. They couldn't find the ball any more. And as with the introduction of round arm ninety years earlier, he did it with a woman's help.

It happened like this. Bernard Bosanquet was a tall, talented Oxford University student proficient in a number of sports. A hard-hitting batsman and quickish bowler, he found the paceman's lot a hard one and experimented with different slow deliveries, spending hours spinning a tennis ball out of the back of his hand to his cousin Louise in his uncle's garden. He became the champion of 'twisti-twosti' – an old name for a familiar dressing room game to kill time when it's raining, which involves bouncing a ball off a table so that your opponent can't catch it.

His dexterity developed into a sideshow at Oxford, where he would take visiting county batsmen into the nets at lunchtime and try to outwit them with his sleight of hand. 'If it pitched in the right place it probably hit them on the knee, and everyone shrieked with laughter, and I was led away and locked up for the day,' Bosanquet wrote with typical self-deprecation, looking back on his career in *Wisden*. No one was laughing when he bamboozled fifteen Sussex batsmen with his variations in a match at Oxford in 1900.

'That's like telling fibs!' exclaims the son.

What he had discovered was a way of making what looked like a leg break (turning from right to left) spin the opposite way by inverting his wrist. This was the origin of the most famous word in cricket, the googly. It's basically a simple conjuring trick. Because the wrist is rotating the same way for the leg break and the googly it's not easy to spot the difference from the batsman's end, 22 yards away. He's therefore dumbfounded when a ball that he's expecting to spin one way suddenly goes the other. The Aussies often call it the 'wrong 'un'. A complex phenomenon is explained simply in the World War Two film *Hope and Glory*:

'This is the leg break,' says the dad to his son, bowling him one. 'And this is the off break.' He spins one the other way. 'Now. A googly looks like a leg break but is really an off break!'

The googly is a phenomenally difficult art to perfect and Bosanquet practised it endlessly before eventually having the confidence to unleash it in a high-profile game, the championship match between Middlesex, for whom Bosanquet played after the university term, and Leicestershire at Lord's in July 1900. 'I dismissed Coe with a particularly fine specimen that bounced four times,' he recalled. 'The incident was treated as a joke but a small beginning marked the start of the revolution.' Quite how a decent batsman, especially one on 98, allowed himself to be stumped off a ball that bounced four times is pretty confounding in itself, but it does illustrate the devilish properties of the googly, and the difficulties of controlling it. Batsmen are saved such humiliation these days. Balls bouncing more than once are not allowed. This could have effectively ended the bowling career of Sir Tim Rice, who admits himself that some of his deliveries are so slow that if he doesn't like one he can go down the pitch and retrieve it.

For a brief period Bosanquet's googly was out-landishly effective. He tried it one evening at Lord's in 1902 against the visiting Australians. 'I had two overs and saw two very puzzled Australians returning to the pavilion.' His greatest coup, however, came that winter, when, on tour in Australia with Lord Hawke's XI, his googly bowled Victor Trumper, a sort of turn of the century Bradman. The match was in Sydney, and Trumper, on 37, was looking ominously good. 'Two leg breaks were played beautifully to cover,' Bosanquet remembers. 'The next ball – delivered with a silent prayer – saw the same stroke played, and struck the middle stump instead of the bat.'

The incident sent shock waves through the Australians, who had won four successive Ashes series, and they spent time unravelling this new technique, made all the more difficult by the fact that Bosanquet himself often didn't have a clue where the ball was going. By the time he arrived with the England side a year later for the 1903–4 Ashes, Trumper and Co had fashioned a response. It wasn't enough to stop England, however. Pelham Warner made masterful use of his mystery spinner – recognizing leg spin's value on hard pitches – and England regained the urn, Bosanquet's googly-laden 6-51 sealing the triumph in the fourth Test. Three of his victims were stumped. Thereafter his delivery was nicknamed the 'Bosie' by the Australians, though 'googly', a word coined previously in Australia for a high teasing delivery that baffled the batsman – literally making him goggle with surprise – became the universal term. The ball itself has gradually attained mystical qualities, and the phrase 'he bowled me a googly' has now become common parlance for politicians complaining about awkward questioning from Jeremy Paxman on *Newsnight*.

The indefatigable Bosanquet ignored claims – mainly from batsmen – that his back-handed ball was unfair and he had one more day in the sun, dismissing eight Australians at Trent Bridge in 1905 in his first Test in England. But after that his bowling declined – clearly it had always been a bit prone to getting the yips – and he returned to being a forceful batsman and joyful amateur. And, as invariably happens, something invented by the English was improved on abroad and revisited on us with interest. Reggie Schwarz played with Bosanquet for Middlesex and studied his methods. He subsequently represented South Africa and not only regularly routed England with his googlies, but taught a whole host of Yarpies how to do so. The Aussies cottoned on too, and have been bewitching England with the stuff ever since, culminating in the devastating emergence of the leg-spinmeister Shane Warne in the 1990s. So in the end you'd call Bernard Bosanquet part victor and part villain.

Saints and Swingers

About this time there was one other bowling innovation. Believe it or not it came from America. Perhaps it's not so surprising when you hear that the invention was swing, though not the Dixieland type. John Barton King was a star of the Philadelphian team from 1893 to 1912, successfully adapting the concept of the curveball from baseball to cricket. Instead of relying on movement off the pitch, he was able to make the ball dip or bend in the air, and developed the 'angler', a delivery that we would know today as an inswinger. He used it to devastating effect one day at Hove, taking 7-13, and in that sense was an early version of Imran Khan, though he looked more like Reggie Perrin and didn't try to woo every blonde sloane in town. One presumably begets the other.

What was revolutionary was that Bart King was the first to protect and shine the ball rather than allow it to get rough and scratched. He used that and the seam as a rudder to make the ball swing in late and uproot stumps. On tour with the Philadelphians in 1908 he took 87 wickets to head the English first-class averages. The fetid air resonated to him bellowing, 'Gimme five!' With his help Philadelphia acquitted themselves well against the counties, but American cricket was already in decline as the baseball boom took hold. After 1908 they played no more first-class cricket in England.

Bart King's impact, however, can still be felt today, if you're facing – or watching – some chap lolloping in to bowl and seeing an initially straight ball suddenly boomerang in towards the wicket. Swing has baffled batsmen, commentators and scientists for a century, but there's no denying its potentially lethal effect. Even though they often used dubious methods to maximize their swing, the sight of the Pakistanis Wasim Akram and Waqar Younis in the 1990s demolishing teams in perfect batting conditions was one of the most exhilarating the game has ever seen. Unless you were one of the batsmen.

Yorkshire were one of the chief beneficiaries of Bart King's innovation. They achieved a hat-trick of championship titles in the first years of the twentieth century, largely because of their bowling. Two bowlers in particular, Wilfred Rhodes and George Hirst. Both left arm, one slow, one fast. Both from Kirkheaton – a village in *Last of the Summer Wine* country near Huddersfield – they routed nearby village Slaithwaite for 9 and soon became cricketing legends. Hirst, an ultra-competitive type with dry-as-a-bone humour, bowled nippy left arm and batted with fleet-footed panache. Rhodes, more studious, excelled with his left-arm spin, his main assets being excellent control and command of flight. Over a thirty-two-year career it brought him the small matter of 4,204 first-class wickets, by a street the most in the game's history. A doughty fighter with the bat, he also worked his way up from a no.11 rabbit to eventually open for England.

Hirst began playing for the county in the 1890s. His bowling was brisk and straight but not devastating. At only 5ft 6in he was also short for a quickie and his run-up began with a peculiar hop, step and jump, but he hurled himself through the bowling crease with great energy and vigour. He batted no.10 at first, but earnt a reputation for stout defence and gradually worked his way up the order, earning England selection in 1898, although a dodgy knee meant his bowling became less effective.

The turning point was 1901, when he borrowed Bart King's methods and developed late inswing, often releasing his fast left-armers from round the wicket with three close fielders on the legside. It was early 'leg theory' and it was some transformation. It was like

Greta Garbo discovering her voice. That year Hirst took 183 wickets, was equally destructive the following year and in Yorkshire's three championship-winning seasons also scored over 5,000 runs, pulling and hooking with abandon. As a brilliant, fearless fielder as well, he was practically a one-man team. (He and Rhodes once bowled out Australia between them for 36.)

Hirst regularly did the double of 1,000 runs and 100 wickets in a season (as did Rhodes), which just doesn't happen in the modern game (last instance, Franklyn Stephenson in 1988). Before you conclude that English cricketers were just better then, remember that county teams in the early 1900s often played thirty-two matches (twice as many as today) as well as bowling about 1,000 overs an hour.

The pinnacle of Hirst's career was yet to come, though. In 1906 he was thirty-five and nursing a chronic knee injury when he became the one and only cricketer ever to score 2,000 runs and take 200 wickets in a season. It's a staggering performance when you think about it. Never mind having the concentration and skill needed to score 2,000 runs, few men have managed 200 wickets and most of those are spinners (and no one has got near it since 1957). Complaining to his doctor about sore feet, Hirst got a blunt reply: 'Don't you realize, Mr Hirst, you've given your legs more use than five ordinary men in a lifetime.' He got through the rest of the season by massaging them morning and evening with neat's-foot oil. His dry humour emerged later when he was asked how someone might feel if they ever emulated his unique double. 'Bloody tired,' he replied, matter of factly.

With an obvious and deep passion for the game, he was one of the most committed cricketers there has ever been. How else can you explain a man who played first-class cricket until he was fifty-eight, walking to the wicket more than 1,200 times and bowling 25,000 overs? 'His smile used almost to meet at the back of his neck,' his captain, Lord Hawke, said. And the secret of his everlasting spirit? A tea-time tipple of a gin and sherry cocktail. Guess today that would be a vodka Red Bull.

Rhodes Scholar

In the pantheon of great English bowlers, Hirst's old colleague Wilfred Rhodes is sometimes forgotten. Perhaps that is how he wanted it. He was a modest, unostentatious chap, who went about the business of wicket-taking in an efficient, unassuming way. He was a classic left-arm spinner, but his demeanour was as far removed from the excitable Monty Panesar's as it is possible to go. Then again, if he'd celebrated every one of his 4,204 wickets as Monty does, he would have quickly died of exhaustion.

From his early beginnings as a slow left-armer, Rhodes had a simple philosophy: 'Give 'em nowt'. He rarely did. An incredible 9,518 of his 30,000-plus overs were maidens (though many of those overs consisted of only five balls). The determined set of his chin reflected his ingrained Yorkshire tenacity. As with many out-standing cricketers, he learnt to play the game solo, bowling for hours in a barn and on a home-made turf pitch laid against a haystack to stop the ball. He quit his job as a railway engine cleaner to play for Kirkheaton, but was soon lured away to pro in Scotland for Galashiels. His success there was written off: 'they never were any good at cricket,' said his Kirkheaton club chairman. But aged twenty he was fast-tracked into the Yorkshire team in 1898, to replace the left-arm spinner Bobby Peel whom Lord Hawke had sacked the previous year for being drunk and weeing on the pitch. (You often wonder how the players of yesteryear would fare in today's game. And what old Hawke would have made of an England all-rounder being drunk in charge of a pedalo.)

Rhodes was an immediate phenomenon, taking 154 wickets in his début season and earning an England call-up. His first Test, against Australia at Nottingham, in which he took seven wickets, was also fifty-year-old W. G. Grace's last (he retired after this, saying 'the ground was getting a bit too far away'). In 1900, Rhodes's astonishing 261 wickets piloted Yorkshire to the championship title. He had a photographic memory, and after he got a batsman out once, it was inevitable he would do it again. Mind you, that was partly because he was always bowling. After five years in county cricket he had 1,251 wickets.

The great, if occasionally flowery, cricket reporter Neville Cardus describes Rhodes's art:

Flight was his secret, flight and the curving line, now higher, now lower, tempting, inimical; every ball like

134

every other ball, yet somehow unlike; each over in collusion with the others, part of a plot. Every ball a decoy, a spy sent out to get the lie of the land; some balls simple, some complex . . . and one of them – ah! which? – the master ball.

Cardus hadn't been drinking. That's how they wrote in those days.

Believing that you should never play the cut before the end of May, Rhodes's stolid tailend batting – first glimpsed when he and Hirst nudged England to nail-biting victory in 'Jessop's match' – gradually flowered and for a while superseded his bowling. He was one of the first to use a two-eyed stance, left shoulder pointing to mid-on. He later opened for England with 'The Master', Jack Hobbs. If you think Hirst had stamina, get this. Rhodes did the double of 1,000 runs and 100 wickets in a season sixteen times. Wherever he went, he applied a permanent tourniquet to the scoring (with bat and ball). He was as perennial as the speed restrictions on the M62.

If war hadn't interrupted his career, he would probably have taken 5,000 wickets. Instead he worked in a national ammunitions factory rectifying shell cases. He was paid £2 a week. That was augmented with wartime Saturday appearances for Yorkshire. Resuming his first-class career in 1919, Rhodes became the first player to appear in fifty Tests. He had taken twenty-two years to achieve this landmark. Marcus Trescothick, by contrast, took 3½ years to reach the same number (by which time he'd also played about 4,237 one-dayers – no wonder he was burnt out). Rhodes was still wheeling away in his England cap in 1929, aged fifty-two, and remains the oldest man to play a Test match. He was a walking cricket record – the bowling machine that never wore out.

Rhodes announced his retirement in the summer of 1930, about the time a new young Australian, Donald Bradman, was reeling off scores of 131, 254, 334 and 232 in his first Test tour of England. The obvious time to quit, really.

The *Daily Express* lamented: 'Was Wilfred Rhodes' parting too silent?' and there was a case for saying it was given his achievements, which rank him, statistically anyway, as the greatest all-rounder ever. Imagine what it would be like now. He'd have had a farewell guard of honour at every ground he played at, eight-page pull-outs in all the papers, tribute programmes, three-part autobiographies, fitness DVDs, honorary degrees in bio-chemistry from Umist, a lifetime's supply of Yorkshire puddings, a statue outside the Kingsgate shopping centre in Huddersfield, and an invitation to partner a Spanish salsa champion on *Strictly Come Dancing*. As it is there is one solitary book about his life – *Wilfred Rhodes* by Brian Croudy (compared to about twenty-five on W. G. Grace) – and that's it. Still, as the consummate professional, he probably preferred it that way.

The Greatest?

Before we move on from these golden years, where county matches drew 10,000 spectators and the sun shone all day and every batsman 'walked' and no wife ever complained if their husband left the toilet seat up, mention should be made of a couple of other significant characters.

Two years ago, compiling an all-time best England XI for the *Daily Telegraph* in a lunch hour, I selected a fast-bowling attack of Trueman, Willis and Botham. Not bad, I thought. More than 1,000 Test wickets between them, a few Ashes triumphs and good for a laugh on a rainy day too. I was politely ticked off by Messrs Boycott and Benaud for omitting a certain S. F. Barnes. And having learnt more about him I can see why.

Sydney Barnes is unique, as a star England bowler who actually played most of his cricket in the northern leagues rather than for a first-class team. A taciturn, independent man, he couldn't be doing with the tread-mill and meagre pay of county cricket – £3 a week in 1900. So after a short spell with Warwickshire in his early twenties, he plied his trade in the thriving Lancashire leagues. At first Rishton and later Burnley, where he could earn £8 for an afternoon's work.

Tall and strong, he was brisk rather than outright quick but, using his high action and immensely supple fingers, he achieved extravagant movement both in the air and off the pitch. He not only cut the ball but actually spun it too at a speed probably equivalent to an ageing Glenn McGrath, and with an equal repulsion of batsmen. At the time, most bowlers moved the ball pre-dominantly *in*. Barnes honed a finger-flicking method of making it move away. In essence he bowled fast leg breaks, interspersed with off-cutters. Occasionally he

137

would veer wide of the crease to bowl a ball that angled in before cutting viciously away off the pitch. He was just as much a pioneer as Grace or Bosanquet.

Exceptionally accurate, he was lethal on damp or bouncy tracks. Mirroring the way Waqar Younis was discovered by Imran Khan in the late 1980s, Barnes so impressed the England captain Archie MacLaren in the Old Trafford nets one day in 1901, he was asked to go on tour to Australia and accept a contract with Lancashire. He received the offer by telegram relayed to him in the field with Burnley. At the time he had taken 13 first-class (i.e. county) wickets spread across seven seasons. It was a gamble with a capital G. It'd be like calling up a club trundler from the Birmingham League to play in the 2006–7 Ashes. (Actually, given England's abysmal bowling in the last three years, they'd have been better off with a club trundler from the Birmingham League.)

A matter of weeks later Barnes, like Waqar, burst on to the international scene. Within two overs of his Test début at the Sydney Cricket Ground he had caught and bowled Trumper, the greatest batsman in the world, for 2, and he added four more scalps before the innings was done. In his second Test, in Melbourne, he took 13 wickets, including Trumper cheaply twice more.

The exertion of 64 overs in the second innings was too much, however, and he was subsequently injured. After that he earnt a reputation as a bolshy mercenary. He didn't see why he should be paid the same as others who did far less work – invariably the amateurs. It might have been a Golden Age for them, but it was a grind for the professionals. Barnes fought a one-man class war. He was Arthur Scargill in disguise.

He put selectors' backs up and missed a number of Test series. He also played only two seasons for Lancashire before returning to the leagues again. But he was so good he couldn't be ignored and reappeared intermittently for England for the next ten years, mostly abroad.

With the cold face of an assassin and a complete disregard for anyone else, he once said, 'There's only one captain of a side when I'm bowling. Me.' He was impossible to get the ball off and, armed with superb stamina, frequently bowled more than 30 overs in an innings in enervating heat, cutting down his pace to conserve energy. His productivity was astonishing. In virtually every one of his twenty-seven Tests he took 5 wickets in an innings and had an average (16.43 per wicket) bettered only by George Lohmann in the entire history of Test cricket. His strike rate (a very low 41 balls per wicket) puts him in the same devastating bracket as Waqar.

How did he do it? With a broad repertoire of deliveries, each one cleverly concealed, he always attacked, forcing the batsmen to play. 'I never gave 'em rest,' he said. Against lesser batsmen he often moved the ball too much and had to endure a sequence of playing and missing, after which he'd grunt, 'They aren't playing well enough to get out.'

On the matting wickets of South Africa in 1913–14 his lift and spin were utterly unplayable, and he took 49 wickets in four Tests (still a record by any bowler for a Test series). With England having already won the series 3–0 he declared himself unavailable for the fifth match after a financial dispute and never played for his country again.

Instead he put his upright McGrath-like action back to use for minor-county Staffordshire and in the leagues, and was still successfully pro-ing when he was sixty-five. He remained a grim tormentor of batsmen to the end. A plaque stands outside the museum at Edgbaston chronicling his final achievements which a fastidious statistician, Leslie Duckworth, calculated as an amazing 6,300 wickets in all serious cricket at the ridiculous average of 8.33. He was born to bowl.

Richie Benaud, a man who has witnessed over 500 Test matches, comfortably more than anyone else, actually saw Barnes in action. It was at Stoke-on-Trent in 1953, when Australia played the Minor Counties, and Barnes was invited to bowl the first ball of the match. It landed perfectly on a length and was played defensively. Benaud was so impressed (well, Barnes was aged 80 at the time) that he selected him in his all-time greatest XI. There can be no higher accolade than that.

Two other legendary players emerged in the first decade of the twentieth century: the master batsman Jack Hobbs, discovered on Parker's Piece in Cambridge, who was to eventually break virtually every run-making record under the sun. And Frank Woolley, cricket's first great left-hander, about whom it was said, 'When you bowled to him there weren't enough fielders; when you wrote about him there weren't enough words.' More of them anon.

Running Amok

With Bosanquet and Barnes's influence there evolved greater diversity in the bowling than ever before, with speed, swing, cut and spin all being deployed to counter the flatter pitches. Every county team had a leg-spinner. Overs had been extended to six balls (1900) to give the purveyors of leg spin more scope to develop their strategy. There was also still a legacy of the nineteenth century in the form of George Simpson-Hayward, the last of the 'lobsters' – not a reference to his ruddy complexion, but the fact that he bowled slow underarms. It sounds absurd but he was picked for England after taking a stack of wickets for Worcestershire, and bamboozled the South Africans with his spinning moon balls. But C. B. Fry ridiculed this type of bowling by hitting it between his legs croquet-style and its like was not seen again until the Middlesex captain Mike Brearley tried to provoke a belligerent Rhodesian, Brian Davison, out of his wicket with a few head-high lobs in 1980.

In spite of the bowling variations, batsmen continued to hold sway. Up and down the country there was an orgy of scoring, led by Surrey's Tom Hayward, Hobbs's mentor, who became the second man after WG to score a hundred hundreds, and there were regular mammoth partnerships. In a club match in County Durham, a Stanley batsman scored 31 with one hit when the ball disappeared down the hill and into a nearby farmyard. (There is also a legend that WG once hit a ball 25 miles after striking a six on to a passing train, but it's unverified.)

Bowlers had their odd day in the sun, notably one June morning at Gloucester in 1907. In forty minutes' play the entire Northants side were bowled out for 12, by Gilbert Jessop's pace and the left-arm spin of George Dennett, who had the crazy figures of 6-1-9-8. It is still the lowest total recorded in first-class cricket and really underlines the point about Northants. They were rubbish then and have been virtually ever since.

The MCC had finally got their act together and set up the Advisory County Cricket Committee to run the county game, and cricket was booming at every level – county, club and village. Crowds of 20,000 were regular at the Roses match between Yorkshire and Lancashire, one of the highlights of the summer.

But the proper organization of the game, and the onset of professionalism, led by Lord Hawke's Yorkshire, didn't please everyone. The traditionalists – well, actually they were Luddites – spoke out. 'Any step that can bring sentiment again into first-class cricket is to be welcomed,' said the writer E. V. Lucas in *The Times* of 4 September 1908. 'A hard utilitarianism and commercialism have far too long controlled it . . . a three-day match today can be a scene of little joy and little enthusiasm.'

For all its aesthetic pleasures and perceived virtues, cricket is always a byword for a general lament that life is not what it was. Or maybe just look at it another way. Cricket is like sex: much more fun to do than it is to watch.

SEVEN

Changing of the Guard

The year 1908 was a defining one for cricket. In April W. G. Grace braved snow on the pitch to play his last first-class match, for the Gentlemen of England v Surrey at the Oval, making 15 and 25. His forty-year career had utterly changed the British sporting landscape. It was now big business. Four months after his first-class farewell, on the other side of the world, at Cootamundra in New South Wales, George and Emily Bradman had a son they called Donald, and whose first words were presumably 'Yes . . . two!'

In between those momentous days, Grace, now pushing sixty, scored his final century – 111 not out for London County v Whitgift Wanderers, a match in which he also took 7 wickets, including a hat-trick. He was the definition of insatiable. It was not a first-class match though, and that is the point. The London County team had already been marginalized by the powers that be (the MCC), anxious to retain the feudal structure of the first-class game based around the old county boundaries, those arbitrary things which had already become irrelevant to modern urban life. Many of the county teams themselves were increasingly based at their city headquarters – Edgbaston, Old Trafford, Trent Bridge and the like – rather than being tied to their more rural outposts.

League cricket was thriving in the north, giving the man on the Rochdale omnibus an opportunity, as it might have said in the Berkeley Homes brochure, to 'perfect his work/life balance' – i.e. work during the week and play for/watch his town/village on Saturday afternoon. This was the moment cricket could really have taken off. County matches were played predominantly during the week to allow the amateurs the weekend off. Attendances were starting to tail off. The Lancashire League, in particular, had evolved in parallel with professional football, for the benefit of the factory worker. It was a decent standard – appealing to the likes of Sydney Barnes – and attracted good crowds. Cricket could at that point have embraced the success of the northern leagues and established a nationwide, city-based infrastructure – like the one proposed in 2008 in fact – playing Saturday matches for the benefit of everyone. But instead it closed ranks.

The gentleman–players divide was at the heart of this impasse. The (mainly southern) amateurs largely despised the professionals – of which Yorkshire had the most – suggesting they were squeezing the charisma out of the game in order to win. 'Average mania is as fatal to cricket as trade unions are to commerce,' voiced one gent. The first-class county game looked down its nose at the leagues with their dodgy pitches and instant results. So the inefficient cartel of county cricket, which now had 16 members (Worcestershire joining in 1899 and Northamptonshire in 1905), remained intact. Even then most counties made a loss, and depended for their survival on local benefactors and members' subscriptions. The working classes could neither afford the subscriptions nor attend the matches, except at holiday-time, causing the usual domestic arguments:

'Where you going?'

'To the cricket at Old Trafford.'

'I thought you were taking the kids to Blackpool so I could go to the hairdressers!'

'But Lancs are second from top, and anyway your hair doesn't need cutting!'

'I haven't had my highlights done since May!'

'Lancashire haven't won the championship since 1897!'

Then, as now (when counties depend on the ECB for their annual £1.5m handout), the economics of county cricket just didn't make sense.

There were a few moves afoot to restrict the dominance of batsmen. One was to widen the stumps, another to make it easier to get an lbw by restricting 'pad play'. Frederick 'The Demon' Spofforth even proposed penalizing batsmen for playing out a maiden over. (The term 'maiden' had been used to mean 'unproductive' or 'virginal' long before its association with a lack of scoring in cricket.) There was one outlandish suggestion to ban left-handers, much to the dismay of the recently emerged Frank Woolley, among others.

Predictably, given that most members of the ruling body were batsmen, it is not surprising that no changes were introduced. In fact just about the only legislative change was a 1910 ruling that a ball hit over the rope without bouncing now counted six instead of four (a six was previously only achieved if the ball was struck out of the ground), facilitating even faster scoring! And an over now consisted of six balls instead of five, making bowlers tire quicker. The only respite was the introduction of a tea interval, but that took months of debate and in the end was restricted to only fifteen minutes – barely time to get your 2lb leather clod-hoppers on and off. It's always been a batsman's game, whatever they may tell you.

The two most prolific batsmen in the history of the game were already making their mark. Woolley, a tall, graceful left-hander, emerged through the Tonbridge nursery and first played for Kent in 1906. Though he began with nought and one for plenty against Lancashire, his luminous batting, steady left-arm spin and safe slip catching were immediately influential in Kent winning their first (official) County Championship. He was a prolific run-scorer, who had, as H. S. Altham put it, 'an unmistakeable air of majestic, almost casual, command'. He was, in many ways, an Edwardian version of David Gower, with a similar tendency to get out to an insouciant shot; in Woolley's case, particularly in the 90s. (Also, he would have certainly not looked out of place in a Scott Fitzgerald novel with his dapper good looks and his dilettante attitude and a pretty blonde on his arm.)

Woolley's panache was manna from heaven for the burgeoning group of writers now covering cricket. Raymond Robertson-Glasgow (known to everyone as 'Crusoe') frequently waxed lyrical about him:

> In describing a great innings by Woolley you had to go careful with your adjectives and stack them in little rows like pats of butter or razor blades. In the first over of his innings, perhaps, there had been an exquisite off-drive, followed by a perfect cut, then an effortless leg glide. In the second over the same sort of thing happened, and your superlatives had already gone.

Compiling the small matter of 58,969 runs in Woolley's thirty-two-year career gave the scribes plenty to hyperbolize about. Sometime in the 1930s he overtook WG's record tally. Neville Cardus was intoxicated by him. 'His cricket is compounded of soft airs and fresh flavours,' he wrote. 'The bloom of the year is on it, making for sweetness . . . His innings are thin spun, seeming too insubstantial for this world.' Again it could have been written about Gower (despite his huge success at Test level).

Bowling at Gower, as I did countless, fruitless times, was an odd experience. With that languid air, he looked nonchalant, as if he didn't care, and you the bowler fancied your chances. But that nonchalance belied predatory eyesight and a sly dominance. He would dispatch balls barely wide or short that other batsmen would defend or leave and make it all look graceful and ridiculously easy. I remember him flicking me lazily for four on the legside one day. The shot defied description. I asked him what it was. 'I suppose you'd call that an underhand pull,' he replied, a touch embarrassed. And that was the worst part: being effortlessly picked off by a bloke who seemed to have only half his mind on the job. One suspects bowling to Woolley was a bit the same.

He was slightly less successful at Test level, and experienced a rude introduction, courtesy of the provocative Australian captain Warwick Armstrong. A bulky 20 stone, with the type of pot belly that the Aussies would call 'an awning over the toy factory', Armstrong was Australia's WG, in attitude if not quite longevity. A bullish batsman and wily leg-spinner, Armstrong was an uncompromising character, who challenged umpires' decisions and thought nothing of running a negligent batsman out at the bowler's end. As Woolley walked out at the Oval in 1909 to make his Test début, Armstrong made an absurd play of warming up, bowling a succession of looseners to the fielders, holding up play for a mind-boggling 19 minutes. Even the umpires were in awe of him.

This was largely responsible for Woolley managing only 8 in his first Test innings before being bowled, and it took him a while to get established. He gradually worked his way up to no.4, but some years later, in 1928, he was omitted from the winter tour of Australia despite having scored the little matter of 3,352 runs that summer for Kent. I suppose these amazing run-scoring feats must be set against the fact that, in those days, fielding was largely an escort service to the boundary. The only dive you saw was when a swarm of bees materialized from a nearby orchard.

He played sixty-four Tests but even in his pomp Woolley seemed more at home amongst the fluttering white marquees and foliage and bonhomie of Canterbury Week, a cricketing institution that dates from 1841 and originally featured cricket during the day and theatrical performances at night. For that reason one of the marquees is still hosted by the 'Old Stagers'. It was in this convivial – often inebriated – atmosphere that Woolley ran amok. 'There was,' waxed Crusoe, 'all summer in a stroke by Woolley, and he batted as if sometimes shown in dreams.' One should not forget either his 2,068 wickets and 1,018 deft catches, mostly at slip, comfortably the most by an outfielder in the history of the game. A stand named after him commands the long-on boundary at Canterbury, though it is looking a little dog-eared these days.

Jack Hobbs, the other great run-machine of the Edwardian era, was a contrast. If Woolley was the artist, Hobbs was the pragmatist. Perhaps that's why there are only a couple of books dedicated to his life (although he ghost-wrote several himself). And if you Google Jack Hobbs you actually get more references to a nondescript footballer on loan from Liverpool to Leicester.

The great batsman, christened John, was shortish and nimble, his footwork was precise and his shots were smooth and controlled. He began life with a distinct advantage. His father was a net bowler at Fenners, Cambridge, later a groundsman and then an umpire. A perfect combination.

10.30am: 'Here, son, I'll bowl you a few . . . hope you like the pitch I've prepared for you – flat as a pancake

149

. . . [whispers] Hey, don't forget to get your pads in the way at my end . . .'

11.24am: 'That's not out, bowler! My lad's . . . correction, the batsman's pads are too far outside the line. Unlucky, try again. [mouths] Keep going, son!'

The first of twelve kids, Hobbs also eventually had an entire team of brothers and sisters to act as fielders if he fancied a middle practice.

Of course, he didn't get where he did without practice – no one does except heirs and lottery winners – and he spent inordinate amounts of time hitting a tennis ball with a stump in a fives court. It's a great way for boys to improve hand–eye co-ordination and footwork and also distracts them from monopolizing their parents' computer or masturbating too much.

Hobbs played cricket and sang in the choir at a church school in Cambridge. His hero was the Surrey and England opening batsman Tom Hayward, also a Cambridge man, who took him under his wing. Hobbs played for Cambridgeshire in his late teens, and his services were offered to Essex, the nearest first-class county, but they were rejected. You can imagine the conversation:

'Not a bad-looking player, what d'you think, Alf?'

'Nah, plays too many shots. 'E won't last a minute against Hirst or Lockwood.'

You wonder how they felt when, after Hayward got him qualified for Surrey, he took 155 off the Essex attack in his first championship game. (Presumably, similar to how the Durham wicketkeeper Chris Scott felt when he dropped Brian Lara on 18 during his run-spree in 1994. 'I suppose he'll go on and get another hundred now,' muttered Scott to the slip cordon. Sure enough Lara did . . . er . . . he made 501 not out.)

A self-made player who confessed he never had any coaching, Hobbs was something of a dasher early in his career. The benign pitch at the Oval helped. In one match the visitors Hampshire racked up 645-4 on the opening day. Hobbs and his opening partner Ernie Hayes responded by putting on 371 in less than three hours (Hobbs made a chanceless 205). Bowling was clearly as much of a forlorn business in Kennington then as it is now.

He got a chance with England on New Year's Day 1908 (another notable incident in that year). This, however, was only because some players, including C. B. Fry, were unhappy with the financial incentives MCC were offering for the tour to Australia. Or in the case of Fry, it was actually his wife Beatrice who complained, the first impact of Wagdom on the British sporting world. Hobbs slotted in, made 83 in his first Test innings and soon formed a productive opening partnership with the more circumspect Wilfred Rhodes. Initially he was flummoxed by the googlies of the South African Reg Schwarz. But, using his pad as an important line of defence outside off stump – giving this rather disapproved-of method credibility (you couldn't be out leg before then if the ball pitched off the stumps) – he returned to conquer him and his colleagues with a powerful 187, his first Test century. By 1911 he had eclipsed Trumper as the best batsman in the world. He was also panther-like in the field, regularly running out unsuspecting single-seekers.

Hobbs's latter-day equivalent is Graham Gooch – who actually went on to overtake Hobbs's colossal run aggregate, if you count his one-day performances as well – and there are similarities between the two. Though capable of adventure, both were functional rather than flowery batsmen, both excelled on the back foot, rose to the demands of a tricky pitch or an awkward situation and were utterly self-effacing. Without ego, each had a waspish sense of humour, which in Gooch's case was often at the expense of Mike Gatting. Remarking on the 'Ball of the Century', Shane Warne's first in an Ashes contest which cleaned up a bemused Fat Gatt at Old Trafford in 1993, Gooch said, 'If it had been a cheese roll it would have never got past him.'

With a light and compact build, Hobbs had a high, flowing backlift and great balance at the crease, and he moved into position nimbly. Bowlers said he seemed to instinctively know where the ball was going to be as it was delivered. He was virtually in position waiting for it. He reeled off centuries almost in his sleep (197 in all). Although, as Wilfred Rhodes once pointed out, he was a bit inclined to mentally nod off once he had the bowlers at his mercy: 'He could have made 397 [hundreds] if he'd wanted, but when Surrey were going well he used to throw it away – give his wicket to one of his old pals, hit up a catch and go out laughing.' Hobbs, who perpetually shunned the limelight and later turned down the opportunity to be England's first professional captain, was the definition of English self-deprecation.

After Hayward retired, Hobbs and Andy Sandham, a ferocious puller and cutter, formed an equally prolific opening alliance for Surrey. Having had a fruitless morning bowling to the pair at the Oval, the writer R. C. Robertson-Glasgow, who played for Somerset, said, 'It's like trying to bowl to God on concrete.' Surrey boast more members of the hundred hundreds club – Hayward, Hobbs, Sandham, John Edrich and now Mark Ramprakash – than any other team, though they only equal the number of *Strictly Come Dancing* titles (1) held by Yorkshire players (Darren Gough).

For England, Hobbs and Herbert Sutcliffe became the acme of opening partnerships. Here was a perfect combination, southern polish and northern grit, and they developed a superb understanding, sharing in 15 century opening partnerships in Tests. In the 1920s their names were as inextricably linked as Torville and Dean or, well, Gough and Kopylova. Their second-innings opening salvo of 172 in the 'Timeless Test' on a sticky track at the Oval in 1926 was instrumental in England regaining the Ashes for the first time since 1912. The brave and combative Sutcliffe's Test record was phenomenal, and he became the only Englishman to finish with a Test average of over 60.

Despite his achievements, which included twelve centuries against Australia – more than anyone else – Hobbs kept a low profile. He married his teenage sweetheart (whom he took on tour to Australia, the first professional to do so), they had three sons and he was happy after matches to eat a simple meal at a Lyons Corner House on the Strand. He was a regular church goer, and remained teetotal – celebrating his long-awaited equalling of W. G. Grace's tally of 126 centuries with a glass of ginger ale.

There is Pathé archive film of this event at Taunton in 1925. With Hobbs 91 not out overnight, a huge crowd assembled to see him triumph and play was delayed for half an hour to get everyone in. A film cameraman was deputed to capture the moment. Such is the awkward nature of one-camera cricket coverage, however, that he missed it. The vital stroke – a pull for one – was re-enacted after play in hackneyed slow motion with the fielders loitering around in feigned anticipation. It's the worst bit of acting after Liz Hurley in *Austin Powers, the Spy Who Shagged Me*. Hobbs sent a proud telegram to his wife, who was on holiday in Margate, and received hundreds of congratulatory wires, one addressed simply to 'Superman, Taunton'. He promptly eclipsed Grace's record with another century in the second innings of the match.

Generally he was a less ebullient batsman after the war, playing predominantly off the back foot with masterly precision though he also possessed a flowing drive. He had an uncanny knack of being able to leave an awkward ball alone. He had 'regal control', it said in his *Wisden* obituary, from the 'twiddle of the bat before he bent slightly to face the attack' to 'the beautifully timed push to the off to open his score, the push was not hurried, did not send the ball too quickly to the fieldsman, so that Hobbs could walk his first run.' Everything about his batting had poise and certainty and commitment. Everything about his life in fact. 'He was a man of the highest integrity who believed in sportmanship in the highest sense, teamwork, fair-play and clean-living,' Herbert Sutcliffe said. 'His life was full of everything noble and true.' No one has a bad word to say about him.

The Hobbs Gates were erected at the Oval in his honour – and a pavilion named after him on Parker's Piece in Cambridge, where he learnt to bat. Despite his plea that they should 'stop all this nonsense', he was knighted in 1953 and in 2000 was voted third in the *Wisden* poll (behind Bradman and Sobers) to declare the greatest cricketers of the twentieth century.

Rude Interruptions

Hobbs's career straddled two distinct eras, so we have to rewind a bit to pick up the story. On 15 April 1912, just off the coast of Canada, the world's largest ship sank on its maiden voyage: 1,517 drowned, and the corny remark 'It went down well didn't it?' 'What?' 'The *Titanic!*' was coined. On 23 August the same year, the world's first-ever triangular cricket tournament, played in England, met a similarly watery end. The weather was dismal throughout the nine (mainly three-day) Test matches featuring England, Australia and South Africa played that summer. The event was the brainchild of the newly formed Imperial Cricket Conference (ICC) but in such damp conditions neither of the tourists were any match for an England side featuring Hobbs, Rhodes, Fry, Woolley, Jessop and

Barnes, among others. And, in keeping with the elements, the public response to the multi-nation tournament was so lukewarm that the ICC didn't try it again until the first World Cup in 1975.

Some interesting players emerged, though. One was the Warwickshire captain Frank Foster. A bristling hitter and skiddy left-arm fast bowler, he borrowed George Hirst's method of angling the ball into the batsman from round the wicket, and upped the ante by making the ball bounce up at the body with a number of close legside fielders. Although slow bowlers had, from W. G. Grace onwards, often aimed exclusively at or outside the leg stump, Foster was the first quickie to consistently do so.

Foster formed with the wizardly wicket-taker Barnes the first all-seam opening attack, enabling England to win the Ashes in 1911–12. Foster took 32 wickets in the series, and Plum Warner, in his end of tour report, said, 'His bowling makes such haste off the pitch that even such accomplished players as Mr Trumper and Mr Armstrong have not had time on occasions to play their stroke.' Aiming the ball consistently on or just outside leg stump, and often hitting the batsmen on the hip, Foster was in effect the originator of Bodyline, though it was then called 'leg theory'. The England captain Douglas Jardine consulted him about his approach and field settings before the infamous 1932–3 tour of Australia. Foster, whose own career was terminated by a motorcycle crash during the First World War, could not have envisaged what a kerfuffle it would cause.

There was also J. T. Hearne, who preferred to be

known as Jack, not surprisingly since he was christened John Thomas – I mean, really, what are parents thinking when they do that to a kid? The archetypal English trundler, he bowled for Middlesex (and England) from 1890 to 1914, taking wickets aplenty with his nagging cutters and swingers. In one season he bowled 10,000 balls (which equated to 2,000 overs in the 5-ball-over era), something that only one other bowler in history – the arch run-stopper Alfred Shaw – had ever before managed. It would take most modern county bowlers about five seasons, a hundred massages and twelve back scans to get through that many deliveries.

With the evolution of new bowling styles, wicket-keeping also came to the fore. The smooth Warwickshire gloveman Dick Lilley donned the England gauntlets for most of the twentieth century's first decade. He was succeeded first by his own protégé E. J. 'Tiger' Smith and then the twinkle-toed Surrey man Herbert Strudwick, who was one of the first keepers to stand back to medium pacers, though he was also happy to stand up to anyone, withstanding the bruising to his hands by religiously soaking them in a chamber pot every morning. And so began the English tradition of producing talented wicketkeepers with bizarre habits, notably placing a block under the car accelerator pedal raising the foot to avoid undue Achilles strain when driving on congested roads (Alan Knott) or lunching on Weetabix stewed in milk for exactly twelve minutes (Jack Russell).

In 1914, England held the Ashes and had just thumped

South Africa 4–0 away under the leadership of the blue-eyed blocker J. W. H. T. Douglas (christened Johnny Won't Hit Today Douglas by the Aussies). It was of course illegal for anyone to captain England unless they had at least three initials and owned 20,000 acres of the finest grouse moor in Scotland. So cricket supporters began the summer of 1914 in optimistic mood. Europe was in turmoil – Germany invaded Belgium, Austria was tangling with the Serbs, who were backed by the Russians, Ireland was on the verge of civil war, and Britain and France were engaged in their annual bout of verbal fisticuffs – yet county cricket went on as normal.

For a time. Those who believe, however, that the influence of the 66-year-old, straggly-bearded WG was over were mistaken. By mid-August, although war was underway on several fronts, many thought it would be only a minor affair. Not Grace. On 27 August a letter he had written to the *Sportsman* was published. It read:

> The fighting on the Continent is very severe and will probably be prolonged. I think the time has come when the county season should be closed, for it is not fitting at a time like the present that able-bodied men should play and pleasure seekers look on. I should like to see all cricketers set a good example and come to the aid of their country without delay.

Was W. G. Grace actually God? Very probably. He certainly looked like him.

The rest of the season was promptly cancelled, and the County Championship awarded to Surrey with two games to play. A high proportion of county cricketers (210 of them) signed up to the armed forces and most of the rest were involved in some way or another. Even Grace did his bit, bellowing with rage at the Zeppelins when they floated over his south London home. A friend pointed out that the fast bowling of the Australian Ernie Jones had never bothered him as much. 'But I could *see* him!' Grace fumed. A year later, he died of a heart attack after an air raid. Even in death his impact was massive as the nation mourned his passing. Cricket, and life, would never be the same again.

EIGHT

War Games

Because there were few major matches, most cricket histories make only passing references to the game during the First World War. In fact there was a fair amount of cricket played. The County Championship was suspended, and the pavilions of many first-class grounds were converted into military bases and hospitals, but a few counties still played weekend games, some northern leagues continued for a time and public school cricket actually expanded.

Abroad, impromptu games were conceived in the trenches. Well, you can take the man away from cricket but you can't take cricket away from the man. There was no equipment of course, but at Vermelles in France, just out of sight of the front line, officers played a game using a rafter as a bat, a tied rag as the ball and a cage containing a dead parrot as the wicket. There is no mention of whether the parrot had been gassed, blown up or was hit by a vicious delivery. Perhaps it wasn't dead, just pining for the fjords . . . The game was abandoned when falling bullets landed on a length, which brings to mind the Australian all-rounder Keith Miller's famous quip after surviving life as a fighter pilot in the Second World War. Asked why he was so cool under pressure in a Test match, he replied, 'Pressure? Jeez! A Messerschmitt up your arse. That's pressure!'

Typically inventive, a few Australians played cricket while being shelled at Gallipoli in 1915, using it as a decoy while most of the force were secretly evacuated. Gallipoli, a thin, rocky peninsula in western Turkey, played a defining part in the relationship between Britain and Australia. Winston Churchill (then First Lord of the Admiralty) was one who believed taking the peninsula would create an effective supply route into Russia. A large Allied force was sent to invade it, including thousands of Australians and New Zealanders.

But the men were woefully ill-equipped for such hostile territory, there were no coin-operated barbeques and the British commanders were seriously incompetent (one slept through the initial stages of the invasion). They were sitting targets and the mission was a disaster, costing the Allies 43,000 dead. The Australians suffered 27,000 casualties, including 7,500 dead. As it was their first experience of war, it left a bitter taste, and strengthened their desire to be independent from Britain. It certainly spiced up their cricket. They won eight Tests in a row against England straight after the war, and their regular visits to Gallipoli on the way to England for an Ashes series are partially motivational.

Elsewhere in the Great War there were instances of

men throwing a cricket ball out of the trenches to initiate the advance over the top, apeing the famous action of the England rugby captain Edgar Mobbs who, having recruited his own rugby-playing battalion, punted an oval ball out of the hole for him and his men to pursue at the Battle of Ypres. The consequences were inevitably tragic. Most of Mobbs's 400 recruits were mown down, himself included. Seventy first-class cricketers perished during the fighting, including the outstanding Kent and England left-arm spinner 'Charlie' Blythe (2,503 wickets in his career) and the young Australian Norman Callaway, who made a double century in his only innings for New South Wales, and thus has the honour of the highest average in cricket history.

In the region of 750,000 British men lost their lives in those four brutal years, and, naturally, the nation was a pretty sombre place for a time, although as there were now three females for every one eligible male the blokes were on a pretty flat track. In cricket, however, the gaiety and self-expression of the 'Golden Era' had been replaced by a rather more introverted type of player with his cap pulled down and his shirt collar turned up. The County Championship stuttered back into life in 1919 with two-day matches, and Test cricket began again the following year.

Predictably, England were no match for the Aussies, whose cricket strength had not been similarly decimated. In fact the improvement of their pitches and the introduction of eight-ball overs launched a new generation of prolific run-makers (and suicidal bowlers): the Victoria team twice scored more than 1,000. In one of these innings, the New South Wales leg-spinner Arthur Mailey notched up the memorably atrocious bowling figures of 4-362. 'It was rather a pity Ellis was run out at 1,107,' he said afterwards, 'because I was just striking a length.'

The Aussies also had the 'Big Ship', Warwick Armstrong, as captain, who, it might be said given the times, took no prisoners. The true originator of sledging, having subjected the young Jack Hobbs to such a barrage of abuse in a Test before the war that he shouldered arms four balls later and was bowled, the corpulent Armstrong would do anything to provoke a batsman into submission. This might be by deliberately frustrating them with negative bowling outside the leg stump, intimidating them with words, or other inflammatory tactics. He also apparently 'allowed' ordinary batsmen to make runs for their counties against the Australians so duping the England selectors into picking them for Test matches. It still happens.

Irritatingly Armstrong was also a rather good player who once spent an afternoon at an Ashes Test match padded up in the members' bar drinking whisky with friends and then strode out and made 158. 'He made a bat look like a teaspoon, and the bowling weak tea,' said Edmund Blunden. He imbued his compatriots with their now infamous ruthlessness, and, spurred on by the first of the great fast-bowling pairs – Jack Gregory and Ted McDonald – they walloped England 5–0 in 1920–21, a total humiliation not repeated again until the most recent Ashes series in 2006–7.

England, captained by the Hon. Lionel Tennyson (grandson of the great poet), were thumped 3–0 at home by Armstrong's men a few months later and then, led by another triple-initial man, Arthur Gilligan, lost 4–1 in 1924–5. So much for amateur captaincy, which at that very moment Yorkshire's Lord Hawke was championing with his 'pray god' speech (see pages 101–2).

This prompted more ludicrous debate about the whys and wherefores of gentlemen and players, most of the newspapers coming to their senses and siding with the players, accusing Hawke of being a 'snobocrat' with 'Stone Age views' and telling him to 'play the game'. But the selectors remained in their ivory towers and England weren't to have their first professional captain (Len Hutton) for another thirty years.

At least, after the devastation of the war, they were starting by the mid-1920s to develop some players again. County cricket was back on track to the initial delight of an enthusiastic audience who, still literally rather shell-shocked, welcomed the relative peace and quiet of the game. Glamorgan became the seventeenth first-class county (although they had finished only sixth in the minor-counties championship), and while the northern (professional-laden) counties dominated, the (amateur) administrators justified their positions by incessantly tinkering with the points system. Amazing how history keeps repeating itself, isn't it?

This was the era of some truly great players. Hobbs, Sutcliffe and Woolley were in their pomp, the cavalier Walter Hammond was emerging, someone whistled down a Nottinghamshire pit and up popped a chap called Harold Larwood. Middlesex paraded the diminutive run thief Patsy Hendren – the first to wear primitive side flaps as head protection – and Hampshire had Philip Mead. When I first started watching county cricket in the 1960s I knew of the exploits of all these players. But one name fascinated me above all others. A. P. 'Tich' Freeman.

A Kent supporter married to my 1968 *Wisden*, I noticed his name appeared in the 'most wickets in a season' list five times. In the season of 1928 Freeman bowled 1,976 overs for Kent (comfortably exceeding the 10,000 balls sent down in 1896 by Jack Hearne) and took 304 wickets. Three hundred and four!! That's just absurd. It's incredible stamina and consistency too. People have played for a decade and not taken that many. You do wonder if the batsmen of the time must have lacked a little selectivity. I mean, how could they be so consistently out-foxed by a dwarf, who came rolling in to bowl and tossed up these inviting little spinners travelling at about the speed of a milk float? What were they thinking about, eels and whelks for tea?

That, though, was Tich's art. He looked totally un-prepossessing but each ball, accurately pitched, carried a little bit more spice than it appeared. With small, strong hands he spun his leg break sharply – undoubtedly aided by a decision to make the ball slightly smaller (and there-fore harder to hit) in 1929 – floated in a well-disguised top-spinner and bowled an occasional googly. Of modern bowlers the closest to him in style would have been Sussex's Pakistani Mushtaq Ahmed. Tich was, as the statistics suggest, impossible to get the ball off.

The old Middlesex opener-cum-scorer Harry Sharp used to talk in reverent tones about 'Tich', often after witnessing Mike Gatting's latest destruction of some mediocre county spinner. ''E'd 'av 'ad you, Gatt,' Sharp used to say, sipping his after-match whisky. 'You'd 'av never been able to get down the wicket to 'im!' In fact, although 'stumped Ames bowled Freeman' appears in scorebooks more than almost any other bowler/fielder double act, Freeman actually took almost half his incredible 3,776 wickets (second-most of all time) bowled, lbw, caught and bowled, or hit wicket – in other words without any help from the field.

At 5ft 2in, surely the smallest man to play for England, he had only moderate success at Test level. He teased out a few of the West Indians – newly anointed as the fourth Test-playing country in 1928 – but found the Aussies harder to crack. He was unlucky that they had just unleashed a wave of irrepressible batsmen with nimble feet and insatiable appetites. So he continued to bamboozle half a dozen county batsmen a day, immediately after which he was collected from the ground by his large and rather terrifying wife, Ethel – who couldn't abide him enjoying an after-match drink and smoke, taken home, fed and put to bed. It wasn't a romantic life off the field. He took more than 250 wickets in six successive seasons, and the Middlesex coach of the 1980s, Don Bennett, was fond of telling any complacent youngsters that in 1936 Freeman took 103 wickets . . . and was promptly sacked for his impudence.

You Do the Maths

In the late 1920s, English cricket encapsulated Britain's stark division into bourgeoisie and proletariat. The 'haves', fictionalized in the novels of P. G. Wodehouse, whose central character – the valet Jeeves – was based on a Warwickshire player of the same name, guzzled champagne, danced the Charleston (England captains Arthur Carr and Percy Chapman) and cavorted with women (Wally Hammond). The eccentric Nottinghamshire batsman George Gunn epitomized their spirit. The non-striker in what he assumed was the last over before lunch in a match against Hampshire, he walked off with the clock showing 1.30. The umpire called him back saying, 'Not yet, George. Lunch is at two o'clock today.' Somewhat irritated, Gunn took guard for the next over, then stepped aside to let the first ball hit his wicket. 'I take my lunch at one-thirty,' he said adamantly, striding off. Like Chapman, Carr and many others, Gunn still played cricket as if it were the Golden Age.

Meanwhile the 'have nots' scrapped for their lives. British export revenues had plummeted, unemployment was raging and the average professional cricketer might earn £300 in a season if he was lucky, which at least was triple the pay of a cotton worker. Benefits, surprisingly granted tax-free status in a House of Lords ruling in 1927, provided the pro who had given up the best years of his life to serve a county side a valuable lifeline (even so, Roy Killner's £4,000 benefit was a record until the late 1940s).

A general lack of disposable income, midweek

matches and a proliferation of draws caused county cricket's popularity to wane, and, again in the north, the leagues filled the vacuum, playing matches on Saturday afternoons and hiring exciting players from the new Test-playing countries, like the brilliant West Indian all-rounder Learie Constantine and later the incomparable George Headley.

The Great Depression of 1929 was the economic downturn brought about by excessive consumer spending and over-dependency on American banks. (Substitute 'Icelandic' for American and you have the fundamentals of the credit crunch of 2008.) Two words might also have described the feelings of bowlers world-wide at the arrival of a certain Donald George Bradman.

Reared in Bowral, a small inland town eighty miles south-west of Sydney, the seven-year-old Bradman spent hours throwing a golf ball at a water tank behind his house and hitting the rebound with a stump. He made his first century for Bowral High School aged twelve (an undefeated 115 out of 156 all out). The next year (1921), acting as a scorer for the local cricket club, he was pressed into the team when one player failed to turn up. He went in at no.10 and scored 37 not out. A teammate gave him his first bat as a present.

He left school at fourteen and took a job as an estate agent's clerk. He became a regular in the Bowral Town team. A short and dapper seventeen-year-old whose pads seemed to reach to his navel, he made 234 not out in one match in 1925, 300 in another and 320 in another. All these innings were played on a concrete pitch covered with a coir mat. His father took him as a treat to watch an Ashes Test match at the Sydney Cricket Ground. 'I shall never be happy,' the kid said, 'until I play on this ground.'

He didn't have to wait long. A hundred for the Southern Country Week team in his first outing on a grass pitch was followed by an invitation to join St George's, a prominent Sydney club, and then, in 1927, selection for New South Wales. After an arduous two-day train journey from Sydney to the Adelaide Oval – the place that would become his adopted home – he made his first-class début. Of course, he made a century, scoring 118, batting at no.7. He registered a duck on his first visit to the SCG, but weighed in with 134 there two matches later.

Even if you don't know the Bradman story, you can guess what happened next. Runs surged off his bat in huge waves. Nothing could staunch the flow. Bradman was a walking tsunami. In his second first-class season, 1928–9, aged twenty, his tally of 1,690 runs in 13 matches (including 3 Tests) is still a record for Australian first-class cricket. His first Test produced only 18 and 1, after which he was dropped, but it was his one and only faltering step. He made 79 and 112 on his recall two weeks later. There followed a 340 for New South Wales and, a few weeks later, an innings of 452 not out against Queensland at the SCG, trumping the quadruple centuries of the contemporary Victorian Bill Ponsford who, in effect, had laid down the standard which Bradman sought to emulate. It remained the highest individual first-class score ever made until over-taken by Hanif Mohammad (run out on 499) in 1959.

Bradman seemed to have a shot for every ball and no

obvious weakness. For the hapless bowlers, the concept of eight-ball overs – ill-conceived anyway in a place where the temperature often exceeds 40°C – can never have seemed so flawed. Their only recourse would have been to order him to go back to batting with a stump as he had in childhood.

Nothing, however, can eclipse the orgasms of run-making he produced on his first tour of England in 1930. After a six-week boat-train odyssey to London via Perth, Colombo, Cairo, Rome and Paris, the Australians arrived on 23 April. On 30 April they played the traditional opening match at Worcester. Worcester were soon bundled out for 131. By the close of play on the first day, Bradman, in his first innings outside Australia, was 75 not out. After just three hours batting the following day, he had improved that to 236. In the next match, against Leicester, he made 185. Then there was 252 against Surrey (a useful retort to the Surrey captain, Percy Fender, whose comment that Bradman was 'unwilling to learn' is up there with Tony Greig's 'we'll make them grovel' and Nancy Reagan's 'Fancy building a castle [Windsor] so near the airport!' as one of the most idiotic comments ever made) and 191 against Hampshire. He had 1,000 tour runs before the end of May.

I'll excuse you while you stifle a yawn. But the statistics have to be seen to be believed. And we haven't even got to the Test matches yet. OK, here goes: in the five Tests of that summer, Bradman's scores were 8 and 131 (Trent Bridge), 254 and 1 (Lord's), 334 (Headingley), 14 (Old Trafford) and 232 (the Oval).

That's 974 runs in seven innings, average 139. The Aussie wicketkeeper Rodney Marsh, who was fond of later denouncing English bowlers as 'pie throwers', would have had a field day.

In fact the English bowling – featuring Larwood and Maurice Tate amongst others – wasn't half bad. Bradman simply had an unerring eye, immaculate balance, dexterity bar none and an instinctive understanding of the bowlers' plans. Also, as an antisocial type, he had an inherent desire to remain out there on his own in the middle rather than loiter in a noisy, cloying dressing room. Well, given the choice, wouldn't you rather be in the fresh air acknowledging the crowd's applause than dodging the barrack-room insults, burps and farts of a bunch of smelly cricketers? His 252 at Lord's and 334 at Headingley, 309 of which were made on the first day, are often proclaimed as two of his greatest innings.

There is plenty of black-and-white footage of Bradman from the 1930s. It reveals a short, compact player, bat resting unusually between his feet in his stance, the movements smooth and unhurried, the drives and pulls and dabs loaded with certainty. There is nothing fancy or uncontrolled. (In his torrent of runs in 1930, he hit only two sixes, neither in a Test match, one of them off a no ball.) Watching an Australia–India Test match in his eighties, Bradman was captivated by Sachin Tendulkar's batting, remarking that there were parallels with the way he used to bat. In Tendulkar's easy movements and controlled shots, the ball apparently laser-guided into spaces, you can see definite similarities, if not in the 3lb railway sleeper of a bat Tendulkar wields as opposed to Bradman's 2½lb wand.

Why didn't the bowlers emulate Armstrong and try barracking Bradman, you wonder? The answer is they were all too tired or gobsmacked to do so. Take the Somerset spinner Jack White, who bowled the first ball to Bradman in the Lord's Test. It was taken contemptuously yards down the wicket and thumped boundary-wards on the full. 'When he finished the stroke,' wrote Cardus, 'he was close enough to J. C. White to see the look of astonishment on the bowler's face.'

It probably wouldn't have worked anyway. Bradman was a strangely elusive loner who irked his teammates by disappearing to his room at the close of play to listen to music or write letters home. He never bought a round of drinks, and stubbornly justified himself when confronted about it. Despite his prowess he was not a popular team member.

One man was especially miffed about Bradman's grand entrance. That man was Wally Hammond. In any other era, Hammond would have been top dog. He was the cricketer of your dreams. Debonair, dashing, devastating, with women all over him. Or should that be with him all over women? A majestic batsman in the classic style, he played innings of regal, destructive power, sweeping mere bowlers aside with a flash of his blade. He had forearms like legs of pork. Striding about the crease grandly, he was Caligula with a bat.

In the summer of 1927, the 24-year-old Hammond drilled to the boundary the first five balls of the day bowled by the fearsome Australian Ted McDonald, who was playing for Lancashire, and he went on to a brilliant 187 in just three hours. Most of his innings were like that. Fast bowlers bounced. Hammond hooked. Spinners tossed up. Hammond drove. In the winter of 1928 he took the Australian bowlers to the cleaners with a sequence of scores the like of which had never been seen before. In the match that marked Bradman's (disappointing) Test début, Hammond made 251 and he finished the series, which England won 4–1, with 905 runs, average 113. He could bowl and catch at slip too, and drink and shag as well. He was the ultimate all-rounder, and he knew it.

Now, in 1930, he had been upstaged, and cursed his luck, often to be heard muttering, 'Bloody Bradman', while playing for Gloucestershire. But in a way Hammond created Bradman. He was the catalyst. Whatever Hammond did, Bradman, imbued with a strong sense of his own importance, exceeded it. It was ruthless, it was remorseless, it was a superiority complex writ large. Subconsciously Bradman believed it was his duty to explore the limit of human endeavour. With Australia now themselves blighted by economic depression, he was a purist in a contaminated world. He owed it to his people to seek perfection. Oh all right, enough of this psychological claptrap. ''E joost liked battin',' as Geoff Boycott would say.

To get a result, English Test matches had now been extended to four days, and of course Australia won the 1930 Ashes series – the leg-spinner Clarrie Grimmett, who invented the flipper (back spinner), playing a valuable supporting role. But it was really all about one man: 'a team in himself', as Jack Hobbs commented. The *Evening Standard*'s headline was an apt epitaph:

BRADMAN BATS AND BATS AND BATS

The crowds flocked to see this amazing run-machine and the press eulogized him – 'Bradman is living witness to the very important truth that men are not equal,' proclaimed *Christian Renewal* magazine. But there was a latent resentment in English cricket about the way this intruder had taken the game on to a different plane, cold-bloodedly nullifying everything that had gone before – Hambledon, Grace, all the charisma of the Golden Age. His inexorable run-making seemed to be questioning the right of anyone else to be with him on that stage. I suppose a modern equivalent could be the way the remorseless Pete Sampras and the relentless Andre Agassi crushed the panache and artistry of 1980s tennis.

Bradman had the impact of two men. 'A menace to English cricket,' the *Daily Mail* called him. Not only that but he had single-handedly confiscated the post-war *joie de vivre*. 'Why isn't cricket fun any more?' headlined the *Daily Herald* and other papers followed suit. They resented the teetotal, apparently joyless Bradman for everything: England's defeats, unemployment, the exorbitant price of meat, even the mouldy weather. The expression of that resentment was Bodyline.

Stop the Bleeding!

Watching all these developments was Douglas Jardine. Born in Bombay to a Scottish lawyer, Jardine had a complex upbringing involving prep school in Oxford, holidays in Scotland, where he lived in a vast empty house with his aunt, boarding school at Winchester College and university back at Oxford. At Winchester he developed a reputation for extreme courage, excelling at the bizarre game of Winchester football, particularly in the 'hot' (scrum) in which you had to stand still while opponents booted the ball at you. Now you know why most people who went to Winchester have a nervous tic.

He played for Oxford University and Surrey and, though he was a bit of a grinder, was good enough to be chosen for England's victorious 1928–9 tour of Australia, where he scored 341 runs in the series, average 42. The seeds of his acrimony towards Australians had been sown on that tour, where his habit of wearing a striped Harlequin cap and a white silk cravat in the field drew predictable insults from the bleachers. 'Where's your butler to carry your bat?!' they yelled, and, when he was seen flapping at flies round his head, 'Don't kill them, they're the only friends you've got!' They despised his posh accent and his superior air. The antipathy was mutual. 'All Australians are uneducated, and an unruly mob,' Jardine proclaimed.

After the debacle of 1930, England then lost to South Africa that winter. In a rare burst of initiative, the MCC decided on a bit of a clear-out and recruited Pelham

Warner to assemble a fresh team to win back the Ashes. Announcing that England needed to find 'a new type of bowler, new ideas for Australia', Warner persuaded Jardine, whose trenchant batting style was admired but whose only experience of captaincy had been at school, to have a go at leading the side. Also he had only two initials. Still, he had three Tests against New Zealand, on their first tour of England in 1931, and one against India the following summer to bed in.

Little did Warner realize what he had unleashed. Watching the 1930 series from afar, Jardine's anti-Aussie stance had hardened. Recognizing that Bradman was the main obstruction, he spent over a year formulating his plans. There have been less comprehensive war strategies. He studied footage of the 1930s series, read reports, consulted various trusted players, like the left-arm leg theorist Frank Foster and Jardine's friend and Surrey captain Percy Fender, who had studied Bradman at close quarters. Both believed they had spied a weakness. He was vulnerable to short-pitched bowling on leg stump. Or, as Jardine put it, 'He's yellow.'

The next step was to convince the bowlers of the idea. He summoned the two quickest, the burly-shouldered Harold Larwood and his Nottinghamshire left-arm opening partner Bill Voce, to a clandestine meeting at the Piccadilly Hotel in August 1932, a month before departure. In this sense the amateur/professional division worked. The hired hands were used to being told what to do and accepted it.

With Larwood he was preaching to the converted anyway. He had already discomfited Bradman with some leg-stump bowling at the Oval and was fed up with his dominance. 'Bradman didn't break my heart in 1930,' he said, 'he just made me very, very tired.' Voce, who with Larwood had taken a stack of county wickets that summer with similar methods, was a little more blunt. 'If we don't beat you,' he told Australia's Viv Richardson early in the tour, 'we'll knock your bloody heads off.'

England's tactics seemed to be working shortly after they arrived in Australia. In two games against an Australian XI and one against New South Wales, Bradman looked ill at ease against the England quickies and failed six times. Once he was bowled by Larwood trying to make room to cut, another time he was bowled middle-stump by Voce going too far across and attempting to pull. The stand-in captain for the second of these games, R. E. S. Wyatt (Jardine had gone trout fishing), systematically moved more and more close fielders to the legside, other batsmen took blows on the body and after the match Bradman complained to the Victorian cricket officials about the approach. Jardine fanned the flames by declaring to his team before the Test series began that Bradman should be regarded as 'the little bastard'.

Bradman wasn't universally popular with his own cricket board either – after disagreements over him writing newspaper articles – and he missed the first Test through illness (probably stress). Despite Stan McCabe's fearless 187, England won this match handsomely, almost by an innings. Larwood took 5 wickets in each innings. With a smooth, accelerating run-up, a whirling action and powerful shoulders, a legacy of his work down t'pit, he was not only the fastest bowler around but very accurate with it. To lapse into modern parlance, he was superb at 'executing plans', and stuck to them, irrespective of what people thought of them. His favourite song was Frank Sinatra's 'My Way'. Also, as he was only 5ft 9in – the same height as the 1980s West Indian paceman Malcolm Marshall – his short balls skidded at the batsman's ribcage and, like Marshall's, were difficult to avoid.

In the second Test at Melbourne, Bradman was back, but the impact of leg theory was immediately evident. A national hero, Bradman entered to vast, unrelenting applause from a record-breaking crowd and the bowler – the tall but hardly terrifying Bill Bowes – had to wait for it to subside. He used the time to reposition a couple of legside fielders. Obviously expecting a bouncer, the Don stepped uncharacteristically right across his stumps to his first delivery and attempted to pull it, but his timing was all wrong and he could only deflect it into his wicket. It was the only first-baller of his Test career.

On a desperately slow pitch, he made amends in the second innings with a three-hour unbeaten hundred, countering attempted leg theory by swaying outside leg to hit short balls through the offside, something he'd practised extensively during his layoff. Australia, with the feisty leg spin of Bill 'Tiger' O'Reilly to the fore, promptly levelled the series. All Australia was euphoric, and every woman under fifty wanted to kiss 'The Don'. Bradman, however, was more interested in making a formal complaint to the Australian Board about

'Bodyline bowling', warning it would 'kill cricket if allowed to continue'. All the harassed board did was leak it to the press.

Snivellers

So in the third Test, in Adelaide, everything really kicked off. Emotions were already running high two days before the match when spectators hurled insults at Jardine as England practised, and the session was curtailed. He had also had a row with his fourth fast bowler, the Etonian Gubby Allen, who had refused to adopt the Bodyline methods and called Jardine 'a perfect swine', and the Nawab of Pataudi, who had made a hundred in the first Test but was reluctant to field in leg theory positions. He was unceremoniously dropped.

The first day, during which England made 236-7, was uneventful. But after lunch on the second the Australian captain Bill Woodfull was felled as a short one from Larwood slammed into his chest, provoking a furious reaction from the 50,000 crowd, and a provocative 'Well bowled, Harold!' from Jardine, deliberately within earshot of Bradman, the non-striker. Acknowledging that Larwood was more potent when riled, Jardine stopped him in his run-up and ostentatiously moved several fielders over from the offside to leg. Another short ball to the partially recovered Woodfull knocked the bat out of his hand. The crowd were apoplectic and threatening to invade the field. 'Hey, George,' said one

English fielder to umpire Hele, 'if they come over the fence leave me a stump!' 'No way,' replied Hele, 'I'll need all three myself.'

Bradman, who, as old footage illustrates, was jumping nervously across his crease, often overbalancing, promptly fended a Larwood throat ball to short leg and departed for eight. Woodfull eventually followed. So did McCabe, and though Ponsford made a defiant 85, this was only by virtue of wearing extra padding so he could withstand numerous blows to the body. At a drinks break, one of a thousand Jardine-haters yelled, 'Don't give him a drink, let him die of thirst!' Australia ended the day well behind in the match, much to the chagrin of the departing masses, lacking a few bikini-clad women in their midst to deflect their anger, as happens at the Adelaide Oval these days.

Perhaps the most inflammatory incident happened after play, however. Warner, the self-appointed team manager, visited the Australian dressing room with his assistant to see if Woodfull was OK. It was more than a touch disingenuous, given that Warner had singularly failed for the preceding two months to dissuade the England bowlers from their tactics, and the Australian captain knew it. Towelling himself down after a shower, he famously replied, 'Mr Warner. There are two teams out there on the field. One is playing cricket, the other is not. That is all I have to say. Good afternoon.' How dignified their displeasure was in those days, eh? It's surprising he didn't add, 'And do pass on my regards to the fragrant Mrs Warner.'

Of course, the story was fed to the press – apparently

by Bradman, whose Machiavellian side had become increasingly obvious – and by the resumption of the match after a rest day was all over the papers. The situation was compounded by the Australian wicketkeeper Bert Oldfield top-edging a Larwood thunderbolt on to his head and retiring hurt ('It's not your fault, Harold,' he mumbled chivalrously), and Jardine posting himself on the boundary to really incense the barrackers. He was pelted with orange peel – about as effective as throwing tissues at a charging rhino – and a riot was brewing. Mounted police reinforcements were summoned, and the mood calmed as, over the next two days, England, led by a stonewalling Jardine, ground out a huge lead.

By the end of the fifth day (all Tests in Australia were timeless) the hosts were slipping to a heavy defeat, despite a counter-attacking 66 from Bradman which ended when he tried to loft the spin of Hedley Verity for a second successive six (his first in Tests). 'I wanted to hit one bowler before the other hit me,' he said afterwards. The sense of outrage sat heavily on the Australian Cricket Board delegates, and, after hasty consultation, they wired the MCC in protest. They called 'Bodyline bowling' a 'menace' to the game causing 'intensely bitter feeling' and declared it 'unsportsmanlike'.

Again, the press responded before the power-brokers. The story made front-page news for several days, sidelining Hitler's rise to power in Germany. One of the first out of the blocks was Surrey's Percy Fender, who, remember, was partly responsible for concocting the whole strategy. With more than a hint of satisfaction he dismissed the Australian complaints in the *Daily Telegraph*, pointing out that leg theory was hardly new: England had previously had to endure something similar from the Australians Gregory and McDonald. The only difference here was in the emphasis on legside field settings. (There were often six close fielders on the legside, which wouldn't be allowed now.) It was, he wrote, a bowler's job to discover a batsman's shortcomings, 'and to play on them to his discomfiture', and it's hard to disagree with that. It's what the game's all about. Other papers were even more forthright. The *Daily Herald* accused the Aussies of 'Undignified Snivelling'. 'Cheapest Possible Insult,' declared the *Star*. *The Times* denounced a suggestion that an English captain would stoop to anything that was 'not cricket'. No one wrote that a cricket ball can hurt if it hits you, and if you don't like that idea, take up badminton. Maybe they should have.

Jardine made a brief public statement after the match, which England won by the colossal margin of 338 runs, giving them a 2–1 lead in the series. 'What I have to say is not worth listening to,' he said. 'Those of you who had seats got your money's worth, and then some. Thank you.' If only all press conferences were like that, rather than endless and laden with 'We're in a good place right now' and 'We put the ball in the right areas', which I always think sounds like they're landing it in Knightsbridge or Mayfair. While questioning England's tactics, the Australian papers accused their board of a 'hysterical' reaction and their players were advised to get on with it.

Affronted by the 'unsportsmanlike' slur, the MCC committee, consisting of a viscount, several peers, the Speaker of the House of Commons and a former governor of Bengal – representative of the British public as usual – eventually rejected the Australians' protests. 'We deplore your cable,' they replied some days later. 'We have fullest confidence in captain, team and managers and are convinced they would do nothing to infringe the Laws of Cricket or the game.' Craftily, they added that if the Aussies wanted to cancel the remaining matches they would agree 'with great reluctance', knowing that the series was a box office phenomenon and it was the last thing the Australians would actually want. Predictably the Aussies retracted their 'unsporting' accusations and the tour continued.

There was a three-week gap before the Brisbane Test, which was an anti-climax. The row had blown itself out and a benign pitch and excessive heat during the Test drew the England bowlers' sting – Voce was injured anyway. Fortified by the odd glass of champagne supplied by Jardine, they still explored the Bodyline route and Larwood dismissed Bradman twice more, once caught at deep cover, the only fielder on the off-side. By virtue of more dogged batting and the courage of the Lancashire left-hander Eddie Paynter, who, suffering acute tonsillitis, twice dashed from hospital by taxi to make crucial runs, England won the Test by 6 wickets and thus regained the Ashes.

In the final Test, in Sydney, Larwood took 4 first-innings wickets – including Bradman's – contributed 98 with the bat as nightwatchman, and, despite injury, clocked the Don on the shoulder in the second innings (the only time he was actually hit in the series) before breaking down. Jardine ignored Warner's request to desist from Bodyline as an act of good faith, saying, 'We've got the bastards down there and we'll keep them there.' He wouldn't allow Larwood off the field until Bradman was out (bowled Verity for 71). The illustrious pair walked off the field together. Incredibly, Larwood never played for England again.

Sticky Fingers

After a month in New Zealand, the England players arrived back in dribs and drabs. Gubby Allen actually stopped off in Hollywood to fraternize with various film stars and didn't return until mid-May, as was the amateur's wont. Larwood, freed from his contract, spoke out, declaring that Bradman had been frightened. 'He was scared by my bowling,' he said. Jardine, in a one-off interview, denounced the term Bodyline as 'meaningless', arguing that it was a media creation that 'would have died a natural and speedy death' if not taken up by the Australian Cricket Board. Courageous to a fault, occasionally sadistic, Jardine defended the whole issue simply and succinctly with this little refrain:

> Australia's writers showed their claws,
> Her backers raged, her batsmen shook,
> Statesmen consulted – and the cause – ?
> Our bowling was too good to hook.

The matter didn't end there of course. There was a ceremony at Trent Bridge for the victors in early summer, and Jardine and Larwood made emotional speeches in front of a large and ecstatic crowd. But, anxious to maintain good relations with the remnants of the Empire (in other words keep getting Australian lamb at a good price), the British government got involved. Prompted by the new MCC President, Viscount Hailsham, who was also Secretary of State for War, the Nottinghamshire chairman asked Larwood to sign a letter apologizing for the way he had bowled in Australia. 'Over my dead body,' retorted his mother, or words to that effect, when she saw the request, and a severely affronted Larwood refused. The Cabinet minister and Dominions secretary Jimmy Thomas ensured he was never again considered for England selection.

That summer the West Indian fast bowlers Learie Constantine and Manny Martindale attempted to give England a taste of their own medicine. Jardine had always maintained that it was up to the batsman to sort out a way of dealing with this tactic, and at Old Trafford he withstood a number of blows to score 127, his only Test century. England won that series, and the one in India that followed (the first Test match on Indian soil was played at Bombay Gymkhana, a sentimental moment for Jardine returning to his birthplace). After this Jardine, sensing political unease, resigned the captaincy. Warner, enjoying the afterglow of Ashes recovery while voicing his disapproval of Bodyline, was relieved. 'When Jardine sees a cricket ground with an Australian on it, he goes mad,' he said.

Warner was the classic English paradox: desperate to win but in as polite a way as possible. It was appropriate that he was knighted. He was the epitome of a hypocritical Englishman. And, in the winter of 1933, with another Australian series looming, the MCC belatedly conceded that 'a direct attack by the bowler upon the batsman would be an offence against the spirit of the game.' Eventually they issued a ruling declaring that fast, short-pitched deliveries persistently aimed at the batsman's body were 'unfair'. And everyone got on with the game.

It was a different game, though. The gloves were off. Bodyline tactics were even witnessed in the traditional Varsity match between Oxford and Cambridge. Looking at the issue seventy-five years on through the prism of numerous accounts, Bodyline wasn't just about cricket, or indeed just about sport. It reflected the emotions, and political ambitions, of the time. England had been reconstructed after the Great War, and was just establishing itself again as a proud and powerful nation when the Depression, and Bradman, struck. It was a rude wake-up call, exposing the inadequacy of Britain's aristocratic/amateur-led effortlessness. The former colonies were asserting themselves in new and alarming ways. Bradman's clinical dominance symbolized the rapid fragmentation of the Empire.

England's response – personified by the proud, institutionalized Jardine – was forthright and ruthless. The short-term aim – to cut Bradman down to size – had been achieved. He averaged only 56, still the second highest in the 1932–3 series, mind, but it was less than half his output of 1930. The Ashes were reclaimed, but in a way that signalled a new era of calculation and grim determination. Sheer god-given talent and privilege were not enough. You had to get your hands dirty. In more ways than one. Just across the Channel, Hitler, despite the reported loss of one of his testicles in the Battle of the Somme (prompting the favourite playground song 'Hitler has only got one ball, the other is in the Albert Hall'), was now on the warpath.

NINE

Nazi Delivery

We are at 1934. The year the Loch Ness monster was first sighted, the year the outlaws Bonnie and Clyde went on their sex'n'steal ride around America, the year Percy Shaw invented the cat's eye when his car headlights picked out a startled moggy on a fence in Halifax, and if it had been running away he'd have invented the pencil sharpener. The average price of a house in Britain was £515, which in 2008 is the average price of paying someone to come and fix the boiler. And that's only if they turn up.

Mid-summer '34 saw the Night of the Long Knives and all sorts of other disturbing goings-on in Germany, but the British were otherwise occupied debating the Reconstitution of the LBW Law. The saga had begun five years earlier when a glut of runs worldwide, and extensive use of the pad, persuaded the authorities to tweak the law and allow leg befores even if the ball had hit the bat first. That had little effect, so then it was mooted that you could be out lbw to balls pitching *outside* the off stump. Previously you could only be out lbw to a ball pitching *in line* with the stumps. Bowling was a mug's game then, Jesus!

After much procrastination, involving the MCC and other bodies, and general whining from batsmen (apart from Bradman, who was nobly in favour of making it easier to get him out), it was agreed to try this amendment the following season. It was reasonably successful, though it's a shame they didn't go the whole hog and allow lbws to balls pitching outside *leg* stump as well, an initiative that would have arrested the rapid decline of leg spin in English cricket.

A collective guilty conscience was to blame for England relinquishing the Ashes again in 1934. Unfettered by Larwood, Bradman was back to his best (758 runs, average 94) and the British public took him to their hearts as if he was one of theirs (which he was in a way – his grandfather was brought up in Suffolk). Spectators swarmed around him wherever he played, and there is a delightful picture of him in *Wisden* trailing a gaggle of idolizing schoolkids, staring at him as if he had descended from Mount Olympus. Or maybe they were just getting him to sign their Player's cigarette cards. When Bradman was taken seriously ill at the end of the tour, even King George V got involved, demanding regular medical bulletins. 'I want to know everything,' he declared. A heavy smoker, the King died himself soon afterwards of bronchitis and emphysema. He must have had some great cigarette card swaps.

By the mid-1930s, most households had a wireless, and the BBC broadcast their first Test match commentary in 1935 with the Oxford rugby blue

Howard Marshall at the microphone. That and the rapid advance of newspaper circulation (the *News of the World* and the *People* sold a combined 10m copies by the end of the decade) helped to further popularize cricket. Test matches – now played by six countries with the addition of West Indies (1928), New Zealand (1930) and India (1932) – were the main attraction, but though county cricket consistently lost money, it had glamorous appeal (yes, really!) and a rash of teenagers signed up to join in.

Wally Hammond was England's star turn. A grandiose batsman of supreme power, his determination not to be entirely upstaged by Bradman resulted in an incredible 336 not out against New Zealand, the new highest individual Test score, and including ten straight sixes, three off fast bowler Jack Newman in one over. He was the obvious man to captain the side, but he was a professional, so, underlining the absurdity of this division, was overlooked. He filled the void by bedding a lot of eligible women. It was said that Hammond had two ruling passions. His cricket bat and his genitals. The conscientious objector Gubby Allen was made captain instead for the 1936–7 tour of Australia. Harbouring a dislike of northern professionals, Allen left behind Sutcliffe and the young thruster Len Hutton, chose southerners like Arthur Fagg and Laurie Fishlock instead, and the Southern Softies lost the series 3–2, after being 2–0 up. Just to rub salt in Hammond's wound, Bradman was now captain of Australia.

Eventually Hammond sacrificed his match fees, became a director of a Gloucestershire tyre company and was at last made captain. He led England against the 1938 Australian tourists. Still preferring the company of his nearest and dearest, Bradman persuaded the Australian board to allow wives on tour for the first time. Not only was he the best batsman the world has ever seen but he was also the originator of the WAGs. The women probably regarded it as a punishment since the series was a stalemate and Gucci hadn't opened yet. Bradman traded centuries with Hammond, culminating in an English runfest at the Oval, where Hutton batted for thirteen hours to make 364, the new highest individual Test score. When he was out at 770-6, the Yorkshire wicketkeeper Arthur Wood, coming in at no.8, famously said, 'I'm just the man for a crisis.'

This was the second Test ever to be covered on TV – the first was the Lord's Test of the same year. It was transmitted by the BBC only in the London area to a few thousand receivers, though a large crowd built up outside an electrical shop in south London to watch the set in the window. Given that England's innings of 903-7 declared was ground out over three days, they must have wondered if they were actually watching moving pictures. It would have been a struggle for solo commentator Henry Wakelam. 'Oh I say, that's another dot ball to Hutton, his 552nd. He's doing awfully well though to keep those dashed colonials out.' He could at least have had a laugh at the bowling figures of Australian chinaman* bowler Laurie Fleetwood Smith: 87 overs, 1 wicket for 298. So much for the new bowler-friendly lbw law.

* The explanation for the term 'Chinaman' concerns Ellis 'Puss" Achong, a tricky left-arm spinner of Chinese extraction who played for the West Indies in the early 1930s. Achong dismissed England's Walter Robins with one that spun unconventionally from off the leg, after which Robins exclaimed, 'Fancy getting out to a bloody Chinaman!'

Hammond led England in South Africa in 1938–9, a largely tedious series culminating in the incredible 'timeless' test in Durban. This, the original insomnia cure, was a ten-day affair in which England, seeking an improbable 696 to win in the last innings, were 654-5 when foiled by rain. (In which case how can it be called 'timeless'?) Then against the West Indies in the summer of 1939, Hammond finally overtook Bradman's tally of Test hundreds with his twenty-second.

His enjoyment was shortlived. A week later Germany invaded Poland and on 3 September Neville Chamberlain declared that Britain was at war. The air-raid sirens sounded and excited children rushed outside to watch the action, hoping to see that grumpy Mrs Burton's house over the road get bombed and ignoring their parents' orders to 'Get inside the shelter, you brats!' They needn't have worried. The first bombs didn't fall on Britain until July 1940.

The final county match before the outbreak of war had been a poignant one. Yorkshire beat Sussex at Hove to make it a hat-trick of County Championships, and a total of 12 titles between the wars, underlining their dominance. The left-armer Hedley Verity, who many believed was the finest left-arm spinner ever to play for England, finished off Sussex with an extraordinary spell of 7-9 in 6 overs. It was his last appearance in first-class cricket. Serving with the Green Howards in Sicily in 1943, he was shot and captured by the Italians and died of his wounds shortly afterwards.

Some counties wanted to stage the championship in 1940, but it soon became clear as everyone joined up that there would be no players, and, as rationing had been introduced, no shoulders of lamb for lunch. Lord's remained available for matches (and lunches), and there was a fair amount of cricket played between services personnel on leave and county players based at home, and some old players like Frank Woolley coming out of retirement for an England XI against the Dominions.

One match at Lord's in 1944 between the Army and the RAF illustrates the British indefatigability that characterized the war effort. The former England captain Bob Wyatt was about to bowl to the elegant young Middlesex batsman Jack Robertson when they heard the drone of a doodlebug approaching. All the players fell to the ground, but the flying bomb missed Lord's, detonating 200 yards away in Regent's Park. Still clutching the ball Wyatt scrambled to his feet and delivered it. Overloaded with adrenaline, Robertson smote it for six into the Grandstand, and the match continued uninterrupted.

The Oval, commandeered – but never used – as a prisoner of war camp, was badly bombed during the blitz. There was a hidden agenda here. During a tour of England in 1930, the German cricket team went to watch a Test match at the Oval. But some jobsworth excluded them from the covered stand. You can hear the conversation now:

'Oi! You need special tickets to sit there!'
'Was?? Ve hav got tickets!'
'These are not the right ones.'
'Verdammt nochmal. Vere does it zay zat?'

'Right here. Look, can't you Krauts read?'

'*Um Gottes Willen*, zere are plenty of free zeats 'ere.'

'Rules are rules. And hand over those sausages too. No food allowed in the ground except from official suppliers.'

'But zese are not sausages, zese are genuine Bratwurst!'

'They look like sausages to me and they are not allowed.'

'*Das ist unerhört*! Ze Führer vil hear about zis.'

Cricket had been introduced to Germany by British residents in the 1880s, and soon kids were playing games against lampposts in Berlin streets. Many clubs formed in and around Berlin, Frankfurt, Hamburg and other cities. The Reich Sports Leader, Hans von Tschammer und Osten, was entertained at Lord's and the Oval in the 1930s, and was so captivated he requested some English professionals to help further the game. They never materialized and football eventually squeezed German cricket virtually out of existence.

You can only speculate how history might have been different had the Nazis become diverted by cricket instead of obsessing over other issues. I mean, look at the cricket-loving PM John Major, whose Utopian dream for Britain in 1993 involved 'the long shadows falling across the county ground, the warm beer, the invincible green suburbs, dog lovers and pool fillers, and old maids bicycling to Holy Communion through the morning mist . . .' He was quite persuasive and it all nearly came to pass until he admitted having an affair with Edwina Currie.

It Ain't Half Hot, Mum

While first-class cricket was suspended in England during the war, it continued, at least for a time, in the former colonies. Bradman reeled off more ridiculous sequences of scores for New South Wales in 1939–40, and appeared (mainly unsuccessfully) in other inter-state matches afterwards to raise money for the war effort. There was some inter-island cricket in the West Indies, though none of it featuring Jamaica, which interrupted the fabulous career of George Headley – known as the black Bradman – and with good reason as he had mastered the England bowling like no other, and in swashbuckling style.

In India the Ranji Trophy – founded in 1934–5 and involving about twenty-five regions – was actually invigorated in the war years, producing some massive scores and drawing large crowds. It was also an influential unifying force in the subcontinent, as compared with the other main Indian tournaments, the Quadrangular and the Pentangular, which were more secular, pitting teams of Hindus, Muslims and Parsees against Europeans.

These competitions did, however, lure top cricketers from overseas – notably Denis Compton – and are credited with inducing the rapid rise in Indian cricket. Compton made stacks of runs for Holkar, and was well remunerated, though not always. Before one match the team's patron, a rich merchant, offered Compton a bonus of 50 rupees for every run he made after 100. As he left the field, dismissed for 257, he was calculating how much the merchant now owed him. Entering the dressing room his elation was soon doused by a note on his chair. It was from the merchant. It read: 'Well played, Mr Compton. Very sorry, called away on urgent business.'

Cricket also took off in other surprising locations. A large quantity of first-class players from England, South Africa, Australia and India were stationed in Egypt, including Hammond, and played matches of high quality in Cairo and Alexandria. The same sort of thing happened in Papua New Guinea, and the natives took to it as a useful diversion from eating each other. One or two Middle East nations discovered cricket around this time too, notably the United Arab Emirates, who later appeared in the 1996 World Cup (though the team was mainly made up of expat Pakistanis). The UAE's major city, Dubai, is now, rather incongruously, the official centre of world cricket: the International Cricket Council's headquarters are located there. Many people assume this is for tax reasons. There is no truth in the claim that it's because ICC executives like stocking up on cut-price Rolexes.

You might well wonder how a place like UAE, which is basically just sand and oil sheiks, got into cricket. A letter I received a few years ago from a retired British airman, John Butcher, explains. His enlightening story is worth hearing because it undoubtedly echoes how cricket got a footing in many parts of the Empire. It is 1943 and Butcher was stationed at an air base in Sharjah, adjoining Dubai, awaiting instructions.

I was the watchkeeper one morning in the transmitting station, deeply immersed in the newly-arrived 1943 *Wisden*. I was therefore disconcerted by the roar from the M.O. doing his rounds and suggesting that I was not exerting myself. I leapt to attention waiting the storm. Instead he said, in soft Irish, 'What's the book?' '*Wisden* sir,' I said. He begged me to lend it to him when I'd finished and we talked cricket for half an hour. He visited later, borrowed the book and when he returned it, told me to get a team up from Signals.

On the airfield, a gunpost stood in the centre of the only patch of hard sand. Twenty men removed the gunpost. Arab labourers painted 1000 petrol tins white to form the boundary, palm fronds were woven into sightscreens, a native carpenter produced a scoreboard. Someone told the labourers it was rain-making equipment and they worked with a will. Equipment appeared from the weekly Dakota – a beautiful short-handled Gunn & Moore, a massive teak creation from India and four Israeli bats which lasted only six overs before the delicate relationship between the handle and the blade dissolved.

Then came the mat. Balls would not last on sand and we only had six. The M.O. remembered seeing a 22 yard mat in the officer's mess in Bahrain. Early in the morning one of our rusty Vincents took off, and later the mat appeared. No questions were asked or answered.

Unseasonal rain apparently delayed the first match for a fortnight, but before long a league had begun amongst ten teams drawn from 200 men, part British servicemen, part locals. There was not a lot of war action in Sharjah, so the assembled crew needed something to pass the time, and the Wii hadn't been invented then.

Butcher continues:

> The BOAC Indians won the first league. Seven elegant Hindus, coached to perfection in good schools, provided the runs and the keeper. Their scores were limited by a reluctance to run more than a single [well, it was 44 degrees in the shade]. Bowling was the job of the labouring class Muslims. They played in full robes. Little black hands peeped out from yards of muslin and the ball spun towards you.

From such little acorns, the sprawling oak of Sharjah cricket grew, to the extent that it now encompasses a multitude of club and school competitions and stages major international events at the stadium, built on the site of that first improvised pitch. Dubai is very much the hub of world cricket operations (though the Indians might dispute that). There is a room full of TV monitors at ICC headquarters simultaneously showing every major cricket match in progress around the world, checking on players and umpires. It's like a scene from the James Bond movie *Tomorrow Never Dies*, in which Jonathan Pryce plays a sinister media mogul monitoring the world via a video wall. It's very Big Brother. And all because a young airman was caught reading *Wisden*. How the Muslim world might be different if he'd been caught reading *Beach Volleyball Monthly*.

The airman's story has a touching end:

A general duties airman who had had a trial for Surrey was rumoured to be on the next Dakota. I told the Signals officer to get hold of him. He met the plane, but the Armoury officer pulled rank and put the Surrey man in his team against us that afternoon. They made 80, about par for the course. We prepared to face the Surrey demon. His resentment might have been directed at Hitler for interrupting his potential career, or at the RAF for sending him to the 'White Man's Grave' or at the officer who'd put him in charge of latrines, but we were soon 12-7.

I was joined by AC2 (aircraftman) Danny Barratt, a sturdy Yorkshireman. Somehow he survived the first over from the demon. The next hour was a complete blank. We were awakened by a shout: 'John you've got 40, Danny's got 28. We've won!' The gods of cricket had smiled upon us.

Next day the Signal's Officer visited the transmitter for the first time in living memory.

'Good morning LAC Butcher and AC1 Barratt!' [LAC stands for leading aircraftman.]

'Er wrong sir, I'm AC1, Barratt's AC2.'

'You heard what I said!'

'But aren't we supposed to pass a Board?'

'Fuck the Board. We won the match!'

We decided a few more matches like that and we'd be Air Marshals!

Cricket, you see, refreshes the parts other careers cannot reach.

Aye Aye Captain

George Orwell defined sport as 'war minus the shooting' (Andrés Escobar, the Colombian footballer who was murdered after his World Cup own goal in 1994, may be the exception). The baronet Sir Home Seton Charles Montagu Gordon used cricket as a metaphor for conflict at the beginning of the Second World War. 'England has now begun the grim Test match against Germany,' he wrote. 'We do not wish to win merely the Ashes of civilisation. We want to win a lasting peace with honour and prosperity to us all.'

As we all know, it was a long old game lasting 2,073 days and costing 450,000 British lives, though that was nothing compared with Germany's seven million deaths. Churchill's great speeches had inspired the nation, though his off-hand comments were equally galvanizing. When asked by a south Devon beach Home Guard commander what to do if the Germans landed, he replied, 'Hit 'em on the head with broken bottles', adding as an aside, 'it's about all we've bloody got!'

The Nazis left one major legacy to cricket. From 1945 whenever a ball was trickling agonizingly towards the boundary, the batting team would shout as one, 'German General!', meaning '*Goeball(s)*!' to urge it over the line. (As you can tell, county cricket dressing rooms are zones of great wit and sensitivity.) I have an old book of German–English translation from the period and this use of 'Goeballs' isn't in it. There are some intriguing phrases though, including 'Vorsicht! der

Derdel ist gekommen' ('Look out, the flying bomb is coming!') and 'Ich habe einen Gefangenen eingeliefert' ('I have brought in a prisoner'), which, though of dubious value for today's tourist, gives you an insight into what life was like then.

The war changed Britain drastically. The economy was devastated, Britain having to borrow $3.75bn from the US, a loan finally paid off only in 2006; and from bomb-razed urban areas sprang up pig-ugly estates with stairwells reeking of piss. The country was desperate for rejuvenation and a good wash.

It was a great opportunity too for cricket to advance itself and join the modern world. As usual, the chance was spilt. Seeking a brighter, more dynamic game, the MCC assembled a working party under Yorkshire's Sir Stanley Jackson to come up with a blueprint for the county game. But the idea of two-day matches was rejected; so was Sunday play and one-day/limited-overs cricket ('a danger to the game'). Raymond Robertson-Glasgow argued that a one-day cricket match would reduce the game to the level of other sports which are 'just ninety minutes of mud and energy, a boiled face over a tea-cup or beer mug, and a hurry for the station'. Cricket's superiority complex lingered on and the concept of a cricket cup, eagerly championed by the press as a rival to football's FA Cup, was not deemed necessary. All proposals ended up in the waste bin except, *Eureka!*, allowing a new ball every 55 overs (previously you could only have a new one after 200 runs had been scored).

A mere ten days after VE Day (8 May 1945) the

England side reassembled for the first of six Victory Tests against the Australian Services (sort of Australia minus Bradman, who didn't fight in the war). Three-day championship cricket began the following year, Yorkshire winning the first post-war title. About the same time, the eccentric Australian batsman Sydney Barnes continually complained about the poor visibility during a match, and a law was brought in requiring the batsmen to be 'offered' the light. Typical. Cricket and the world take one step forward, then two back. Offering the batsman the light is equivalent to inviting children to take a day off school. *Well, what do you think they're going to say?* Players going off for bad light is cricket's self-destruct button. All right, if it's Armageddon outside. Then you can understand it. But rushing off the field at the first sign of a bit of cumulonimbus? It's a bit like a round the world yachtsman complaining that the sea was too choppy.

At least the summer of 1947 was a blissful one (except for the bowlers) and the Middlesex twins Denis Compton and Bill Edrich made hay. Compton racked up a colossal 3,816 runs with eighteen hundreds and Edrich a hardly less enterprising 3,539, especially good since he was already on about his fourth wife. Middlesex, of course, won the championship, and MCC ultimately christened the two Nursery end stands at Lord's after the pair. Compton's batting had pizzazz: it was full of flashy drives and nifty legside shots – he is generally regarded as the inventor of the sweep shot, after going down the wicket to the spinner Tom Goddard, tripping himself up and still managing to cross-bat the ball to the square-leg boundary; Edrich's play was more punchy and resilient. That summer their names were as inseparable as Gilbert and Sullivan.

It was all the more remarkable, then, that neither went on tour to the West Indies that winter. In fact they boycotted the tour, along with other leading professionals like Hutton and Lancashire's Cyril Washbrook. It was the pesky business of England captaincy again, which, for unaccountable reasons, was handed back to Gubby Allen, now 45 years old, whose dislike of northerners, professionals and other perceived hoi polloi remained undisguised.

The tour was a disaster. They didn't win a single game, and the party-pooper Allen was fond of making everyone go to bed at 9.30, so they didn't have any fun either. It was of course a triumph for the West Indies, led for the first time by a black man – George Headley – and signalled the emergence of the famous three Ws – Frank Worrell, Clyde Walcott and Everton Weekes. More of them later.

Captaincy has always been a confusing issue in cricket. Because of the game's duration and complexity, the captain of a cricket team has more diverse responsibilities than the captain in any other sport. He is, in a sense, composer, first violinist and conductor all rolled into one. But do you pick the team and then put the person you think most responsible in charge? Or do you identify someone with special leadership qualities and then build the team around them?

The Indians took the latter to extremes on their first tour to England in 1932, putting the Maharajah of

Porbandar in charge. He was a tailender who didn't bowl, and he managed 6 runs all tour. In other words he was a passenger. Going to the opposite extreme, England made their best player, Ian Botham, captain in 1980: aged twenty-four, with no leadership experience and little intuition. England didn't win a single Test under him, his game suffered and the biggest headline he made was when he was accused (wrongly) of thumping a provocative bloke in a Scunthorpe alley.

Surrey's selection of their captain for the 1946 season really took the biscuit, however. Alec Bedser, who with his twin brother Eric was starting to make a name for himself at the Oval, retells the story in a tone of utter disbelief:

> After the war Surrey were trying to find an amateur captain and there was this chap Major Leo Bennett that used to play for the BBC, he was pretty good at cricket. They offered him the captaincy. But before the season started another Major Bennett walked into the Oval. 'Ah, we've been looking for you,' they said, and they asked him to be captain. They got the wrong Bennett. He was Major Nigel Bennett, an ordinary club player. He must have had quite a thick skin because he accepted. But he was an absolute twot. They soon found out but they couldn't take it off him and we had our worst season ever, came 11th.

When you hear stories like this, you wonder how England ever competed at anything, be it cricket, manufacturing or war.

Quite a Useful Deliveree

If Harold Larwood was the antidote to Bradman before the war, Alec Bedser became his nemesis afterwards. Well, sort of. By England's tour of Australia in 1946–7, the 28-year-old Bedser had already led a colourful life. Part of an RAF squadron, he and his twin had survived being strafed by German planes in occupied France in 1943 (they were picked up by a Surrey member driving a rickety van who recognized them) and helped rescue villagers caught in the eruption of Mount Vesuvius while serving in Italy in 1944. On his Test début at Lord's in 1946, coinciding with Brian Johnston's unveiling as a TV commentator, Alec took 7 Indian wickets with his big inswingers in the first innings and 4 in the second, making light of lugging his kit on two trains and a bus to the ground every morning from his home in Woking.

He was an automatic selection for the subsequent tour of Australia. Sitting in the same house sixty years on, he has a clear recollection of that series and his impact on it. He is indebted to his coach, the old Surrey all-rounder Alan Peach, for showing him an invaluable trick. 'He had taught me to hold the ball across the seam to stop it swinging in,' Alec said, brandishing a ball in his huge right mitt:

> I didn't try it in England, but at the second Test in Sydney I was bowling to Sid Barnes and I'm thinking I can't swing it in to him, he's a fine legside player. So I held the new ball across the seam and it pitched and

went away like a leg break. Barnes came down the wicket and said, 'What the hell's going on?' Peter Smith was at mid-on and he said you can't hold a new ball like that and I said, 'Why can't I?' and I ran up and did it again. And that's when I found out I could do it. And I spun it. People don't believe me but I actually spun it.

The fast leg-cutter, bane of top order batsmen's lives and relatively dormant since the days of S. F. Barnes, was reborn.

By the fourth Test at the Adelaide Oval, Bedser had perfected it. He'd already removed the Australian opener Merv Harvey with it when in walked the Don. It was his home pitch. There were a few minutes left for play and the air of expectancy was immense. 'The ball was swinging in a little bit,' Bedser recounts. 'I denied him his favourite legside push to get off the mark for a few balls, and with my ninth ball I held it with that new wider grip. It swung in and pitched leg, cut away and hit off.' There was a collective groan as the crowd realized their great hero had been bowled for a duck. 'Bradman said afterwards that it was the best ball that had ever got him out.'

It caused Bradman to initiate a special net session afterwards, in which he instructed the bowlers to focus solely on imitating Bedser's deliveries. But in six subsequent Tests, Bedser dismissed him a further five times, often caught at leg slip. No other Test bowler ever had such sustained success against him.

Bedser's delivery is not, of course, the most famous ball ever bowled to Bradman. That honour belongs to the Warwickshire leggie Eric Hollies. The story has passed into cricket legend. In 1948, Australia, with the new fast-bowling pairing of Ray Lindwall and Keith Miller as irresistible as any, had arrived at the final Test unbeaten in all matches. They had already retained the Ashes.

At the Oval, England, batting first, were swept away for 52 by the slingy Lindwall. Australia's openers, Sidney Barnes and Arthur Morris, put on 117, before Barnes was caught behind. The stage was set for the Don who, it was widely known, was playing his farewell Test in England, probably anywhere. His Test average, at that point, stood at 101.39. He needed to make just 4 runs to reach an aggregate of 7,000 and guarantee an unprecedented average of 100.

To a standing ovation he strolled slowly out, as was his wont. The English team gave him three cheers when he arrived in the middle. He admitted afterwards he felt a mixture of nostalgia and anxiety, desperate to finish on a high. Hollies was bowling around the wicket. Bradman tentatively blocked the first ball, and poked clumsily at the second. It was a perfectly pitched googly which spun in and grazed the inside of his bat before hitting the top of off stump. Without a moment's reflection, Bradman swivelled on his heel and was gone for nought. Sensing the moment, the crowd, briefly silent, gave him a rousing send-off.

Australia won the match by an innings, so he never got a second chance. You'll know he finished with an average of 99.94 – in its way more of a story. It was 50 per cent higher than anyone else had ever managed –

put another way, he was effectively playing with a bat 1½ times wider than the rest – but it was final proof that he was mortal. He wasn't finished with English bowling though. He signed off with three consecutive centuries (the last, 153 at Scarborough), and a hurricane 123 against Scotland before bidding farewell. The speed and certainty of his scoring remained astonishing to the last. He was a true phenomenon, dominating his own sport for two decades as no one else in any other sport has ever done.

His 1948 team, unbeaten throughout their tour of England, were christened 'The Invincibles', and are often championed as the greatest cricket team of all time, although they lacked a decent spinner. Then again, so did the all-conquering West Indies team of the 1980s, who, for the brilliance of their batsmen and unrelenting ferocity of their fast bowlers, just shade it in my view. But any side with Bradman in it would have a massive head start: in other words a hundred on the board from ball one. (Well, OK, 99.94 if you're going to be pernickety.) As that mediocre batsman Jack Hobbs put it, 'Bradman was a team in himself. I think The Don was too good. I do not think we want to see another one quite like him. I do not think we ever shall.' And he was right. We haven't.

TEN

It's All Black and White If You Ask Me

Britain was looking a bit dishevelled in the first years after the war. Well, you would be if you'd just been bombed for five years and had nowhere to live. It didn't help that there was a grave coal shortage so those who had baths could only fill them to a depth of five inches. There would have been a lot of very pongy bowlers in that hot, sun-drenched summer of '47. Hungry ones too. Everything was rationed and Britons survived on a largely peasant diet of bread and potatoes.

The spirit of camaraderie lured people to cricket in their thousands, however (or maybe it was just a good chance for the men to get out of doing the dishes in lukewarm water). The gates were often closed for Middlesex matches at Lord's, and overall 2.2 million people watched county cricket in 1947. That's an average of 2,500 per day's play. These were the good times. (A daily average of only 880 attended County Championship matches in 2002, though obviously more went to one-day cricket.)

It was all an illusion. The enthusiasts were slowly driven away by grassy pitches barely distinguishable from the outfield producing a glut of nagging medium pacers swinging the ball in (of which Alec Bedser was the supreme example). Mainly unadventurous batsmen were restricted to pushes and deflections on the legside. Off-spin, essentially a defensive form of bowling spinning into the body, was also prominent. The result was a boring sequence of draws, prompting a complaint about 'professionalism' and a renewed clamour for more charismatic amateurs.

In fact there was just a dearth of talent in England. Age and the war had sidelined most of the great old names and no one had yet stepped in to take their place. They were giving débuts to teenagers like the eighteen-year-old cricketing masochist Brian Close. As a result England struggled in Test cricket. Freddie Brown's team was heavily defeated in Australia, failed to get a result in four Tests against New Zealand, even though Test matches had now been extended to five days, and lost a home series to the flamboyant West Indians. The West Indians' victory at Lord's in 1950, by a colossal margin, was their first in England, facilitated by the teenage spinners Sonny Ramadhin and Alf Valentine and the batting of the three Ws.

There was the colossal power of Clyde Walcott, who bludgeoned bouncers wide of mid-on with a flat-bat pull, the deft strokeplay of Frank Worrell and the dazzle of Everton Weekes, whose dynamic batting was not echoed later by his TV commentary. Summarizing for the BBC during the West Indies tour of 1980, he was sitting next to Tony Lewis as Joel Garner dramatically uprooted David Gower's middle stump. 'Fantastic bowling by Garner!' exclaimed Lewis in his Welsh lilt. 'What d'you think of that, Everton?!' 'Well,' Weekes droned, 'Garner bowled de ball, Gower missed de ball and he was out.' It was still more insightful than the dross spouted by any of the modern army of Sky TV football pundits, but he didn't last long in the job.

All three were products of that tiny island of Barbados – 21 miles long and 14 miles wide – which, up to 2008, has produced a gobsmacking seventy-three Test cricketers. It's roughly the same size as the Isle of Wight, which, despite its twenty-seven cricket clubs, can boast only a couple of Hampshire 2nd XI players in the same period. True, frolicking with the bat on the warm, cocaine-textured surface at Mullins beach and diving into the azure Caribbean to fetch a pull over mid-wicket is infinitely preferable to lumbering in to bowl beside lumpen families eating greasy chips on the cold, rippled mud-flats of Ryde beach, but it's still a remarkable achievement. Never mind Lord's, in the context of Test cricketers produced per square inch of terra firma, Barbados is the Home of Cricket.

The 1950 series in England, which the West Indies won 3–1, was enthusiastically supported by the first wave of post-war Caribbean immigrants arriving in droves to find work. Their presence lifted the atmosphere from its traditional culture of polite clapping and 'pass the spam, Cynthia', and thankfully the authorities resisted the temptation to confiscate whistles and drums. It must have all come as quite a shock to the regular cricket crowd to see so many black faces though. Immediately after the war, when soldiers from the colonies had been sent back home, the entire non-white population of Britain numbered only 30,000. (Fifty years later, in 2001, it was four million.)

The West Indies team was dominated by black players but still, apart from George Headley's brief reign, captained by white men. (Slavery was abolished in 1833 but it wasn't until 1960 – in the West Indies' eighty-fifth test – that Frank Worrell became their first officially appointed black captain.) The tradition of the (white) amateur captain held sway in England too for a few more years, but the success of the professional Tom Dollery in leading Warwickshire to the County Championship in 1951 signalled its death throes. A few months later the MCC finally took the plunge and put Len Hutton, the backbone of England's batting, in charge for the 1952 series against India. The general view was that they had taken leave of their senses. Not only was Hutton not an amateur, he wasn't even a captain (Norman Yardley was the man in command at Yorkshire).

Hutton's elevation produced instant results with a thumping series win over India, but his promotion also brought about some strange dialogue the following summer as the former captain Freddie Brown was recalled to the Test side as a bowler for the Ashes. Hutton and others continued to call him 'skip'. You can hear it now:

'Eh oop, skip, can thou take next oover top end?'
'All right, skip! Ta very much.'

'Would thou like a deep square, skip?'

'I would. But skip calling me "skip", skip!'

'Right ye are, skip.'

The Australians were unable to capitalize on this confusion, and Hutton's simple mantras – sell your wicket dearly and bowl your overs slowly – enabled England to hold the Aussies at bay for the first time in two decades. He had some important allies. There was Trevor 'The Barnacle' Bailey, embedded in his own crevice at the wicket (he once took six hours to make fifty – the slowest half-century in Test cricket – making runs like a glacier gains inches) and not averse to bowling deliberately down the legside to stop the scoring (imagine what it would have been like if he'd bowled to himself).

There were the nagging leg-cutters of Alec Bedser, who, during the series, became the leading Test wicket-taker in the world with 218 scalps. (The secret of his perennial fitness, he said, was digging. 'I was always helping my dad, on allotments or with his building work. And if you dig properly it exercises everything you got, particularly your lower back.') There were the nifty sideburns and wagging tongue of wicketkeeper Godfrey Evans. There was the crafty spin duo of Jim Laker and Tony Lock, whose faster ball was slipperier than most club quickies (he had been called for chucking and the Aussies complained that they had been 'thrown' out).

The first four Ashes Tests of 1953 were drawn, destroying the campaign for 'brighter cricket' initiated by the MCC purists, and justifying the Chancellor of the Exchequer's decision to exempt cricket from 'entertainment' tax. Insomnia cure more like. Then, rather like in

2005, everything hung on the final Test at the Oval. This was when England played their trump card. Step forward the inimitable Frederick Sewards Trueman, the 22-year-old tyro whom the surprisingly enlightened selectors had fast-tracked into the team the previous year. Trueman's reaction to getting an England call had been typically understated. 'Booger off!' he exclaimed in disbelief when he was informed on the phone at the RAF camp where he was doing his National Service. His Test début – on his home ground at Headingley – was similarly restrained. He took 4 wickets in India's first innings, and with a bouncer, a slower ball and a fast low full toss was chiefly responsible for reducing them to 0-4 in their second.

With bowling as sharp as his language was blunt, he stormed to twenty-nine wickets in that three-Test series but was then injured for much of the following summer and was only fit for that final Ashes denouement at the Oval. There, despite some dropped catches, he blew away the Australian middle order in the first innings, paving the way, after a Lock'n'Laker double act in the second, for England's eight-wicket win.

It was the first time England had grasped the Ashes for eighteen years – another parallel with 2005 – and thousands of ecstatic supporters invaded the field after Denis Compton had hit the winning runs. The cloak of post-war gloom and austerity had finally been lifted. Yet Pathé footage depicts Compton, having briefly shaken hands with some of the opposition, wandering off with his partner Bill Edrich as if ambling down to the bookies to put a bet on. Such was the nonchalant way sportsmen celebrated their achievements then. These days you'd see more emotion from a kid who's just conquered the T-Rex level on their Nintendo DS.

Three Lions . . . Well, Two and One Leopard

Compton was Britain's first truly commercial sportsman. His exuberant exploits with the bat satisfied the nation's need for a post-war sporting hero, but the fact that he capitalized on his fame was largely an accident. Famously disorganized, Compton frequently arrived at matches without essential items of kit and, having been awoken from a doze to be told he was next in, would grab the nearest bat and go out and make a scintillating hundred (once he actually did so using a relic from the Old Trafford museum). His comment to an astonished young teammate after one such episode is beautiful in its simplicity: 'If you can play, son, you can use the leg of a chair.'

He was also an accomplished footballer for Arsenal and he carried around with him a suitcase full of unanswered fan letters, which, one day, he offered to his pal, the sports journalist Reg Hayter, to sort out. Inside were a number of promotional opportunities, none of which had been followed up. Hayter introduced Compton to a publisher, Bagenal Harvey, who promptly terminated his former employment to manage Compton's affairs. Harvey negotiated his groundbreaking £1,000 a year Brylcreem deal – his client's slicked-back hair was advertised in newspapers and on billboards for years – and became the first-ever sports agent. With Compton and Ted Dexter, he was also to have a big hand in the evolution of one-day cricket a decade later.

Compton's chaotic lifestyle remained, epitomized by his appalling running between the wickets. He once calculated he'd been involved in at least 275 run-outs, most of which were his fault. His calling was, his Middlesex colleague John Warr ascertained, just a basis for negotiation. In his brother Leslie's benefit match, he ran him out before he had even faced a ball. Another Middlesex teammate, Ian Peebles, wrote, 'Whereas the methodical runner is like a traveller who consults weather, routes and timetables, Denis was more akin to a lover of nature who, seeing a glimpse of sunshine, snatches up his hat and sets out just for the joy of life.' And, he might have added, soon finds himself naked in a cold draught.

Compton was a crowd pleaser, an instinctive risk taker who was a throwback to the pre-war era. He walked up the wicket to fast bowlers and tried unusual things against spinners. Once, when hit on the head by Ray Lindwall, he downed a stiff brandy and spanked 145. There was a free-spiritedness about the way he lived his life – often rather the worse for wear when he arrived at the ground after a night out, still in his dinner jacket, legend has it – that endeared him to the nation. His batting was a party piece. Full of wit and dancing feet. But importantly he delivered too, even when he was incapacitated by a chronic knee injury. He made his highest score – 278 against newly created

Pakistan – in 1954 aged thirty-six when he could barely run. Well, most probably *because* he could barely run. Just think how many he might have made in his career if he hadn't been tempted to leave his crease.

Compton retired as a pro in 1957, but carried on playing occasionally as an amateur until 1964. He always had an amateur ethos. He was a born entertainer. In his dotage he could be found, florid-faced, either on the players' balcony at Lord's or lunching at the Cricketers Club in Marylebone, or, combining his two loves, watching play at John Paul Getty's beautiful Wormsley ground while sipping vintage champagne. Denis Compton was cricket's Dom Perignon.

Bowlers – the hops of cricket – win Test matches, though, and two outstanding ones kept the Ashes in English hands for a couple more series. No motorways had yet been built in England, but Frank Tyson, who as a kid was obsessed by Harold Larwood, broke all speed limits with his huge muscular physique. With a long galumphing run and an explosion at the crease he shattered Bill Edrich's jaw with a bouncer at Lord's in 1954, his first full season for his adopted Northamptonshire after being passed over by Lancashire, causing the England selectors to take notice and Compton to slip himself further down the Middlesex batting order. He was generally reckoned to be the fastest bowler in England.

His radar was less reliable, however, and he owed his surprise call-up for the 1954–5 tour of Australia to Trueman's exclusion for his ill-discipline in the West Indies the previous winter. The captain Hutton told Tyson on the boat over that he was likely to be surplus to requirements. This has been regarded in some quarters (chiefly Yorkshire ones) as a motivational master stroke, but Hutton wasn't known for his amazing foresight. Well, certainly not after the first Test anyway. There in a hot and sultry Brisbane he won the toss and put Australia in, citing ideal bowling conditions. It was the equivalent of giving the Brazilians a free passage to the penalty area. The Australians scored 600 and won by an innings.

But something stirred in Tyson, having been battered for 160 off 29 enervating overs at the Gabba. He visited the emigrated Larwood at his Sydney home. Larwood, recognizing a kindred spirit, told him he should always try to bowl as fast as possible. Tyson cut his run for the Sydney Test and increased his pace. Further inflamed by being struck on the head by a bouncer from Lindwall, he ripped out the Aussie lower order, with the help of the equally hostile Brian Statham, to give England a narrow 38-run victory. He was even more devastating in the third Test in Melbourne, bowling downwind on the fifth day to take 7-27 and blow Australia over for 111, after which dull old Frank was renamed 'Typhoon'. Both Richie Benaud, who was playing, and Don Bradman, who was watching, have called it the fastest spell of bowling they have ever seen.

Can this be so? Possibly. The trouble is, judging the speed of a bowler is so subjective. We have speed radar to measure it now, but there is plenty of dispute about whether that is reliable, and often a paceman's fastest ball – his bouncer – doesn't register a reading at all, because the detecting gadget, focused further up the pitch, 'loses' a delivery dug in very short.

The evidence of the 100-metre sprint, the 2,000-metre row and the Heaviest Deadlift With Little Finger (95kg by Norwegian Kristian Holm in 2007) suggests that humans are getting faster and stronger (and madder) by the decade. Diet is better, training is more meticulous. The pace of every international sport is quicker (apart from Japanese golf), the hits in rugby and American football and Sumo wrestling bigger than ever before. So it stands to reason that bowling is faster now than in the 1950s.

Tyson's speed was actually measured at 89mph by the Royal Aeronautical College in Wellington, New Zealand, though he claimed he was still swathed in sweaters and hadn't warmed up. You can assume he bowled some balls over 90mph but deliveries of that speed are relatively commonplace now. The 100mph barrier was broken in the 2003 World Cup by Shoaib Akhtar. Yet that delivery was nudged to square leg with ease by England's Nick Knight, underlining the well-known fact that it's not just what you've got but what you do with it.

In the end speed is less important than deception. The straightforward actions of some pacemen make their deliveries easy to see from the hand (though not necessarily easy to play). Those of others are harder to pick up as they emerge through a whirl of arms and legs. The Pakistani Wasim Akram was a classic, shimmying up – often behind the umpire – to jump out and let you have it in a blur of activity and dust. He had a wicked change of pace. As the batsman, your reactions against such bowlers are more rushed and jerky, making many balls *look* even faster than they perhaps are. Direction is obviously vital too. Devon Malcolm was undeniably fast. But often the person beating the hastiest retreat from one of his missiles was the short leg not the batsman.

Tyson's powerful frame, huge gather at the crease and muscular delivery made him almost certainly the fastest bowler the game had produced at that point. Black and white footage suggests he might have threatened the 95mph mark. But his prowess was short-lived. Injury and expectation caught up with him. And soon, by his own admission, he was only going as fast as city traffic. Which, in Northampton, is not very fast at all. The Typhoon had blown itself out.

Australia's other great tormentor of the mid-1950s was a much more inconsequential-looking fellow. Jim Laker was a cool-headed Yorkshireman of bushy eyebrows and sly grin, but few words, an irony given his subsequent distinguished career as a TV commentator. He began in the Bradford League as a batsman and fast bowler but turned to off spin while stationed in Egypt during the Second World War (spinners have always preferred pitches like deserts), continuing quite a tradition of Yorkshire-born off-spinners.

After the war he was snapped up by Surrey to form a perfect and perennial right-arm/left-arm spin partnership with Tony Lock. With strong fingers and unerring accuracy, Laker utilized any help he could find in a pitch, spinning the ball sharply and landing it persistently on the proverbial sixpence. Fielders said they could hear the ball whirring as it travelled (which was also true of Shane Warne, though you wouldn't put it past Warne to often add to the sound effect himself). Floating the ball into the breeze, Laker also had the gift of the ball that drifts away from the right-hand batsman, a subtle version of the *doosra* that batsmen know and hate today.

On spinning surfaces he hypnotized batsmen, taking wickets in clusters at paltry cost. Once in a Test trial he took 8-2 in 14 overs. He did the hat-trick four times in six years. He was unfazed at bowling with five men round the bat. There was something oddly detached about his method. He wasn't quite mechanical. But he was a passionless exterminator. He was also lucky to have emerged at a time when the lbw law had been adjusted to allow dismissals to balls pitching outside off stump. He exploited batsmen's lingering habit to thrust their pad at the ball spinning in from the off. If he had been playing in the early 1930s he might well have been just plain James Laker the club batsman and local bank manager (he trained with Barclays as a teenager).

Then again, great sportsmen invariably have an ability to adapt to their environment. Laker made the most of what he was given. At Old Trafford in 1956 this was already a bare surface (pre-ordered by the chairman of selectors, Gubby Allen), before England piled up 459 against Australia in their first innings. Then rain fell (well, it was Manchester) on the uncovered pitch. The following day the soil was tacky. It was like bowling on springy putty. Laker was on in the ninth over. The effect of the heavy roller took a few minutes to wear off. An hour and a half later he had skittled the Australians for 84. He took 9-37.

That was amazing enough. What followed defies any kind of sporting possibility. It is like a footballer dribbling through the opposition to score himself again and again and again. And doing so without hogging the ball. It was not just the fact that Laker took all ten Australian wickets in their second innings, but that he bowled 51 overs in doing it. That means someone else bowled at least 50 the other end. It was Lock (he actually bowled 55), a thoroughly decent spinner in his own right, and on a surface now as unstable as gunpowder. He didn't even get a sniff of a wicket.

Bowling around the wicket, Laker made the ball spin and pop and, despite often having six men round the bat, never let the mesmerized Aussies get after him. Even the normally aggressive Keith Miller offered just a dead bat. Laker conceded only 53 runs in those 51 overs. He got half his wickets caught in the leg trap. The rest were bowled or lbw. After each one he turned nonchalantly on his heel and, hands in his pockets, chatted to the umpire until the next batsman arrived. There were no high fives or any of that malarkey. Even when he took his record-breaking tenth, he only reacted as if he was a man on a street corner who'd spotted a vacant taxi.

Laker's 19 wickets in the match, two more than any bowler has managed in any form of the game before or since, say three things. One, he was remorseless and peerless on a helpful surface. Two, Lock must have urinated on a gravestone or something because he bowled 69 overs on a raging turner and got just one wicket in the match. Three, the 1956 Aussies were utterly useless against off spin.

Laker's 19-90 are numbers as fantastical in sport as Mark Spitz's seven Olympic golds in Munich, and Torvill and Dean's twelve perfect 6.0s for their *Bolero*. In their individual disciplines, their performances were as near to perfection as it is possible to get. No one else has got close. And no one else probably ever will.

Shameful Behaviour

Elvis and rock and roll were all the rage in America in 1956. In England there was petrol rationing and the 150th anniversary of the Gentleman v Players fixture. God vented his mild wrath on this anachronism by raining on it, rendering it a dull draw. The gentlemen had anyway found it more and more of a struggle to compete in this match, their numbers having dwindled. There were 175 amateurs out of 450 county cricketers in 1949, but they constituted less than half that a decade later. The 'leisured' classes were in decline as inflation rose and dabbling in the stock market with your old man's money became a less sustainable way of life.

The loss of the amateur was bemoaned for his 'unfettered spirit of high adventure' (proclaimed the cricket historian Diana Rait-Kerr) – in other words the modern professional had had a charisma bypass. Having met a few of them hanging around county ground committee rooms over the years, it is hard to argue with that. There was much hankering for the

Golden Age. The historian C. L. R. James wrote, 'the prevailing attitude of the players of 1890–1914 was daring, adventure, creation. The prevailing attitude of 1957 can be summed up by one word – security. Bowlers and batsmen are dominated by it.'

The essential distinction is one of attitude. There was an independence of spirit about the amateur, a freedom associated with their lack of reliance on cricket to make their living. The professional was more constrained by protocol, doing things by the book rather than risking disapproval from their employer. Even in the 1990s, there was a special exuberance about the play of Kent's Etonian Matthew Fleming, known affectionately as 'Jazzer' (after jazz-hat, the usual nickname for anyone who went to a posh school because of the loud, stripy caps they wore). He got off the mark with two sixes on his Kent début, and always batted in cavalier fashion. Then again it's a lot easier to be uninhibited when your family own half of a merchant bank (Robert Fleming) with net assets of £800m.

That year MCC attempted to take action (again) to liven up the game – urging shorter boundaries, a restriction on legside fielders (which hastened the decline of leg spin) and a greater urgency on the field. By far the most obvious solution to the dwindling support of county cricket – limiting the overs – was rejected.

Some counties recruited overseas players to boost interest. The dashing Barbadian batsman Roy Marshall played for Hampshire, the Guyanese Peter Wight, who later became a long-serving umpire, joined Somerset, and there were Australian all-rounders or wrist spinners in several other sides. (Yorkshire, of course, steadfastly refused to play anyone unless they were both born in the county and had 'Ilkley Moor bar tat' tattooed across their chest.)

The measures did nothing to arrest the decline in crowds or Surrey's dominance of the domestic scene. In 1957 they won the County Championship for the sixth successive season. Their skill, ruthlessness, ability to score quick runs and brilliant close fielding remained unmatched. Micky Stewart, father of Alec, was in the vanguard of this, snapping up countless chances at short leg, including a world record seven in one innings against Northants.

It was not a lucrative business being a professional cricketer, though, even a successful one. The pros' dissatisfaction deepened when an MCC sub-committee met in 1958 and decided that 'the distinctive status of the amateur is not obsolete, is of great value to the game and should be preserved', and announced that amateurs would get compensation for loss of earnings in addition to their expenses. And all their income was tax-free. Laker declared that he was considering turning amateur as he'd 'be better off'. He got into trouble voicing such views in an autobiography, *Over to Me*, published the following year.

England's shamateurs toured Australia in 1958–9 with, on paper, one of the best teams they had ever fielded. The batting was in the 'gentleman' hands of Bailey, May, Graveney, Cowdrey and Dexter; the bowling featured the 'players' Trueman, Statham, Lock and

Laker. They were thumped 4–0. It can't have helped that one group were being lavished with tax-free perks while the other got paid a pittance and had to cough part of it back up. They were united in common grievance against the victorious Australians though, because some of their bowlers were chuckers. Ian Meckiff even admitted it. They also made the most of the back-foot no-ball law, allowing pacemen to 'drag' their way over the front line and release the ball from about 18 yards.

The growing influence of professionalism was harder and harder to ignore. Quite apart from the blokes with the dodgy actions, there were more and more instances of poor 'behaviour', with time wasting, orchestrated appealing for lbw and, that sin of sins, not 'walking'. The thing is, once your livelihood is potentially enhanced by remaining there when you've thin-edged it, or by paying cash for a £20,000 kitchen extension and avoiding VAT, you do it. Anyway, if the greatest of them all, Bradman, didn't walk (he stood for a bottom edge on 28 at the Gabba in 1946–7, was given not out and went on to make 187), how can you expect anyone else to? Most serious cricketers now subscribe to the original Australian mantra: 'You only walk if the car runs out of petrol.' Which means the number one priority for batsmen aiming to reach the top isn't superb hand–eye co-ordination but the art of overcoming a guilty conscience.

The amateur ethos was declining inexorably and, when you think about it, they were all non-walkers too, accepting money for playing and not paying tax on it. By the early 1960s the Advisory County Cricket Committee had sensibly voted to abolish the distinction between amateurs and professionals: all players would now be known simply as 'cricketers' (though 'professional' is still a word used for the star player in the northern leagues). So ended the ludicrous 157-year class delineation of Mr this and three initials that which was so absurdly rigid that Brian Close was reprimanded by his Yorkshire captain for not addressing an opposing gentleman as 'Mister', and the Lord's announcer once declared that the 'scorecard entry F. J.Titmus should read Titmus F. J.' (Pros had their initials after their surname and amateurs before.) The last Gentlemen v Players match, in 1962, ended in a cloudburst. God had had the final word.

Trooping of the Colour

The slow death of the 'gentleman' was equated with the backward state of the country. The Labour leader Harold Wilson made political capital out of it, suggesting that the Conservative government, run by landed gentry like Alec Douglas Home, were like amateurs 'in a world of players'. The European Union was forming without Britain, which was fading as head of the Commonwealth, and over-obsessed with helping America douse the flames of communism in Russia and Cuba, and listening to the cheesy sounds of Cliff Richard.

In cricket, the real action was also taking place outside England. Australia were regaining their strength under the artful Richie Benaud, India and Pakistan were breeding prolific batsmen and holding each other to incessant draws, and West Indies were an emerging force, centred on the brilliant all-round talents of Garfield Sobers. One of six kids, he was born with an extra finger on each hand. One came off when he was nine, the other, he declares blithely in his autobiography, he cut off with a sharp knife when he was about fifteen. English adolescent boys squeeze their spots, and West Indians slice off their spare fingers. By then he was already an outstanding natural sportsman. He excelled at cricket, first playing with a piece of timber and a lump of tar as the ball, then progressing to tennis ball games on any bit of ground he and his friends could find.

As a fifteen-year-old he played for the Police Cricket Club as a left-arm spinner and lower-order batsman and was invited for trials to represent Barbados. He made his Barbados début aged sixteen, having to borrow a pair of white trousers because he had only ever played in shorts. He took 7 wickets in the match against the Indian tourists and made 7 not out. A year later, he made another appearance for Barbados against the England tourists. It earnt him a call-up for the fifth Test of the series in Jamaica. His Test début was his third first-class game. He took 4-75 and batted usefully at no.9.

That was in April 1954. Sobers was seventeen. Over the next four years his performances at Test level were unspectacular but he gradually moved up the batting order to no.3, learning masses from touring, and partnering his idol, Everton Weekes. It was in the series against Pakistan in 1958 when he first caused a sensation. In the first Test he had witnessed the ultimate in selling your wicket dearly, as the diminutive run-machine Hanif Mohammad occupied the crease for 15 hours 10 minutes to make 337 (until recently the longest-ever innings in first-class cricket) and steered Pakistan to a draw.

The left-handed Sobers went one better in the third Test in Jamaica. Well, actually 28 better. Coming in at 87-1 towards the end of the second day, he was still batting in mid-afternoon on the fourth, 300 not out. It was his first Test century. (Somehow you just can't imagine an Englishman having the uninhibited ambition to convert a maiden hundred into such a huge score.) His partner, Clyde Walcott, then informed him that he needed 65 runs to make the record Test score and as it was a six-day game there was plenty of time to go for it. 'I decided to get my head down,' Sobers recalled.

When he got to 363, Hanif Mohammad came on to bowl. Sobers took a single off the first ball, and was back on strike for the third. Hanif asked if he could bowl it left-handed. Sobers said he could bowl two-handed if he wanted. He pushed the ball into the covers and they scrambled a single. He had broken Len Hutton's record which had stood for twenty years (and taken 3½ hours longer). Surprisingly, in view of the famous big-hitting record Sobers later set, his 365 not out contained not a single six.

More than 13,000 spectators descended on the pitch. It was, in one way, the West Indians' defining moment, Jamaica – the most populous island in the Caribbean –

celebrating a black Barbadian eclipsing the individual feats of all the old white masters. The 21-year-old Sobers received a hero's welcome when he returned to his native island. His reaction to his achievement in his life story is amusingly frank. 'The innings undoubtedly changed my life but not my bank balance,' he wrote. Sobers has always had a reputation for being a bit of a mercenary.

Sobers' batting style embodied all that professional English batting was not. It was expressive, audacious and lucid. It wasn't technically constrained. The backlift was extravagant. The feet danced and the arms swung free. His body was a lithe blur of rhythmic movement. An 80mph ball was an opportunity not a threat. Maiden overs were a personal affront. Sober? It was anything but. He credits the extra bounce of the tennis balls he grew up playing with for making him, like many other West Indians, a superb hooker and cutter. It is the source of their flamboyant back-foot shots, flaying good-length balls 'on the up'. He never bothered to wear a thigh pad.

(I once spent some time with some Guyanese kids, playing cricket by the banks of the Demerara river. The rubber ball they used leapt up off the uneven surface. They were quick to stand up tall to wallop it off their chins. English players, brought up with hard balls, are more concerned with forward defence. They tend to stoop towards the ball. English batting is traditionally stodgy, like our beer and puddings.)

Sobers was the antithesis of the other great run-maker of the fifties, Hanif, the relentless accumulator, who, the following year, broke Bradman's record for the highest-ever first-class score, making 499 on a matting pitch, playing for Karachi against Bahawalpur, and being run out going for his 500th off the last ball of the day. Greedy bugger.

Sobers began reeling off centuries everywhere he went. And if that was not enough he came to England to play league cricket for Radcliffe and added fast swingers and chinamen and googlies to his slow-left-arm repertoire. In Tests he could bowl an incisive and decidedly brisk new-ball spell, return later with his orthodox left-arm spinners, or try a few chinamen if he so desired. Factor in his electric fielding, particularly at leg gully, and he was indisputably the most complete cricketer who ever lived. Jack Hobbs might have said Bradman was a team on his own. Well, the Don couldn't bowl a hoop down a hill. Sobers really *was* about six players in one.

The Tru(e)th Hurts

Sobers, like most of the greats, was never coached. He was left alone to find his own way. There is a delicious irony in the manner England's number one match-winner of the time was handled. Fred Trueman, who weighed 14lb 1oz at birth, was always larger than life, and controversy followed him around like a bad smell. He was ill-disciplined in the West Indies, criticizing umpires and acting stroppily, and on tour he could be tactless. In Sydney an Australian official asked him politely what he thought of 'our bridge'. 'Your bridge?'

Trueman snorted. '*Our* bloody bridge you should say – bugger it – a Yorkshire firm – Dorman and Long – built it – and you bastards still ain't paid for it!'

His anti-establishment attitude caused him to be omitted from touring parties. This did not justify the embarrassing scene at his home ground at Headingley when the chairman of selectors, Gubby Allen, laid down a handkerchief in the nets and made him try and hit it in front of a large crowd. He found the incident utterly humiliating but for once kept his counsel.

Perhaps subconsciously it drove Trueman on. Or maybe it was just a general hatred of batsmen (and anyone not from Yorkshire). Trueman's favourite antic was to pop his head round the opposition dressing room door before going out to field. He'd canvass the room for past victims and greenhorns. 'Awreet, I can see five or six wickets for FST today,' he'd crow and stride out. Sometimes he'd be the last one on to the field, advising the steward not to bother shutting the gate after the incoming batsmen: 'Woon o' them'll be back soon!' he'd exclaim in their earshot. He was fond of knocking out the stumps of anybody wearing unnecessary adornments like cravats or stripy caps and dismissing them with 'It were hardly worth gettin' dressed, wor it?'

During overs he had a nice selection of one-liners including, after countless streaky shots, advising, 'You've got more edges than a broken pisspot! And wi' next 'un I'll pin thee to flippin' sightscreen.' His Middlesex opponent J. J. Warr said, 'If Fred was fined £200 every time he swore he'd have financed the national debt.' His bowling doctrine was simple: 'Use every weapon within the rules and stretch the rules to breaking point!' But his reputation for Anglo-Saxon comment and bristling demeanour, earning him the nickname 'Fiery', overlooks the fact that Trueman was a brilliant and versatile bowler. He generated genuine pace from his surging run and colossal miner's shoulders and would make the ball swing away late with his side-on, slightly slingy action. John Arlott described his delivery as 'like a storm-wave breaking on a beach, and he followed through with so mighty a heave that the knuckles of his right hand swept the ground.'

There was an intensity about Trueman's bowling – using well-directed bouncers and yorkers followed up with 1,000-yard stares – that made all but the stoutest batsmen buckle. He had a colossal physical presence. He wouldn't spare his England mates if he was playing for Yorkshire. He once cracked three of Godfrey Evans' ribs with a beamer. 'Sorry about your ribs, Godders – really, I meant to skull you,' he said. 'Anyway, why didn't you put your bloody bat there?' Wayward in his youth, he developed superb control and he was adaptable too, able to cut his pace and bowl fast off-cutters as he did to demolish Australia twice at Headingley in 1961. And he was phenomenally fit, regularly bowling over 1,000 overs in a season and rarely breaking down.

His opening partnership with Brian Statham is legendary. Neither exerted themselves much before the game – Trueman's pre-match 'routine' involved hanging up his jacket and tie on a peg and having a cup of tea, and Statham's was a fag, a cough and a coffee. But put a new ball in their hands and they were hostile and remorseless, the rumbustious Trueman exploring a batsman's reactions and his courage, the whippier Statham their precision and their patience. He was as direct and reliable as Trueman was explosive and mercurial. (England lost only eight out of thirty-five Tests that they played together.) They were neck and neck to 200 Test wickets and Trueman later became the first man to reach 300, during the Oval Test of 1964. And that was despite missing 51 Tests, for a variety of reasons, during his England career. If he had been more tactful and 'they' had been less censorious he would have taken 500. If, if, if . . .

Trueman often claimed, only half jokingly, that he was 'the best fast bowler that ever drew breath' and the statistics absolve him of any hubris. They are on a par with any of the great post-war pacemen. It is impossible to say how fast he was for certain. He harrumphed indignantly on radio when compared in speed to Yorkshire's most recent 90mph merchant, Darren Gough. Given that Trueman had the benefit of the back foot no-ball law, meaning his front foot was a good few inches closer to the batsman, he probably had the edge. Watching some old black-and-white footage of himself bowling out Australia, he remarked, 'I'd have been even quicker in colour.'

But Trueman was more than a tremendous fast bowler. Hailing from a desolate mining community on the Yorkshire–Nottinghamshire border, he was a working class hero, his flapping black mane and jutting chin and shirt-tails flowing from a body in full flight a symbol of what could be achieved, regardless of your background, through determination and dedication in new professionalized, egalitarian Britain.

Trueman stood for total commitment to a cause and uncrackable self-belief. After play he was fond of reflecting on the ways he'd conjured up his wickets. 'You must have bowled the lot, Fred – inners, outers, yorkers, slower ones,' said his Yorkshire colleague Richard Hutton, son of Len, after one such post-mortem. 'But tell me – did you ever bowl a plain straight ball?' 'Aye, I did,' Trueman retorted, 'to Peter Marner and it went straight through him like a stream of piss and flattened all three.'

Age did not wither his pride or his lofty expectations of England bowlers. When the honest Yorkshire-born seamer Neil Mallender was picked against Pakistan at Headingley in 1992, Trueman watched and winced. 'Aggers lad,' he said on *Test Match Special*. 'There've been some great fast boolers 'ave coom down that 'ill . . . [pause for effect] . . . And 'e's not one of 'em.'

With ball or tongue, Fred Trueman was never knowingly surpassed.

ELEVEN

One Day, My Son . . .

'Christine Keeler knickers for sale,' yells the street sales-man. 'Come an' get 'em . . . peephole, see-through, seamless, backless . . . Christine Keeler knickers for sale!'

'Oi you!' a grumpy-looking woman berates him, brandishing some saucy underwear. 'I bought some of those Christine Keeler knickers here last week and I've been done!'

'Aha, another satisfied customer,' says the salesman smugly.

The joke at the expense of the MP John Profumo's mistress encapsulated the new liberty pervading 1960s Britain. Sex and drugs and rock and roll. Well, for Marianne Faithful anyway. The Rolling Stones' brazen first single was 'Come on!' and the Beatles' dazzling first album, *Please Please Me* (1963), included 'Twist and Shout' and 'Love Me Do'. Other artists like the Beach Boys and Chubby Checker offered similar encourage-ment to live it up.

Actually, cricketers already were. Hampshire won a first-ever County Championship in 1961, under the captaincy of the gambolling aristo Colin Ingleby-Mackenzie. When asked afterwards what was the secret of Hampshire's success he replied, 'Oh, wine, women and song.' The reporter persisted, enquiring what sort of rules the team abided by. After a pause Ingleby-Mackenzie replied. 'I absolutely insist,' he said, 'that all my boys should be in bed before breakfast.' (How times change. Twenty-five years later, Middlesex's captain Mike Gatting told us, 'If you're going to get pissed or laid, do it before midnight.' See, we 1980s pros were much more responsible.)

Ingleby-Mackenzie engendered a spirit of fun and bonhomie and was happy to take risks. Ten of Hampshire's nineteen victories came from tempting declarations. Amidst the laissez-faire there was some discipline though, not least the relentless perseverance of the archetypal English dobber Derek Shackleton, his medium pacers as unremitting as the sea at Bournemouth. It was said he only bowled one half-volley a season, and when, in one match, he sent down three it was discovered that the pitch was too short. His accuracy and stamina were unparalleled. 'He'll keep bowling it on the spot till he drops dead,' said one opponent, 'and then he'll fall on a length.' He bowled over 1,500 overs in the summer of '61 taking 158 wickets.

The licentious image of the early 1960s – the miniskirts, the long hair, the free love, the pirate radio stations – passed many of us by. Well, I had an excuse: I was only three at the time. Worse luck. But in keeping with popular culture, there was new scope for self-expression in cricket with the advent of the one-day game. A limited-overs cup, first conceived by the MCC in 1956 to arrest falling county attendances, was finally inaugurated in 1963 when they had dwindled to 700,000.

The Gillette Safety Razor Company underwrote the first competition (the word 'sponsored' wasn't common parlance) for £6,500, about the cost of a night out with Ian Botham these days, and not enough to put up visiting teams in hotels. They had to stay with members of the home side's committee. The tournament was given a nice, succinct title: The First Class Counties Knock-Out Competition for the Gillette Cup, and the matches were 65 overs a side to be completed in a day. They walked faster then. At current over-rates, they'd still be trundling in at midnight.

The organizers hadn't heeded the lessons of 10,000 years of British settlement, which state that if you're going to launch a glamorous new *one*-day trophy, don't do it in Manchester. Therefore the inaugural Gillette match was a watery, *two*-day affair at Old Trafford, between Lancashire, who batted with surprising enterprise to score 304-9, and Leicestershire (including a certain H. D. 'Dickie' Bird opening the batting), who didn't. Gillette's other innovation was the man of the match award (£50), an idea which initially caused much consternation, as the organizers bellyached about the relative values of, say, a fifty and four wickets, but which was soon adopted by other sports. In case you're in need of a really obscure quiz question, I can tell you that Lancashire's Peter Marner was the world's first recipient of a man of the match award for his century and three wickets.

The first winners of the competition were Sussex, and it was where the new England captain Ted Dexter proved himself to be an astute thinker. To defend their total of 168 in the final at Lord's he set strange funnel-shaped fields that no one had seen before. Where most other captains had scattered their fielders randomly around the boundary, Dexter either had his men in close saving a single or deep and straight. 'I told the bowlers a good ball was one that was hitting the stumps. Then I could set a field to it. I had long leg and third man quite fine, and deep mid-on and deep mid-off. If they bowled full and straight they were hit straight.' It is a basic blueprint that has stood the test of time through 60-over, 50-over, 40-over and Twenty20 matches, and will continue to do so even when cricket has been reduced to 12-ball shootouts.

The first Gillette final, which Sussex won by 14 runs, was a huge success. The *Daily Mirror*'s Peter Wilson, the leading sportswriter of the day, marvelled at the atmosphere – 'a sell-out with rosettes, singing, cheers, jeers and countercheers . . . this may not have been cricket to the purists, but by golly it was just the stuff the doctor ordered.' It even captivated the arch conservative E. W. Swanton who wrote in the *Daily Telegraph* that 'this "instant cricket" is very far from being a gimmick and there is a place in it for all the arts of cricket, most of which are subtle ones.'

Dexter's mind, meanwhile, was already whirring. He was famous for his majestic batting style, reminiscent of the Golden Age, which had earnt him the nickname 'Lord Ted'. His defining innings had been at Lord's in that summer of '63, a counterattacking 70 against the fearsome West Indians Wes Hall and Charlie Griffith. 'The openers had gone, and the ball was flying everywhere. I said to myself, "Come on, Dexter, play your game. Better get some while you're here." ' Singlehandedly in the space of 12 overs he transformed the crisis of 20-2 into the comfort of 100-2. 'Griffith didn't know where to bowl.'

His England captaincy was less distinguished, as it was frequently distracted by thoughts of golf, which he'd admit was his real first love. Brought up in Italy, he had learnt to play at the Menaggio golf club, dramatically constructed on a narrow mountain ledge overlooking Lake Como, and it developed into a lifelong obsession. He became one of Britain's finest amateur golfers, winning the Prince of Wales Open at Deal and numerous other prestigious events. Also adept at rackets and rugby, Dexter is on a par with C. B. Fry as the best all-round sportsman this country has ever produced.

He had more than a touch of ingenuity too, seen in the winter of 1962 when he'd outwitted Richie Benaud's tactic of bowling outside leg stump into the rough by playing tip and run, and this newfangled limited-overs cricket had got him thinking. His subsequent ideas changed the game for ever. It is no exaggeration to say that Dexter was the man who shaped modern cricket.

It was his friendship with Bagenal Harvey, the agent who looked after Denis Compton's affairs, that did it. Although county cricket was now fully professional, there were no official matches on Sundays. Harvey had a sponsor, Rothman's cigarettes, interested in the idea of promoting regular Sunday afternoon matches, and the BBC were interested in showing them, as long as play finished by 6pm. Harvey couldn't guarantee this. '"You can," Dexter said, "you limit the overs and restrict the run-ups." So I went away and wrote the rules.' Out of that, the Rothman's International Cavaliers were born.

They were like cricket's Harlem Globetrotters, a virtual world XI touring the country entertaining full houses on a Sunday afternoon, usually for a county player's benefit. As Dexter said:

> We had such an amazing side – Sobers, Compton, Graeme Pollock – I was only able to creep in at no.6 or 7. When we went to Lord's for the first time we told them to be ready, there'd be a big crowd. They said, 'No, no, there won't.' They'd sold out of everything by twelve. We took the place by storm.

Though essentially exhibition matches, they were hugely successful. For the players it was a major contrast from, as Dexter put it, 'the futility of travelling 150 miles overnight to play county cricket in front of two men and a dog at some obscure outpost of cricket's over-expanded empire'. The games were innovative in many ways. In one both Benaud and Compton wore radio mics linked to Brian Johnston in the commentary box and he asked Benaud what he was going to bowl and Compton how he'd respond. Sky TV's publicity machine, claiming they brought every newfangled device into cricket coverage, is a gross exaggeration.

With the Cavaliers, private enterprise had shown the cricket authorities a route to solvency (not for the first time) and the Advisory County Committee pinched the idea. They proposed an official Sunday league. The trouble was no sponsor would support it without TV coverage, and the BBC were happy with the star-studded Cavaliers' entertainment. The MCC hierarchy persuaded the counties to ban players from appearing for the Cavaliers, so that they could get their own competition up and running. They enlisted a rival sponsor. So, amidst a barrage of law suits, the John Player County League was born in 1969. An entire match was shown live on BBC2 every Sunday.

Some teams took a little time to adjust to the restriction of just 40 overs' batting, and initially totals hovered around the 160 mark. In one match the Somerset spinner Brian Langford managed to get through his entire allotment of overs without conceding a run, giving him the bizarre limited-overs figures of 8-8-0-0. Not exactly cricket to get the turnstiles clicking – except to let people out. But interest was considerable, attracted by the guarantee of a finish, the chance to avoid scrubbing Sunday roasting tins and a plethora of fabulous overseas players who'd suddenly infiltrated the game.

The cast list included Majid Khan (Glam), Mike Procter (Glos), Farokh Engineer and Clive Lloyd (Lancs, the first winners), Garfield Sobers (Notts) and the dream team of Barry Richards and Gordon Greenidge at Hampshire. Observing the Warwickshire team that included the West Indians Rohan Kanhai, Lance Gibbs, Alvin Kalicharran and Deryck Murray, Fred Trueman remarked, 'You only need a green 'un and you'll 'av' a snooker set.'

Crowds in the first year totalled 280,000 on Sundays, almost as many as attended County Championship matches the other six days of the week (327,000). My father and I were part of that statistic, lured by Kent's diversity of skills: the belligerence of Luckhurst and Johnson, the elegance of Cowdrey and Denness, the breakneck speed between the wickets of Asif Iqbal, the languid competence of Woolmer, the eccentricities of Knott, the throwing of Ealham, the colossal hitting of Shepherd, the triffid-like action of 6ft 7in Norman Graham, and the mesmerizing control of Underwood.

That Kent side showcased cricket's glorious variety and possibility, all compacted into a Sunday afternoon of eating egg sandwiches and drinking Tizer. The players looked as if they were enjoying themselves and it was contagious. Little did I imagine that, a decade later, I would be out there with them, struggling to come to terms with a compulsorily shortened Sunday run-up and the muscular ambitions of a coachload of magnificent batsmen, and surrounded by a scrum of young autograph hunters whispering, 'Who is he?'

The Sunday League was the uncle of the one-day international (the first was in 1971) and the grandfather of Twenty20 cricket. Renamed the National League it has survived, with one or two modifications, to the present day, to be finally replaced in 2010 by something that hasn't yet got a name (or structure). It has effectively bankrolled the English game for four decades, converting it into the multi-million-pound empire it is today.

Certainly in the 1960s cricket needed saving from itself. Most of the Test matches in that decade were dire. The Ashes series featured a sequence of draws, dominated by the arch Australian blockers Bobby Simpson and Bill Lawry, and against weaker countries both the loveable grafter Ken Barrington and the durable loner Geoff Boycott were sidelined by the England selectors for slow scoring. During one Test, the *Guardian*'s Neville Cardus admitted that he was 'bored to limpness because I had seen Geoff Boycott and John Edrich compile, or rather secrete, 100 runs in 56 overs bowled by game, in-experienced New Zealanders'.

The Indians and Pakistanis made occasional tours but had stopped playing each other after three Test series. Hostilities between the countries was put down as the reason, though in truth it was actually boredom. The last ten matches between them had all been tedious draws. Pakistan were starting to produce some decent cricketers, mainly batsmen, including the elegant Majid Khan, the wiry Asif Iqbal and Hanif Mohammad's younger brother Mushtaq, who played in a Test aged fifteen having made his first-class début at thirteen. ('First class' was a slightly misleading term in Pakistan's haphazard domestic structure. In one match, Railways made 910-6 dec against a makeshift Dera Ismail Khan team who were then dismissed for 32 and 27, giving Railways victory by an innings and 851 runs. This result is up there with Arbroath's 36–0 defeat of Bon Accord and Hong Kong beating Singapore 164–13 at rugby as the greatest mismatch of all time. It was the only 'first-class' game Dera ever played. It's one way of getting in the history books, anyway.)

The South Africans were at least worth watching, especially the brilliant left-hander Graeme Pollock, whose pulverizing drives and capacity for drink were remarkable, and the deadly aim of Colin Bland, who was known as the 'Golden Eagle' for his ability to swoop on the ball in the field and pick off a victim. But for anyone with a conscience, the South Africans' presence was a blight because of their government's stubborn resistance to incorporate any of their multitude of black players into white teams. (Black inter-provincial competitions had flourished there from the 1880s, but it wasn't until 1992 that one of their number – the Cape Coloured Omar Henry – played Test cricket. That was the year South Africa also played their first-ever, yes, *first-ever* Test against a non-white nation. It had only taken them 103 years to condescend to it.)

The best cricket in the sixties came from the West Indies. Their spirit and exuberance were encapsulated by their brilliant fielding in the tied Test of 1960, the diminutive Joe Solomon twice hitting the wicket from an acute angle in the dying minutes to run out Australia's last men. In 1963, Hall and Griffith capitalized on the last year of the back foot no-ball law, rendering the England batsmen black and blue, with their searing pace delivered from over the popping crease. (The new front-foot law was trialled in county cricket that summer.) With Richie Benaud making his début as a TV commentator, BBC viewers would have soon become familiar with his catchphrases 'quite remarkable delivereee' and 'brilliant leg cudda'.

The original hard bastard, Brian Close, was at the forefront of England's ordeal, advancing up the pitch to take withering blows on the body without flinching. But then Close, a fearless short leg, was the guy who, when fielding a yard from the bat for Yorkshire and taking a sickening blow to the forehead, was happy to see the ball ricochet into the hands of first slip. 'But, Brian, what would have happened if the ball had struck you on the temple?' enquired a concerned colleague. 'He'd have been caught at extra cover,' was the nonchalant reply.

The respective countries' attitudes to bouncers encapsulated their differences. To West Indians a fast short ball represented drama and challenge; to an Englishman it elicited fear and loathing. The West Indies won that series 3–1, and the one in 1966, during which Sobers was insatiable and England tried twenty-three different players, including a young, Cape Coloured South African batsman, playing for Worcestershire, called Basil D'Oliveira. Hardly anyone noticed because, that summer, all eyes were focused on Bobby Moore's England instead.

England's return trip to the Caribbean was a much tighter contest. Led by the placid, gentlemanly Colin Cowdrey, they salvaged three draws – one partly due to a riot in Jamaica – then won the fourth Test thanks to an absurdly generous declaration by Sobers setting them only 215 for victory. In the final Test, in Guyana, England had to bat out the last day to win the series.

They immediately collapsed to 41-5. The Kent pair of Cowdrey and Knott resisted valiantly for four hours, but then there was another slump, and when the last man, Jeff Jones, walked to the wicket two overs still remained. With modern tailenders that might be OK, but Jones came from an era of no.11 bloodhounds – they come in after the rabbits. His average of 3.97 flattered him. He was one of a rare species – at the time, he had taken more wickets than he'd scored runs. (Even Devon Malcolm's batting wasn't that bad.) Grace Jones has more batting talent.

Somehow, in fading light and an atmosphere of near hysteria, Jones survived the final over bowled by the off-spinner Lance Gibbs and England stole the series 1–0. It was the greatest nought ever made, and remained Jones's most important contribution to English cricket until, ten years later, he got into bed with his wife Irene and fathered Simon.

Hello and Goodbye, Dolly!

So to the summer of 1968, one of the most important in the history of cricket. First, some context. That year the laxity of Harold Wilson's Labour government was enjoyed by many, notably students, rock music fans, gays, black-power activists and designers of concrete jungles, and deplored by others, especially Enoch Powell, who made his 'rivers of blood' speech, which aired his grievance at Britain's immigration policy and 'the annual inflow of 50,000 dependants . . . Like the Roman, I seem to see "the River Tiber foaming with much blood",' he warned.

Football League attendances were at a post-World Cup peak of 30,107,298 for the season, and the 'fifth Beatle', George Best, was in his pomp with a brilliant opportunistic goal to seal Manchester United's European Cup triumph against Benfica, after which he was named Footballer of the Year and opened a string of boutiques and nightclubs where everyone snogged to the Bee Gees' 'I've Gotta Get a Message to You'.

I alternated games of football in my eight-year-old friend's sitting room with watching fancy new colour images of Colin Cowdrey celebrating becoming the first man to play 100 Tests by scoring a century against the Aussies at Edgbaston. The graceful, if slightly portly, Cowdrey was my early hero. I loved his easy style at the crease, his exquisite driving and his habit of casually pouching catches at first slip and then glancing backwards to pretend he'd missed it having slipped the ball into his pocket. I admired the way he turned smartly for the pavilion when he'd nicked one, without waiting for the umpire's decision. (How was I to know that he was a professional trapped in the body of an amateur and that he was happy to 'walk' when he'd scored a hundred, but not necessarily when he was on 8?) And, of course, he was captain of England.

Basil D'Oliveira played in the first Test of that Ashes

series, making a valiant 87 not out, though in a losing cause. A tour to South Africa was on the horizon and MCC officials were conscious that D'Oliveira's presence in the England side was already putting that in jeopardy. At a dinner before the second Test commemorating the 200th match between the auld enemies, D'Oliveira was asked by the MCC secretary, Billy Griffith, if he would declare himself unavailable for England and pledge his allegiance to South Africa instead. D'Oliveira angrily refused. To the amazement of the Aussies, who rated Dolly England's most effective batsman, he was dropped for the second Test.

This was a shattering blow. From the age of sixteen, when he had made his début for Western Province in the non-white inter-provincial tournament, D'Oliveira had set his heart on playing international cricket. Some of his performances in South African non-white sides were extraordinary. Still a teenager he made 225 in seventy minutes in a Cape Town club match (out of his side's total of 236) with sixteen sixes. In another game he took 9-2. He scored more than eighty centuries in the 1950s and was regarded as the non-white Bradman.

If the standard of the local opposition was decidedly dubious, he distinguished himself playing for and captaining the national (Coloured) side against various East African nations and would have been a shoo-in for the South African Test team. But apartheid blocked any upward mobility and he had to watch official Test matches at the Newlands ground sectioned off with other non-whites in a cramped, poorly located enclosure called the 'cage'. A first tour of South Africa by the West Indies, with matches against representative non-white sides, was called off at the last minute, denying D'Oliveira the wider exposure he desperately craved.

The commentator John Arlott came to his aid. Perceiving Arlott as both liberal and influential, D'Oliveira wrote to him asking for help and finally secured an offer to pro for Middleton in the Central Lancashire League. That was in 1960. Initially he found the weather and the pitches impossible. But he persevered and eventually came top of the league's batting averages, narrowly ahead of none other than Garfield Sobers. He received a hero's welcome back in Cape Town.

He was equally successful the following season (Sobers apparently checked D'Oliveira's scores every week) and was invited on tour to Africa with an International XI that included many of the world's great players. He was not overawed and subsequently, through the benevolence of Tom Graveney, who'd been on that African tour, he had the chance to sign for Worcestershire in 1964. There was one snag. He was thirty-two, a little old to be starting out in county cricket. He lied and said he was twenty-nine. The deal was done.

He spent a year qualifying, absorbing like a human sponge the lessons of the players he'd watched. Utilizing the nimble and compact game necessary to survive on the primitive pitches of the Cape, he took his chance when it finally came. Making his championship début on a treacherous early-season pitch at Worcester, he came in at 58-3 and made 106. The Worcester faithful were taken aback by the assurance of his innings. 'That Dolly Vera, 'e seems mature beyond his years,' they said. They weren't as stupid as they sounded, eh?

He finished eighth in the national batting averages, and Worcester won the championship for the second season in a row. Test selection followed, and a maiden Test hundred against India in 1967. At the time of his Lord's omission in 1968 he was averaging 43 for England and nearing 1,000 Test runs.

So now you have the back story. Think of the absolute dedication of his twenty years in the senior game, the isolation, the uncertainty, the hardship, the banishment, the travel to an alien country, having to live near Birmingham, and the success against the odds, and imagine how he felt when he was dropped from the team for the second Test of 1968. Devastated isn't the half of it. The apologetic England captain, Colin Cowdrey, might have said, 'Before the season is out you'll be back', but D'Oliveira wouldn't have believed it. He went back to Worcestershire but he was so depressed he couldn't make a run.

He still nurtured faint hopes of making the England squad for the South African tour. South Africa's prime minister, B. J. Vorster, a Nazi sympathizer and one of the instigators of the apartheid regime, had let it be known through Lord Cobham, a former president of the MCC, that the tour would be cancelled if D'Oliveira was picked. An ally of Vorster's tried to bribe him into making himself unavailable with the offer of a lucrative coaching assignment in South Africa. D'Oliveira rejected it, but he wasn't in the party for the fifth and final Ashes Test at the Oval, more or less extinguishing his chances of a tour spot.

Two extra bowlers were put on standby for the Test and D'Oliveira was third reserve. As luck would have it, both those bowlers broke down, and Cowdrey asked for D'Oliveira to be called into the squad as the likely 12th man. Incredibly, the day before the game, the opening batsman Roger Prideaux went down with a mysterious virus (he later admitted it was a convenient way of not jeopardizing his own place). Dolly was in the side. The fates had conspired towards him for once.

The rest is history.

Don't you just *hate* it when people say that, assuming that you should know everything and therefore it is not worth repeating? Pure clichéd laziness if you ask me. Of *course* it's worth repeating. The situation was this. It was 1–0 to Australia, so England couldn't regain the Ashes but they could square the series. England batted first and were soon in trouble. Edrich and Graveney stabilized the innings and it was 238-4 when D'Oliveira walked to the wicket. He survived the final tricky half-hour and finished the first day 24 not out.

The following day he was soon in command, easing the ball majestically around. He was missed by wicket-keeper Barry Jarman on 31 (referred to by E. W. Swanton in the *Daily Telegraph* as 'the most fateful drop in cricket history') but otherwise moved faultlessly through to a stylish and superlative hundred. 'Oh, Christ, you've set the cat amongst the pigeons now,' muttered the kindly umpire Charlie Elliott when D'Oliveira reached three figures. He wasn't finished either, taking the attack to the Australians to be finally ninth out for 158.

It wasn't even close to being the highest-ever Test innings, the most dominant or the most spectacular. But no other has been played under such extreme duress, or had such enormous impact. Peter Oborne argues coherently in his award-winning *Basil D'Oliveira: Cricket and Conspiracy* that it is the greatest innings ever played. No other has been 'against an attack comprising Prime Minister Johannes Vorster and South African cricket at its most corrupt, supported by the weight of the British establishment . . . No other cricket innings in Test history, to put the matter simply, has done anything like so much good.'

The real 'good' was, of course, a long time coming. The initial 'good' was to help England win a Test match. To cap an extraordinary match, Australia, 86-5 at lunch on the last day, were facing certain defeat until a cloudburst flooded the outfield. Players began packing their bags. But once the rain had abated scores of volunteers came on to the field armed with mops and towels and the ground was declared fit just before 5pm. They don't even allow people on the field in a heatwave these days. After D'Oliveira had taken the breakthrough wicket, Underwood, bowling on a pitch that was more sawdust than grass, cleaned up. He took the last wicket with five minutes to spare and the series was shared.

With the tour party to South Africa due to be announced a few days later, however, interest immediately focused on D'Oliveira's fate. The England selectors (Doug Insole, Peter May, Alec Bedser and Don Kenyon) debated the issue late into the night with senior representatives of the MCC (Arthur Gilligan, Gubby Allen, Billy Griffith and Donald Carr), Cowdrey the captain and Les Ames the tour manager. As a group they buckled under the pressure of transparent threats from South Africa. D'Oliveira was not selected. He wept at the news.

It is hard to apportion direct blame (the minutes of the meeting have mysteriously disappeared). Not all of the group knew of Vorster's threats (Bedser admitted to me he didn't) and some were swayed by other batsmen's claims, despite D'Oliveira having the second-best Test average of England's entire top six. But Cowdrey, having promised D'Oliveira he would support his selection, was lukewarm about him in the meeting. So a wavering finger points at him. Captains usually get the players they want if they argue forcefully enough. Cowdrey, beneath the distinguished façade a slightly weak character, probably preferred to avoid a political storm.

He got one anyway. Many, though not all, newspapers were outraged. Thousands of protesting letters were written, and a special meeting of the MCC was called. Various bishops and MPs had their say. It all rather overshadowed events in Swansea, where Garfield Sobers, playing for Notts, struck the hapless Glamorgan left-armer Malcolm Nash for six sixes off one over, so establishing an unprecedented feat and simultaneously earning a local supporter an extra £100 for his Morris Minor, which he claimed had been dented by one of Sobers' sixes (actually he lied – it had been damaged by a stone on the way to the ground).

Three weeks elapsed, during which D'Oliveira's disappointment was only slightly diluted by his agreeing to cover the South African tour for the *News of the World*. Prime Minister Vorster took a dim view of this, but that was nothing compared to what he thought of the next development. In mid-September the trusty medium pacer Tom Cartwright was declared unfit for the tour and, to his brief delight, D'Oliveira was announced as a replacement. Justice had been done.

The selectors had a bit of trouble explaining why a player who was mainly a batsman had replaced a bowler, but Vorster didn't. The MCC had offered him a juicy half-volley and he gleefully thumped it through the covers. Ever the voice of reason, he declared South Africa would not accept a team 'thrust upon us', calling it 'not the team of the MCC but the team of the anti-apartheid movement'. He made a guttural noise as he pronounced the word *aparr-taaytt*, as if he was going to be sick, which most people said he obviously was. But not in South Africa. His speech, at the National Party congress, got a standing ovation.

The 1968–9 tour, of course, was off. The issue rumbled on for months. The white South Africa team was all set to tour England in 1970, but by then their rugby tour of Britain had been disrupted by demonstrators, they had been expelled from the Olympic movement and the anti-apartheid clamour had increased, stirred up by the South African-born firebrand Peter Hain and his 'Stop the Seventy Tour' campaign. The MCC went to considerable lengths to protect the Tests, erecting barbed wire around the boundary at Lord's – as if they were protecting apartheid – causing the odd injury to fielders during early-season county matches. (Where are Health and Safety when you really need them?)

It's incredible to think now how blinkered we all were then. Hain, a Young Liberal, was at the time regarded as something of a hate figure in Britain, as he attempted to destroy our cosy little cricketing clique. (The penny only dropped for me twelve years later when, spending a winter playing in Pretoria, I saw the terrible conditions blacks were forced to live in, the appalling segregation and their lack of accepted human rights.) In fact Hain loved cricket and his activities drew South Africa's shameful policies into the public domain like never before. Finally the British government stepped in to prevent the 1970 tour and after that South Africa remained in the sporting wilderness for two decades. It had only taken the sporting authorities seventy-five years to take a stance against blatant discrimination in South Africa. But, through D'Oliveira, they eventually got there.

To this day you still hear people say politics and sport shouldn't mix. It's a bit like claiming that science should never infiltrate art. Or that business should never influence music. Or that dads shouldn't dance at parties . . . well, on second thoughts . . . In the D'Oliveira affair, politics and sport were not only mixed – they were manacled together. And it signalled the beginning of the end of the cruellest regime in the English-speaking world.

TWELVE

The Lilian Thomson Show

Basil D'Oliveira played a further 28 tests for England and was still turning out for Worcestershire in 1980. And he was involved in another defining moment in the history of cricket: the first one-day international. It was in early 1971 and it came about by chance. The first three days of the Melbourne Test were washed out and officials, searching for a way to recoup lost revenue, hastily arranged a 40-over match to take its place. Sir Don Bradman – the Emperor of Australian cricket – gave it the thumbs-up, and the match was staged at the MCG, the ground where, ironically, Test cricket had been born ninety-four years earlier. The Australians were rewarded for their initiative when 46,000 excited fans turned up.

A large proportion of them were about to make a bee-line for the exits when Boycott, in partnership with Edrich, had managed only 8 runs from the first 8 overs of the game. And these were *eight*-ball overs too. But a decent match materialized which Australia, with superior fielding and pugnacious batting from Ian Chappell, won at a canter with 5 wickets in hand. The experiment was declared a major success. The fact that the attendance was somewhat higher than the total number that had watched the five days of the Brisbane Test was a portent of things to come.

This all took pace in the middle of a rather ill-tempered Ashes series. John Snow was at the forefront of it, whistling bouncers round tailenders' earholes, badly sconning one – the leg-spinner Terry Jenner – and inciting a mini-riot after which the England captain, Ray Illingworth, led his team off the field. England regained the Ashes, but it initiated a new era of aggression in Anglo-Australian Tests (and eventually prompted Jenner to seek alternative means of employment, like coaching Shane Warne, which ultimately proved even more damaging to England's cause).

Australia reacted by sacking their captain, Bill Lawry (the first time they'd done so for seventy years), and installing Ian Chappell in his place. Chappell was as uncompromising as the Adelaide sun is unyielding. He was stern, and gimlet-eyed, and never took a backward step, and that was just supping beers in the bar. Aussie pride coursed through his veins. His *raison d'être* was to grind the Poms into the dust, a legacy of the suffering of his grandfather, Vic Richardson, in the Bodyline series. His strategy was simple, as Simon Briggs recounts in *Stiff Upper Lips and Baggy Green Caps.*

'Boycott? Bounce the cunt. Edrich? Bounce the cunt. Willis? Slog the cunt. Underwood? Bloody tight. Hard to get away. Slog the cunt.' It sounds more like a Dudley

Moore and Peter Cook sketch than a captain's briefing.

Chappell's number one ally was a trucker's son from Perth: Dennis Keith Lillee. The christian names were tame, and with his straggly hair, hirsute appearance and medallion he looked as if he'd strayed off stage from a Creedence Clearwater Revival gig. But from the start of his great marauding run to the end of his follow through about three millimetres from the batsman he exuded menace. He was tall, he was strong, he was fast, he was mean. Most significantly of all, he was clever.

He could spot a batsman's weakness in an instant, and had the control, from a superbly robust action, to exploit it. His speed was once timed at 96mph, and he possessed a vicious bouncer, but he'd learnt from John Snow it was best directed at chest rather than head height. He was ruthless with it, exclaiming, 'I try to hit a batsman in the rib cage when I bowl a purposeful bouncer, and I want it to hurt so much that the batsman doesn't want to face me any more.'

More than that though, he could move the ball in the air and cut it off the pitch, and was one of the first utilizers of reverse swing (though it wasn't called that then), discovering, on exceptionally dry surfaces, that an old ball swung unconventionally. He read pitches expertly, generally keeping to a full length and varying his pace intelligently. He was most un-Australian in that sense. And the reason? A season playing for Haslingden in the Lancashire League (1971), which taught him to refrain from bowling too fast – especially when you were liable to slip arse over tit on damp run-ups – and use what assistance the pitch had

259

to offer. Lillee was a good example of why English cricket really began to struggle in the seventies. It was because a legion of overseas stars arrived to use county and league cricket as their own personal finishing school.

Lillee excelled in the drawn 1972 series in England, aided by the extraordinary swing bowling of Bob Massie, who, after an apprenticeship in Scottish cricket, took 16 wickets in his first Test, making the ball boomerang so much it threatened to come back to him. Just as quickly, the art deserted him and his boomerang wouldn't come back. Within two years he wasn't even playing state cricket back home. It was a quicker disappearance than Shergar.

By then, though, Lillee had a much more serious partner. The casual car salesman Jeff Thomson wandered from a Brisbane forecourt into the Australian side via a meagre five games with Queensland and made one of the worst Test débuts of all time, taking 0-110 against Pakistan. It didn't take him long to make a real impact. In his second Test his whiplash action and fearsome speed terrorized the England batting on an uneven Brisbane pitch prepared by the local mayor (yes, really), and with Lillee approaching full fitness again after a serious back injury, England, captained by a Scot (Mike Denness), could sense they were in for a hiding.

They were right. Lillee and Thomson shared 58 wickets in the six Tests and inflicted all manner of physical and mental scars, utterly confounding one Australian woman who thought Lilian Thomson was a new female tennis star. England cricket tours take place

in some of the world's most sought-after holiday desti-
nations, but it's a misconception to imagine the tourists
arriving back looking happy and relaxed. Batsmen
returning from the Caribbean during the 1980s wore a
haunted look for some weeks after their ritual pound-
ing, and it was the same after the 1974–5 Ashes in
Australia. Holidaymakers? They looked more like a
bunch of Vietnam vets.

The pitches were hard and fast and the bowling was
lethal. Lillee was a calculating sniper, Thomson a
random slingshot. His short, unremarkable approach
gave the batsman no preparation for his delivery, which,
after a balletic two-step, seemed to begin with
his right arm braced and practically touching the
ground behind while his left leg was raised so high that
his studs pointed straight down the wicket. It was like a
sapling bent double. One nanosecond later the ball had
been catapulted at you like a javelin flying straight at
your throat (occasionally without bouncing).

Thomson's pace was measured at 99mph at the
University of Western Australia, but he never had much
faith in speed guns. 'I just shuffle up and go wang,' he
once said. He probably bowled some of the fastest
deliveries ever not recorded, and he regularly detonated
stumps, but it was his severe lift that was really devastating. The ferocity with which he slung the ball into the
surface made it rear up viciously without much loss of
momentum and often cut back at the body as well. He
admitted he didn't mind hitting batsmen. 'I like
to see blood on the pitch,' he said. 'Stuff that stiff-upper-
lip brat. Let's see how stiff it is when it's split.'

Two English batsmen evolved different methods to counter him. The 6ft 7in Tony Greig stood upright, bat aloft almost baseball-style as Thomson approached, enabling him to get on top of everything but the highest bouncer. The diminutive Alan Knott stood more front on and changed his grip so he could uppercut the bouncer over the slips. Though both enjoyed reasonable success they might have been better off spiking his drinks. Decent partnerships were few, and the abiding image of that series is of English batsmen airborne with their head jerked back at right angles trying to avoid another Thommo missile.

The battered England players returned with the haunting verse 'Ashes to Ashes, dust to dust, if Lillee doesn't get you, Thommo must' ringing in their ears. Chappell had exacted revenge for the perceived injustices experienced by his granddad all those years ago. England had been ambushed.

Wonderful Summers, Unless You Were English

What was it about the seventies? Despite the world misery of fuel shortages and violence and terrible clothes, it produced some of the best comedy and some of the funkiest music and some of the greatest cricketers of all time. (Perhaps it was *because* of the fuel crisis and the violence and the terrible clothes.) The music and the cricketers have a common denominator. The emancipation of the blacks.

Berry Gordy founded Motown Records in 1959, about the same time the father of West Indies cricket,

Frank Worrell, was made captain of the national side. And in the years that the most influential Motown artist, Stevie Wonder, was recording his seminal hits, Clive Lloyd was establishing himself as the West Indies' unifying force.

Like Wonder, Lloyd was an exceptional all-round artist; he played with distinction for Lancashire for six years before taking on the West Indies captaincy in 1974–5. An instantly recognizable figure with his gangly physique and stooped gait and thick-rimmed NHS spectacles, 'Hubert', as he was universally known, was a gentle giant off the field but a fearsome striker on it. He used bats like clubs with six rubber grips so he could really feel the handle, and he hit the ball with colossal power. (I remember a straight six off the Middlesex and West Indies paceman Wayne Daniel, which, played from a yard down the pitch, never rose much more than eight feet from the ground before cannoning into the sightscreen.)

His first major assignment was the inaugural World Cup, staged in England in 1975, after three years of successful one-day international competitions. Eight teams took part – the six Test-playing countries (excluding South Africa of course), Sri Lanka and, wait for it, East Africa. The matches were 60 overs a side, with two points for a win, though obviously no one had told India because, after England made 334-4, they played for a draw and Sunil Gavaskar occupied the entire 60 overs making 36 not out. The roly-poly left-arm swinger Gary Gilmour terminated England's campaign in the Headingley semi-final, leaving the Lord's final to be contested by Australia and Lloyd's West Indies.

The final began in dramatic fashion with Roy Fredericks hooking the first ball of Lillee's second over for six and stepping on his stumps. (Tony Blair, making a speech at the opening of the 1999 World Cup, attempted to get some street cred by saying he remembered Fredericks 'hitting the first ball of the 1975 World Cup final out of the ground'. Clearly Alistair Campbell hadn't done his homework properly!) Afterwards Lloyd held together a team of disparate but mercurial talents – Greenidge, Kallicharan, Roberts, a young Viv Richards. Lloyd made a virtuoso hundred himself, like Sobers doing so without a thigh pad, then calmly supervised Australia's self-destruction in a chaos of run-outs.

The final margin was 17 runs, but it should have been 18. Last man Lillee was caught off a no ball. The crowd thought the match was over and rushed on. Fredericks tried for another run-out, only to see the ball disappear into the invading spectators. 'Keep running,' shouted Lillee to his partner, Thomson. Finally the umpires, Dickie Bird and Tom Spencer, declared they could have 2 runs. 'Pig's arse,' cried Thommo. 'We've been running up and down here all afternoon!' So they gave them 3. Why can't we have decisions like that now rather than those endless replays to decide whether or not the fielder's eyelash has brushed the rope?

Lillee and Thomson and the rest of the Australians remained in England for a four-Test series, which, from the moment the greying, bespectacled David Steele emerged from the home dressing room at Lord's, had a comic touch. Steele famously got lost on his way out to the middle for his Test début, descending one flight of pavilion stairs too many (which is easily done, I can tell you) and ending up in the Gents. When he eventually made it to the middle, the response was a mixture of surprise and derision. Some accounts suggest Thomson exclaimed, 'Bloody hell, who we got 'ere, Groucho Marx!'; others report that he spluttered, 'Who's this then, Father fucking Christmas?'

Whatever he said, it had no impact on old 'Stainless', the archetypal English blocker, who stood resolutely behind his straight bat and compiled a stoic fifty, and remained very difficult to dislodge for the rest of the series. His lowest score was 39. It was a major advance on the poor young Essex batsman Graham Gooch who – keeping the spectacles theme going – made a pair on his Test début and, after one more chance, was unceremoniously dropped. The third Test at Headingley was abandoned after sympathizers of the armed robber George Davis damaged the pitch. Appropriately, Australia stole the series 1–0. Bizarrely, Steele was voted BBC Sports Personality of the Year. Still, it was a cut above Princess Anne getting it.

So we arrive at the long, hot, noisy summer of '76. It was a summer of contrasts. Concorde began flying to New York and InterCity 125s took to the rails for the first time, creating faster journeys (and more drastic tea spillage) than ever before. But unemployment was high and interest rates were astronomical (14 per cent) and the new Labour prime minister, Jim Callaghan, had a major job on his hands, not least in keeping the leader of the opposition, Margaret Thatcher, at bay. On the radio, the soothing anthems of Abba and Elton John were juxtaposed with the first strains of the Sex Pistols (if you listened to John Peel), the garish Bay City Rollers and the annoying Wurzels. No one was using their 'brand-new combine harvester' because all the wheat was burnt to a crisp. Well, sort of.

It was also the summer of black power. The huge success of Bob Marley and the Wailers' *Natty Dread* album helped the black community's self-esteem. Encouraged by the African nations' boycott of the Montreal Olympics (mainly because of New Zealand's continued sporting connections with South Africa), they were beginning to stand up for themselves. There were Rock Against Racism concerts and student demonstrations. In Soweto resentment turned into rioting and 500 people were killed.

Into this steamy atmosphere waded South African-born voice of tact Tony Greig. Greig, spotted as a teenager in Queenstown by visiting Sussex players – well, he was 6ft 7in – had been England's premier all-rounder for five years and captain for one. He enjoyed considerable success with bat and ball in the West Indies in 1974, but had also aroused controversy by running out Alvin Kallicharan after the batsman had walked off at the end of a day's play. (The incident provoked a riot – another one – and the batsman was later reinstated.)

In May 1976, Greig, as the current England captain, was interviewed on BBC's *Sportsnight* about the forthcoming West Indies series. It was then that he uttered his famous intention to 'make them grovel'. What he actually said, as recounted by David Tossell in his book *Grovel!* was this:

> I like to think that people are building these West
> Indians up, because I'm not really sure they're as good
> as everyone thinks they are. I think people tend to forget
> it wasn't that long ago they were beaten 5–1 by the
> Australians and only just managed to keep their heads
> above water against the Indians just a short time ago as
> well. Sure, they've got a couple of fast bowlers, but really
> I don't think we're going to run into anything more
> sensational than Thomson and Lillee and so really I'm
> not all that worried about them. You must remember
> that the West Indians, these guys, if they get on top are
> magnificent cricketers. But if they're down, they grovel,
> and I intend, with the help of Closey and a few others,
> to make them grovel.

However it was couched, it didn't wash too well with
the West Indies players, who were, anyway, the world
champions. Added to the fact that the words were
uttered by a white South African, it was like loosening
the lid of a boiling cauldron. It took a little while for
England to be properly scorched. Viv Richards made a
scintillating 232 at Trent Bridge, but the pitch was too
flat and the yeoman Steele blunted the West Indies pace
attack with a century. England had also recalled the 45-
year-old Brian Close – just the twenty-seven years after
his test début – to do the same thing. The second Test,
which Richards missed through injury, was also drawn.

In the third at Old Trafford, all hell broke loose.
England were demolished in their first innings for 71

and – after some rather unsavoury intimidation of the old buffers Close and Edrich – were dispatched in their second innings for 126. The margin of victory was a damning 425 runs. England were doing the grovelling. The men invoking Greig's words were Andy Roberts, Michael Holding and Wayne Daniel, plus Vanburn Holder, the amiable chap with the bow legs you could drive a car through.

Roberts, Holding and Daniel. There's a trio to set the heart pumping. Roberts was a cold-blooded assassin with merciless designs on certain batsmen and two bouncers, one that invited the hook and one that took your head off. Holding purred to the wicket from the sightscreen, body swaying rhythmically, and from a beautifully athletic action unleashed rib-ticklers and stump-detonating missiles. And Daniel was 16 stone of pure muscle who thundered to the crease like a black rhino and hurled the ball wicket-wards with all his might. After the tour he was immediately signed by Middlesex and, aptly nicknamed the (black) Diamond, brought the county untold riches over the next ten years. Facing those three you soon realized adrenaline was brown.

The fourth Test at Headingley was a closer contest, but the West Indies won it to clinch the series. Then all roads led to the Oval. Half of south London seemed to have descended on the ground to pay homage to their heroes. There were Jamaicans and Bajans and Guyanese and Trinidadians and Rastas, with their afros and dread-locks and cornrows, and whistles and drums and conch shells, all come to enjoy a carnival of cricket. With its parched, brown outfield the Oval even looked more Kensington (Bridgetown) than Kennington.

Richards (and later Holding) did not disappoint them. Richards' majestic 291 was the culmination of eight months of incredible run-making, beginning in Australia against Lillee and Thomson, continuing at home against the wizardly Indian spinners Bedi, Chandrasekhar and Venkataraghavan, and ending in the mauling of some of England's all-time greats, including Bob Willis, John Snow and Derek Underwood. His 1,710 runs in eleven Tests broke the record for the calendar year, and his 829 in the four Tests against England was on a par with Bradman's meteoric summer of 1930.

Of course, it wasn't just the weight of Richards' runs, but the manner in which he scored them. There was a detached, almost disdainful air about him from the moment he swaggered on to the field chewing, chest thrust out, arse protruding, maroon cap perched jauntily on his head. He resembled a guy moseying along the beach checking the talent.

He would take guard in a gruff, staccato way, 'Two legs, ump?' and casually survey the field, blinking a little, a cat that is barely awake. He would stroll up the pitch and tap an imaginary bump and give the bowler a sly (and unnerving) glance. He would settle into his two-eyed stance, bat turned in, head leaning a little too much to the off. Then, as the ball came down, he would pounce, seizing on any slight deviation of length or line. A fraction wide and it was flayed through the covers on the up with a glorious follow through, the ball leaving a vapour trail across the grass. Too straight and he unfurled his trademark clip through mid-wicket, played with a straighter bat than it appeared (slowing this shot down, you can see it is just a flick of the wrists at the last moment that sends the ball off at an angle, in similar vein to Kevin Pietersen's style). Too short and he'd murder you backward of point or help it over square leg off the front foot in a blur of forearm and wrist. He did this against me once on a juicy Lord's pitch, flicking a fastish lifter for six, the same ball that, the previous over, had broken a Somerset colleague's thumb.

He produced some shots that seem fairly revolutionary even when you see batsmen playing them today – the languid walk across his stumps to flick offside balls to leg, the lay-back to smear leg-stump balls over extra cover, the nonchalant little dink – what is known as the paddle sweep now – to the fine-leg boundary. There was also the exaggerated block – seemingly played at random when the bowler was at his mercy – and the regular withering blow over the sightscreen. Put that together with his big match temperament and Richards was years ahead of his time.

He had always suggested he would be something special from his school days when he was chosen for his island of Antigua at cricket and football. He was the local favourite (once the crowd thought he had been given out unfairly in an inter-island match – they chanted, 'No Vivi, no match', and got the decision overturned) and money was raised in 1973 to send both him and Andy Roberts to Alf Gover's Cricket School in Wandsworth. Even if Gover told him to play straight he didn't listen and was soon making stacks of runs for Somerset (some astute county members had spotted him while on tour in Antigua).

The only thing he lacked was self-control. He is indebted to Somerset's (imported) captain Brian Close and Tom Cartwright for helping him acquire it. There we go again, fine-tuning the talents of foreign players so they can come and ritually slaughter us! He also speaks highly of Clive Lloyd's calming influence. Lloyd was at the other end coaxing Richards to his first Test century (192 not out against India in his second Test) and Richards says, 'In 1974 a lot of us were touring for the very first time. Individuals do need people who can inspire them. He did that.'

Let's not beat about the bush, though. There was more talent in Richards' pinky than in the entire population of Taunton and he was lucky that he was born in a place where no one would try to tinker with it. Too often in England, natural flair has been tampered with and gradually coached out of players. It is better to let them breathe and find their own way. Richards' mantra on batting is simple: 'If a young man have shots I can teach him defence. But ain't no good if he ain't got no shots.'

So Richards made his 291 at the Oval (there was genuine surprise when he was out, clean bowled by Greig, as everyone assumed he was going to go on and break Garfield Sobers' record) and a wicketless Mike Selvey must have wondered what he'd done wrong to make his Test début there, and then Michael Holding took 14 wickets on a featherbed with some of the fastest, straightest bowling ever seen and was christened 'Whispering Death' by umpire Dickie Bird because he couldn't hear him approaching. On the final day Clive Lloyd was presented with the Wisden Trophy, and all of London's Caribbean community clapped and whistled and banged their drums, celebrating the achievements of a fabulous team. Almost simultaneously Stevie Wonder brought out *Songs in the Key of Life*, which I'm not alone in thinking is the greatest album ever made. Phew. It was quite a week. It was quite a summer.

I Come from a Land Down Under

Life around this time wasn't great for the English pro. With the introduction of the Benson & Hedges Cup in addition to the John Player Sunday League and the Gillette Cup, county cricket was now a seven-day-a-week operation run by a professional body – the Test and County Cricket Board. The TCCB shared out the Test match revenue equally around the counties, but it didn't amount to much. Test match tickets were £1 and the income from television and sponsorship was about £400,000 in the early 1970s, meaning each county received about £20,000 from the board (they now get £1.3m). Therefore the average player's annual salary was barely above the minimum wage – roughly £1,200 a year. (A first-division footballer was on about £7,000.) Winning the John Player League might net them an extra £200. A Test match appearance was worth £150. It was a hand-to-mouth existence. It wasn't the sort of job that had you driving around in an Aston Martin unless you were Ted Dexter and he had retired and was now running a successful PR business.

Some of the celebrated overseas players did slightly better, but nothing much to write home about. Copying the activities of other trade unions, the fledgling Cricket Association tried to flex its muscles, but it had apathetic support. No one was prepared to stick their head above the parapet. Cricketers are generally a conservative bunch who like to know where they stand. They like their home comforts and their daily routine and their Little Chefs. They don't want Heston Blumenthal buggering up their English breakfasts with snail jam on camomile muffins. They're not activists or revolutionaries; the game doesn't lend itself to that sort of activity. Therefore they are liable to be exploited.

Although they were by name professionals, they were, in most senses, amateur. They weren't particularly fit – there were plenty of overweight players, many puffed away on the glut of free sponsors' cigarettes, and at Lord's John Emburey and Phil Edmonds used to drive from the pavilion to the Nursery for nets. On 'practice' days they'd stroll in about 10.30am to avoid the morning rush hour traffic, have a gentle net and, after a large lunch, do some light catching practice before heading home to avoid the evening rush hour traffic. There was no video analysis or biomechanical assessment or dietary control (certainly not at Lord's, where Nancy Doyle dished up a veritable banquet every lunchtime). The coach was usually a retired player who looked after the practice balls and barked at young players if

273

they were late or shoddily attired. 'Greasy square, and you're fielding in flats? You prat!' they'd say.

Financially, it was even worse being an Australian player. None of the state players were contracted (unlike county players) and Test match fees were so low the top players all had other jobs (Lillee ran an office-cleaning business, for example). The world game was now studded with brilliant players – Richards, Greenidge, Lloyd and the fast bowlers in the West Indies, Greig, Snow, Knott and Underwood in England, the Pakistanis Imran Khan, Asif Iqbal and Mushtaq Mohammed – the inventor of the reverse sweep – and the South Africans Mike Procter, Barry Richards and Graeme Pollock. None of them had any job security.

Kerry Packer knew all this. He also knew that he liked cricket. And he wanted a piece of it. And when Packers want things, they usually get them. Kerry was the son of Sir Frank Packer, a media tycoon who owned newspapers and TV stations and ran them with an iron fist. Frank was so unforgiving that when the eleven-year-old Kerry arrived at his Melbourne school for a new term without his tennis racket his father ordered him to make the six-hour return journey to Sydney to fetch it. When Frank died he left his entire empire to Kerry because he had fallen out with his other son, Clyde.

In mid-1976, at the height of the Australian team's power, Kerry Packer went to the Australian Cricket Board determined to buy the TV rights for Australia's home games. He wanted to show them exclusively on his Channel Nine, and offered a vast sum, but the board weren't prepared to yield on their gentleman's agreement with the Australian Broadcasting Corporation.

So an enraged Packer picked up his bat and ball and took it home with him: it was then that he decided to stage his own 'Tests' between Australia and the Rest of the World instead. He asked Ian Chappell, who had recently stood down as Australia's captain, to make a wish list of the best Australian players. They were offered a minimum of A\$25,000 a year for three years, an absolute bonanza for players who'd been complaining that they weren't even paid as much as the dressing room cleaners.

While this was all going on, England, still feudally referred to as the MCC on tour, were Down Under to play the centenary Test. Watched by almost 200 ex-players, it was a classic, and, amidst all this modern financial wrangling, something of a throwback. Derek Randall's second-innings 174 was anyway. Daft as a brush, Randall had already captivated 100,000 people at Eden Gardens, Calcutta, on his Test début with his brilliance and jaunty acrobatics in the field (he actually performed an impromptu cartwheel during an official reception) and now he did the same to a huge Melbourne crowd with the bat.

'The sun has got his hat on, hip, hip, hip hooray,' he sang as he walked out to bat, with Lillee pawing the ground at the end of his run. Having been floored by a bouncer he stood up, doffed his cap and made an exaggerated bow to the bowler. After swaying out of the way of another he performed a backward somersault. Fussing and fidgeting at the crease, and constantly talking to himself, some of his innings were pure slapstick.

But Randall's nervous eccentricity and ragamuffin appearance belied a fantastic eye and the silkiest timing of anyone who has worn (and doffed) an England cap. He pulled and hooked with élan and eased the ball dreamily through mid-wicket with a dextrous flick of the wrists. He placed the ball deftly, hared between the wickets, and entertained royally for 7½ hours over two days sustained only by heavily sugared cups of tea. The Australians appreciated his spirit, even calling him back when they felt an edge to the keeper might not have carried. No, I have not made that up. When he was finally out he was so overcome by the standing ovation that he left the field through the wrong gate and ended up outside the royal box. England were finally dismissed for a valiant 417, losing the match by 45 runs, eerily the same margin of victory that Australia had enjoyed in the very first Test exactly 100 years before.

Within a month the Test match scene had been rent asunder. Packer had signed Tony Greig to lead his world XI, and he had been sacked as captain of England. Greig had helped recruit five other England players (Woolmer, Underwood, Knott, Amiss and Snow), and most of the best West Indians, Pakistanis and South Africans as well. All were threatened with bans from Test cricket by the floundering International Cricket Conference (then essentially an extension of the MCC) if they took part in Packer's World Series Cricket. Greig was accused of treason and of 'disembowelling' world cricket. Packer's first round of matches in December 1977 was timed to clash with Australia's official Test series against India.

At the time Packer was regarded as a villain. Subsequently he emerged as a hero. Players' earnings multiplied as a result of new sponsorship of Test cricket (England players' match fees immediately jumped from £200 to £1,000 thanks to Cornhill Insurance). The Test match bans were quashed by the High Court. Floodlights and white balls were introduced into cricket for the first time. (I was going to include coloured clothes in this list of improvements, but, as we've seen, they were common in the eighteenth and nineteenth centuries, and, anyway, the gaudy uniforms of today are not regarded by many except a colour-blind minority as being an enhancement to cricket.) Australia, who decided not to pick their Packer-players, were brought back down to size for several years as they were obliged to field a virtual 3rd XI in Test cricket.

And there was one other development. After Greig's very public fall from grace, the search was on to find a new England all-rounder. Someone who could cure the perpetual selector's headache of whether to pick a full complement of five bowlers and leave yourself a batsman light, or pick six batsmen and manage with just four pie throwers. Someone, in other words, who was competent in both departments. In the third Test of that summer, at Nottingham, about the time Hot Chocolate had got to no.1 with 'So You Win Again', they gave a début to a young, thrusting chap who'd been doing quite well for Somerset . . .

THIRTEEN

Universes Collide

Some things are meant to be. Sid Vicious was always going to die of a drug overdose. Steve Redgrave was always going to win a fifth Olympic gold having previously asked to be shot if he was ever seen getting in a boat again. Elton John was always going to get a divorce.

The date was 28 July 1977. The place was Trent Bridge. It was not only Ian Botham's Test début but also Geoffrey Boycott's first match back after self-imposed exile. Many harsh words were fired in Boycott's direction about his absence, mostly accusing him of deliberately avoiding the emerging battery of pace bowlers around the world. In fact it was more a case of him feeling peeved at having been overlooked for the England captaincy in favour of first Mike Denness then Tony Greig. First a meek Scot then a mouthy South African preferred to a straight-talking Yorkie. His exile was not born of any apprehension. The only thing he has ever feared is a minute's silence.

That day was also Garfield Sobers' forty-first birthday.

He had retired three years earlier, though Botham and he had once met on the field, also at Trent Bridge, when the teenage tyro had bowled to his boyhood idol as he made a farewell hundred, and Botham was then dismissed by him. (Fatalists saw this, in retrospect, as a ritual handing over of the all-rounder's baton. Realists saw it as an old bull refusing to submit to a young buck.)

It was the appropriate day, and place, therefore, for a pretender to the throne to make a statement. The most famous product of the MCC Young Pros at Lord's, where he used to make an extra buck hiring out seat cushions at Test matches, Botham had already given notice of his all-round ability. There was a courageous, match-winning innings against Hampshire after being hit in the mouth by Andy Roberts, a century (at Trent Bridge), several 5-wicket hauls, and a hook to Ian Chappell's chin in a Melbourne bar during a scholarship trip to Australia.

He took the field for his first Test with his county captain Brian Close's words echoing in his ear: 'Don't let those Australians intimidate you.' Still, as the new England captain, Mike Brearley, brought him on first change ahead of Greig, who was still in the team, he admitted to having 'nerves as taut as a drum'. It was the only time Botham experienced any self-doubt in his life, and it showed. After a first swinging delivery that would have resulted in a wicket if he'd had a third slip, he served up an assortment of juicy leg stump deliveries which were dispatched to the boundary.

At lunchtime, Botham was informed by Gerry, his

father-in-law, that a Taunton publican had agreed to sponsor him for £1 a run and a fiver a wicket. Sensing his raw enthusiasm, Brearley gave him a second spell soon after lunch. His first ball, to the Australian captain, Greg Chappell, was a wide loosener. Chappell, seizing on it with undisguised relish, was slightly over-eager. His attempted backfoot thump ricocheted off a bottom edge into the stumps. Botham did the first of his 383 war dances down the pitch, and from then on was unstoppable. In front of the Queen, who had popped in for the afternoon, he took four more wickets in his next 6 overs. It was written in her, and everybody else's, tea leaves: on his Test début against Australia, Ian Botham was always going to take 5 wickets.

It wasn't the end of the entertainment. When England batted, Boycott was soon in disgrace. He called the local hero Derek Randall – playing his first Test at Trent Bridge – for a suicidal single and ran him out. Boycott made amends with the inevitable century and saw England to victory with an undefeated 80 in the second innings, but the yokel from Yeovil had stolen the show. And, with a breezy 25 in England's first innings, he was now £50 better off too.

Continuing this meant-to-be summer, the teams moved on to Headingley. And who d'you think was on ninety-nine first-class hundreds? That's right, the man born just down the road at Fitzwilliam, near Wakefield, and still, aged thirty-seven, living with his beloved mother Jane (Boycott's father Thomas, a pit-worker, had died ten years before from long-term injuries sustained in a mining accident). England batted first. Boycott opened as usual, and towards the end of the first day drove a gentle inswinger from Greg Chappell between the bowler and mid-on, then removed his cap and raised both arms aloft in celebration of his 100th hundred.

It had been quite a journey for the bespectacled teenager spotted playing alongside Dickie Bird and Michael Parkinson for Barnsley. How their paths (and hairstyles) have diverged. You certainly couldn't imagine Boycott ever interviewing someone. He'd never be remotely interested in anyone else. This was obvious from the start. When during a club match he heard he'd been asked to report to Yorkshire nets the next day, he departed in mid-innings, leaving with the words 'I've finished with your class of cricket.' He was extra-ordinarily single-minded, living a life of almost total abstinence – practising harder, eating more fastidiously, going to bed earlier than anybody else – in order to become the greatest batsman in the world. It was why he was both exceptionally successful and extraordinarily unpopular. Asked one day by an exasperated Boycott why people always took an *instant* dislike to him, a Yorkshire colleague replied, 'Well, it just saves time.' Total egocentricity doesn't wash in Britain.

It would be fair to say he achieved his objective. He scored more first-class runs and centuries than anybody post-war and twice finished a season averaging 100. For England he eventually overtook Colin Cowdrey's record aggregate, and after that Garfield Sobers' too, to become, for a time, the world's leading Test match run-getter. He wasn't perpetually boring either. Despite

Middlesex's Phil Edmonds once grunting, 'He won't die of a stroke!' Boycott had shots: the textbook cover drive – left elbow bolt upright – the neat clip off his pads, the elegant backfoot force. He was stronger than he looked, with supple wrists and powerful forearms, and could hook and pull when in the mood. He was nimble on his feet, and excellent against spin. You don't score all those runs without bundles of talent. And, though viewed as an intrinsically selfish player, he mostly benefited the team too. The fact that England never lost a match when he made a hundred (he got twenty-two in all) will confound all those Boycott-haters who believed he was a negative influence. He averaged 147 in the Tests of 1977 and was a member of four Ashes-winning teams.

But it was his immense powers of concentration and self-denial that set him apart from the rest. The Jacobean poet John Donne said, 'No man is an island.' He might have changed his mind if he'd lived three hundred years later. Boycott was not just an island but an atoll in the middle of a vast ocean, the kind of place where they do nuclear testing, self-contained and completely detached from the outside world. When he recorded *In the Psychiatrist's Chair* with Dr Anthony Clare, he was probed about his absolute single-mindedness, but he was defiant. He saw nothing strange in it. Clare found him uniquely impenetrable. It was his strength as a player, and his weakness as a person.

Through his playing career, Boycott remained officially unattached. He had sixteen different opening partners for England. They were his wives. But there wasn't a lot of romance. Dennis Amiss would habitually wish him 'good luck' as they walked out together. Boycott would reply, 'It's not good luck, it's ability that counts.' In his eyes it was still basically each man for himself.

Yet he was never alone. His mum was always there. It emerged through the Anthony Clare interview that he derived most of his values from her. She had particularly stressed the importance of avoiding temptation. '"Stay away from the girls",' Boycott said she told him. '"They get you in the woods, they get you into trouble." I always followed me mum's advice.'

Boycott's mum has become even more famous in his retirement, of course, as he puts a terrible delivery into context, exclaiming on commentary, 'My moom could have hit that for four!' But it was always his way. Even in his playing days she was the benchmark for everything. He recalled the time when two young Yorkshire players, Kevin Sharp and Neil Hartley, came to pick him up to take him to an away match. His mum answered the door. She was not a tall lady. 'Blimey, Mrs Boycott!' Sharp said, grinning. 'You're not very big for all those roons and wickets you've got!'

New Kit on the Bloke

Geoff Boycott is an endlessly fascinating phenomenon who tends to polarize opinion and dominate conversation. You see it has even happened here. I started off telling the story of Ian Botham's Test match début and suddenly the subject of Boycott has taken over. So enough about him for the moment. Let's get back to the story.

In the winter of 1977, Kerry Packer's name still darkened the corridors of power. But, buoyed by winning his case in the High Court, where the English cricket authorities were portrayed as treating the players like slave labourers, he pressed ahead with his plans. Richie Benaud devised the rules of World Series Cricket and on 14 December the world's first floodlit cricket match was staged, on an Aussie Rules football ground in Melbourne with a specially grown 'drop-in' pitch, between 'Australia' and a World XI. Only 2,000 people attended, and WSC didn't draw huge crowds, compelling the fancy new (double-ended!) TV coverage to avoid showing the vast acres of empty seating, a bit like when Sky show a National League match at the Rose Bowl. But the cricket was pulsating, and according to participants like Barry Richards and Michael Holding the toughest they'd ever played (the pride and professionalism of Clive Lloyd's all-conquering West Indians originated in World Series Cricket). The players were amply rewarded with holidays and houses. Holding had only ever had a few hundred dollars in his post office account. When he got home after WSC and checked his account he was astonished at the amount. 'It was the first time I'd seen a comma in that book,' he said.

What Packer ultimately did was prise apart cricket's ancient curtains and let the bright light of the modern world in. In the end it bought him a seat at the dining table, and TV access to the official Aussies in an exclusive deal with Channel 9 which is still running to this day. Unfortunately his recruitment temporarily decimated the Test team and initially they were pretty rubbish. Mike Brearley, nicknamed the Ayatollah for his luxuriant beard, brought a team Down Under in 1978–9 and they hammered Australia 5–1.

England were pretty good. There was 6ft 6in Bob Willis charging in from one end and whistling Bob Dylan songs on the boundary while Botham swung the ball both ways from the other. Botham also had a brilliant slower ball (a well-disguised off break) which I myself copied and found useful for a while until it was dispatched into the upper tier of the Compton stand in the last over of the 1989 NatWest final. Botham's laconic roommate Mike Hendrick was a good accurate foil. The off-spinner Geoff Miller deceived everyone, including himself, to take 23 wickets in the six Tests.

A new blond left-hander, David Gower, stroked the ball about languidly, dovetailing well in the middle order with the more belligerent Graham Gooch, and Randall was indefatigable. He batted just short of ten hours for his epic 150 in stifling conditions in Sydney, turning the fourth Test around and driving everybody nuts with his incessant fidgeting and constant 'C'mon, Rags! C'mon, England!' exhortations to himself.

Randall's input at team talks was priceless. When Australia had been on top, he piped up, 'We must rise from the Ashes like a pheasant!'

'Don't you mean phoenix?' someone said.

'Oh, I knew it were a bird beginning with F,' Randall replied.

Brearley captained astutely, getting the best out of

everyone to such an extent that the Aussies' combative fast bowler and dry humorist Rodney Hogg declared he had 'a degree in people'.

Brearley's opposite number, Graham Yallop, wore the first batting helmet that season. Dennis Amiss, with a motorcycle variety, and Brearley himself, with pink plastic flaps protruding from his England cap, followed suit in the English summer. And with good reason. Well, four good reasons actually. Andy Roberts, Michael Holding, Joel Garner and Colin Croft. The fastest, nastiest quartet of bowlers ever seen.

At 6ft 8in, Garner was the tallest man ever to have played Test cricket. Loping in to bowl off a relatively short run, he released the ball from a height of over 9ft, meaning his delivery arm was way over the top of most sightscreens. Having been coached at school by Wes Hall and Charlie Griffith he wasn't going to give the batsmen much leeway either. They were either fending the ball off their ribs or digging out his yorkers speared in at leg stump. He was also fiendishly accurate, largely a product of three years at Littleborough in the Central Lancashire League (another one!) before Somerset snapped him up.

Garner, who answered to the nickname 'Big Bird', was in fact a gentle giant and quite charming off the field. Colin Croft, on the other hand, was half crazy. Tall, with a powerful, open-chested action, he delivered ferocious bouncers from very wide on the crease which had a nasty habit of following batsmen as they tried to sway out of the way. He clanged heads and fractured jaws and often overdid the short stuff. He also barged an umpire out of the way in New Zealand after a controversial decision went against him. He and Garner both made a mockery of the fact that when a cricket pitch was established as 22 yards long in the eighteenth century, the average height of a man was 5ft 4¾in. Never mind increasing a sightscreen's elevation. What the batsman wanted to do was move it between him and them.

This pace quartet was decisive in West Indies' winning the second World Cup final, against England in the summer of 1979. In contrast to those morale-shatterers, 12 of England's overs were completed by a combination of Gooch and Larkins' little swingers and Boycott bowling his gentle in-dippers from round the wicket still wearing his cap. Those overs were pulverized for 86 runs by Viv Richards and the swashbuckling Collis King as the West Indies totalled 286.

Underlining that England were already playing catch-up in one-day cricket, Brearley and Boycott's opening stand of 129 took up 38 overs, by which time the required rate was above 7 an over. Garner's yorkers finished them off. Richards, the man of the match, encapsulated the differences in approach when he waltzed across his stumps to the last ball of the West Indies innings and flicked a low, straight full toss from Hendrick deep into the Mound stand for six. It was a microcosm of Caribbean exuberance and flair triumphing over grey, conservative England. Richie Benaud, commentating, was almost speechless, and it remains one of the most outrageous shots ever played in a major match.

Richards was helped (slightly) by a recent advance in

bat manufacture, which after a century or so of stasis had begun to evolve. Richards wielded a Stuart Surridge Jumbo, which had extra meat at the bottom but still picked up like a wand. It was a response to the Gray Nicholls scoop and double scoop as used by Gooch and Gower. In keeping with the ice-cream theme, Duncan Fearnley should have named their innovative bat design, featuring a blade full of little holes, a '99'. Instead it was called a 'Run Reaper', and as its most famous user was Bob Willis, who batted like a giraffe on roller skates, it never caught on.

On the domestic front, Essex won their first County Championship title, now sponsored by Schweppes, in 1979. Appropriately their success was based on an effervescent spirit. The team was bursting with characters, from the mischievous Scot Brian 'Lager' Hardie, an uncomplicated opening bat and masochistic short leg, through the lugubrious Gooch and the debonair South African Kenny McEwan to the chirpy left-arm swinger J. K. Lever and the mad antics of the spinners David Acfield and Ray East.

Acfield was nervous and suffered from homesickness (ideal for being a professional cricketer!). East was a natural clown, performing silly walks, acting like a remote-controlled puppet on the boundary, or resuming his innings disguised in a helmet after tea, having been given out lbw in a cap before the interval. Preparing for a match against Hampshire, Acfield and East were spotted standing in the middle and then looking up to the skies and tossing their heads violently backwards. Asked what they were doing, East replied,

'Practising for bowling at Barry [Richards] and Gordon [Greenidge].' They were steady bowlers though, sharing 82 wickets that summer.

This motley crew were held together by the paternal Keith Fletcher, whose gnome-like appearance and inability to pronounce his 'r's' belied a character as hard as nails. Prone to absent-mindedness, 'Fwetch' tended to forget players' names – even his own teammates' – but always remembered how to get them out. His forensic knowledge sealed the title for Essex in mid-August, but ultimately it undermined England. Allan Border, who subsequently played for Essex, noted many of Fletcher's little ploys and used some of them to clinch the Ashes when he was made captain of Australia.

Essex won £10,185 for the championship title and £7,000 for winning the Benson & Hedges Cup and all the players went off and ordered shag-pile carpets and had their Braintree homes double-glazed. It was an exciting time to become a professional cricketer, which I was just about to do. I had been playing club cricket for four years. League matches on Saturdays, 'friendlies' on Sundays, and 20-over evening matches in the Red Cross Middlesex League midweek. (I only mention this to stress that the Twenty20 phenomenon was not a brilliant concoction by the ECB in 2002, but a popular format that was thriving in the north-east as long ago as the 1930s.) But I'd had to pay for the pleasure. Now they were going to pay me. My starting salary was £45 a week. Plus free lunch and tea. Luxury.

FOURTEEN

'E Couldn't Captain a Toy Ship

You could call the first half of the 1980s cricket's second Golden Age. The county game was littered with world-class players, Ashes series were closely fought, the West Indies played cricket of incredible zest (and occasional over-zealousness), India and Pakistan began to show their might, Sri Lanka added their own brand of wristy ingenuity and Dickie Bird gave an lbw. Or he may have been trying to extract a nostril hair. The batsman (Kim Hughes) walked anyway.

The England team began the decade exhausted. Most people assumed this was due to a disappointing three-month tour of Australia. Actually it was because they were lugging caseloads of beer from Australia to Bombay to celebrate Indian cricket's Golden Jubilee. (Indian beer was regarded as totally undrinkable.) Unfortunately they were playing in a Test, not attending a Bollywood party. The star of the eighties, Ian Botham, was already in the ascendant and dragged England from their torpor with a stellar performance. He took

6 wickets in the first innings against a jaded Indian batting order, swinging and seaming the ball extravagantly, rescued the England reply with a rollicking century and then followed up with 7-48 in India's second innings. Thirteen wickets *and* a hundred. It remains the most exceptional all-round performance in Test history.

It is even more astounding when you consider that, on his first trip to India, he was invariably bowling all day having been up half the night stuffing his face with chicken tandoori washed down with most of the grog England imported. Botham has always had an incredible constitution. No Delhi belly ever afflicted him. Appropriately the Indians called him Iron Bottom.

His extraordinary prowess led to him being named England captain in May 1980. Mike Brearley wanted to concentrate more on his psychoanalysis and clearly believed that with its psychos and weirdos the Middlesex team was a better training ground. He was probably right. It contained the lothario Graham Barlow, the sex-fantasist Wayne Daniel, the Bruce Springsteen obsessive Mike Selvey, the human garbage disposal Mike Gatting, the jovial white South African Vince van der Bijl, the black power supporter Roland Butcher, the hardened senior pro Clive Radley and the polite public schoolboy Paul Downton. Trumping everyone was the confrontational, occasionally deranged Phil Edmonds, who always pulled on his sweater declaring, 'Well, I suppose I'm going to bowl immaculately today', while his laconic spin twin John Emburey reclined in an armchair chuckling, 'If you haven't got any fackin' muscles you can't strain anything!' And then there was me, the tactless, tea-spilling, tatty undergraduate.

Filming that lot for a month could have made as good a movie as *One Flew Over the Cuckoo's Nest*. (Jack Nicholson would have been perfect as Edmonds.) Brearley utterly deserved his reputation as a great captain. Through brilliant man-management and crafty tactics, including once placing the fielding helmet at short mid-wicket for Edmonds to try and induce the batsman to hit against his spin in an attempt to pick up 5 (penalty) runs, he led this unruly mob to two County Championships in three years.

Botham meanwhile was winning nothing. He may have been the greatest all-rounder England ever had but he was the worst captain. This may have been partly because he was the youngest for a hundred years, but he didn't help his cause by being narrow-minded and intolerant. The following winter, for example, when England toured the West Indies, he noticed Graham Gooch tending to nod off at evening socials. Gooch was a habitual early-riser, beginning his day with a run along the beach. Botham called a team meeting and declared a ban on early-morning jogs. When Gooch argued that it was his way of getting himself fit and ready for the match, Botham retorted, 'Yes, but it makes you go to sleep in the bar!'

Botham's record as England captain was appalling: P12 W0 L4 D8. He didn't have an easy ride. Nine of those twelve Tests were against the immense West Indies, and he had the trauma of a replacement player,

Robin Jackman, being refused entry to Guyana because of his South African links, and then the death of his idol and team manager Ken Barrington. At least his record was a good deal better than Sunil Gavaskar's efforts in charge of India. Gavaskar presided over thirty draws (out of forty-seven Tests as captain), which was partly responsible for driving the Indian fans away from Test cricket. In the perpetual argument over whether you should pick the captain first and then the team, or vice-versa, it is pretty clear from both cases that the best players rarely make the best captains.

Emphasizing Britain's growing multiculturalism, which included chicken curry and rice for lunch at Lord's on Mondays, Botham's England selected their first black player in the late summer of 1980. The chosen one was Middlesex's Roland Butcher, born in Barbados and arriving in England when he was four-teen. He was an enigmatic player, capable of outrageous backfoot strokes and astounding catches: he was nick-named 'Hoover' for his ability to dart in from cover and suck up the ball one-handed while running at full tilt. His England career was shortlived, however. He often looked as if he was batting still half asleep, and he was the world's most annoying roommate, stinking the place out with chicken kiev, leaving the remains on the floor for you to tread in when you arrived back late and then getting up at the crack of dawn to noisily clear his sinuses in the bathroom and use up all the hot water.

County seasons were relentless then, with teams regularly on the road at the end of a game to get to another one starting the next day. After winning the championship at Cardiff, Middlesex had to make a mad, slightly woozy dash across the country to be at Canterbury for the final three-day match. It was quite a nostalgic moment for me, playing at the old ground where, twelve years earlier, I had gazed in admiration at the diverse skills of the Kent players. Now I was encountering them up close.

Actually rather too close for my liking. First, on a dust heap, I had to negotiate 'Deadly' Derek Underwood, still rolling in to bowl wearing his heavy-duty 1960s boots, dropping the ball on a perfect length and closing on 300 Test wickets. Desperate to keep out his devilish quicker ball, I jerked hurriedly at every offering, only succeeding in punching slower and loopier deliveries out of reach of the close field, urged on by calls of 'You'll get him in a minute, matey!' His accuracy and disguise were exceptional.

After being put out of my misery, I, the youngest member of the team, was directed to squat at 'boot hill' (short leg) for the spin of Edmonds and Emburey. It was quite fun until Alan Knott came in. He attempted to sweep every ball. With a supreme eye, he got down low to paddle full deliveries fine and thwack shorter balls square. I was cowering, helmeted, two yards from the bat feeling the wind of balls flying past one or other ear or between my legs. All this in spite of three outfielders positioned for the shot, two behind square and one in front. Yet he never missed or gave a chance and, on a September minefield, finished up 85 not out. His superstition of touching the bails at the beginning of every over clearly worked.

Knott was a pioneer in many ways. When he first arrived on the scene, most keepers kept in the pads they batted in. They were large and cumbersome. Knott customized a pair of junior pads which came just over the knee and allowed better freedom of movement. He also adapted his gloves, tailoring each finger to his individual needs and keeping them warm at all times (even storing them under the pillow at night). He took exceptional care of his body, always exercising and stretching between balls, starching his upturned collars so he didn't get a draught down his neck and even, as I've mentioned, propping up his feet on blocks of wood when driving so he wouldn't strain his Achilles.

I knew most of this. I wasn't prepared, however, for his unusual practice technique. Play at Canterbury was delayed by rain one morning. Knowing the Kent players were a little weary of his unusual antics, Knott persuaded me to come into the showers with him. No, he wasn't like *that*. He wanted to hone his one-handed catching. Partially dressed and wearing one keeping glove, he stood in a cubicle and asked me to stand about five yards away. On his prompt I would underarm a low catch and he, initially unsighted, would pop out from behind the curtain and take it. He did ten minutes with one hand, then changed position and did ten minutes with the other. Then he thanked me and went and ate his lunch of quail's eggs and fried mung beans or whatever it was. He was a brilliant all-round cricketer and a ground-breaker. He was also a bloody nutter.

At the end of the 1980 season, Middlesex were invited on a short tour of newly independent Zimbabwe, who had been playing in the South African Currie Cup as Rhodesia since the Second World War. Robert Mugabe had just become president. It was a beautiful country then. The streets of Harare were lined with blooming jacaranda trees, the cricket grounds were beautifully laid out and surrounded by fluttering white marquees, and the steaks for lunch were vast and succulent. The (mainly white) players were strong and talented. Everyone was healthy and happy.

Zimbabwe's captain was the combative all-rounder Duncan Fletcher, who gave the ball a hearty clump with the bat and bowled abrasive outswingers. He cultivated a team that was hard to beat, and waiting in the wings was the fourteen-year-old Graeme Hick, who had scored his first century aged six. I couldn't even *count* to a hundred at that age.

The aim of the tour was to forge a relationship with a new state and help their cricket development. It was a fruitful and enjoyable trip, not least because I ended up in a palatial hotel room which turned out to be the honeymoon suite. Honeymoon . . . Zimbabwe? A classic oxymoron. You wouldn't send your worst enemy there now.

My first sortie into the world of professional cricket ended in Calcutta. Brearley had assembled an 'International XI' to celebrate the golden jubilee of the Bengal Cricket Association. (The Indians love their commemorations. I suppose it's a legacy of British rule.) Calcutta was the diametric opposite of Harare then – poor, teeming and fetid. There is a joyful spirit about the Bengalis though and they turned out in their droves.

The colossal Eden Gardens was half full every day to watch an out-of-practice visiting team get politely thumped by a select Indian XI. There was no sign of the locals' disenchantment with five-day cricket. Maybe that's because Gavaskar wasn't playing.

Did He Really? Yes, He Did

The year of 1981 was all about three people: Prince Charles, Lady Diana and Ian Botham (Diana always said her marriage felt a bit crowded). Diana was like Botham, in just a few months captivating the public and becoming a British icon – certainly in the view of the Norwegian football commentator Bjørge Lillelien, who included her in his impassioned list of Great Brits after Norway beat England 2–1 in Oslo. Remember the others? Here's his hysterical celebration: 'Lord Nelson! Lord Beaverbrook! Sir Anthony Eden! Winston Churchill! Clement Attlee! Henry Cooper! Lady Diana! Maggie Thatcher! . . . You boys took a helluva beating.' It has been voted the greatest piece of sports commentary ever.

The commentary doesn't exist of an outstanding sporting moment that began the year and tends to be eclipsed by the memories of Botham's Ashes. It was the third Test between the West Indies and England in Barbados and it featured Michael Holding, the Rolls-Royce of bowling, against Geoff Boycott, the Morris Minor of batting (slow, but it goes on for ever). The pitch was like greased lightning and so was Holding.

Holding recalls that everything felt right that morning. Clive Lloyd had given him choice of ends and he was loose and confident. A packed house at Bridgetown was expectant as Boycott and Gooch came out to bat. Holding glided in to bowl his first ball, intent on letting it go as fast as he could. It landed on a perfect length and flew past Boycott's tentative prod and into Deryck Murray's gloves still climbing. The same thing happened to the next two express deliveries. The slips took a step backwards.

The fourth ball rammed into Boycott's thigh pad as he jerked his bat at it. The fifth, a little shorter, soared at Boycott's throat and he did well to fend it down to Joel Garner in the gully. The sixth was full and rapid. Boycott, back on his stumps expecting another short one, poked hopefully at the ball but it was too quick and too insistent and it ripped out his off stump to the undisguised glee of the fielders and the crowd. After a veritable working over, Boycott, the master technician, had been bowled for a duck. It was one of the most sensational overs in Test cricket history. Even watching a poorly filmed version on YouTube, you want to do it from behind the sofa.

England lost that series in the Caribbean but Botham remained captain for the summer's Tests against Australia, who in February had stooped to a new low. In the third final of the Benson & Hedges one-day series against New Zealand, with the Kiwis needing a six to tie off the last ball, Greg Chappell told his brother Trevor to bowl an underarm. It was like an extreme version of your older brother telling you to pull your sister's hair.

It's cowardly of him to suggest it and weak of you to do it (the reaction's quite fun though).

Chappell junior did as he was told. First informing the umpires of his change of action, he ambled to the wicket and rolled down a grass cutter of true crown green quality. The batsman, Bruce McKecknie, blocked it, then flung his bat away in anger and marched off. It was a despicable act greeted with whistles of derision by the Melbourne crowd and was serious enough to arouse the ire of the New Zealand prime minister, Robert Muldoon, who said it was appropriate that the Aussies had been wearing yellow. For days the Australians were in disgrace. The Kiwis ultimately saw the funny side of it, and when Greg Chappell walked in to bat in a one-dayer in Auckland a fortnight later, a lawn bowl delivered by some wag in the crowd accompanied him to the middle. Deliveries bouncing more than once are now outlawed in all cricket.

The Aussies arrived in England in May, minus Greg Chappell, who was suffering from illness and fatigue. In other words the selectors were sick and tired of him. Kim Hughes was now in charge. They went one up in the series in a low-scoring match at Trent Bridge, the first Test in England to include Sunday play. The second Test at Lord's was dogged by bad weather and boring cricket, and Botham, returning to the pavilion for his second duck of the game, was greeted with dead silence by the members. This was interpreted as a lack of faith in the England captain, but in truth they were probably just all asleep.

It heralded Botham's lifelong dislike of London in

general and Lord's in particular, and he resigned the captaincy straight after the game. At 8.30pm the chairman of selectors, Alec Bedser, phoned Mike Brearley from a pub. Unable to get the coins in the slot, he was immediately cut off. This happened several more times. Eventually he reversed the charges. He was ringing to ask if Brearley would take over the England captaincy. The answer was yes.

The Headingley Test was nine days away. Middlesex had no first-class cricket in the interim so Brearley was obliged to play a match for the 2nd XI against the RAF. On the eve of the Test he used his psychology expertise to ask Botham if he wanted to play. To his relief, Botham was bursting for action. 'I think you'll get 150 runs and take 10 wickets,' Brearley said.

Things didn't go too well for England initially. They lost the toss and Botham, having slightly remodelled his action, seemed toothless. Riled by Brearley dubbing him the 'sidestep queen' he reverted to his old style and took 6 wickets, but Australia totalled 401. England, despite Botham's breezy 50, capitulated for 174 and followed on. Gooch was out immediately. They were 6-1 when bad light ended play on the Saturday night. The odds against an England win were 500-1. Lillee and Marsh, who both liked a flutter, had a little wager each, harking back to the days of Lord Beauclerk and his aristocratic friends who actively bet on matches they were playing in.

Sunday was a rest day but it was obvious England were going to lose so most of the players checked out of their hotel on the Monday morning. At 135-7 in mid-afternoon, England were still 92 runs behind, and the decisions looked shrewd. Botham was in and playing cautiously (for a not out, he said later, tongue not entirely in cheek), but the end was near. It was Graham Dilley who got England going again, standing on leg stump and swinging (and frequently missing) hard.

Invigorated, Botham joined in. Using Gooch's bat ('He hasn't used it much,' he said), he scored some outlandish boundaries over the slips but some audacious ones as well, driving Alderman over mid-off, thrashing him past cover and dancing down to hit him straight for six. 'Don't even bother looking for that one,' Richie Benaud exclaimed. 'It's gone into the confectionery stall and out again!' They put on 117 in eighty minutes, but when Dilley was out England were effectively 25-8.

Chris Old now joined Botham. 'Chilly' (derived from C. Old) was a fine striker of the ball but didn't like the quick stuff. He coaxed himself into line and they added a rapid 67 as Botham advanced to a mercurial hundred. There is a famous shot of Brearley applauding his achievement then gesticulating for him to keep his head down and stay in. He cleverly farmed the strike with Willis to add a precious 31 and at the end of the day England were 124 ahead with one wicket left.

There was a standing ovation as Botham walked off the field, and later when he entered Bryan's fish and chip restaurant – where the 'baby' haddock laps over the plate both sides, though Mike Gatting always eats two – to join the rest of the team for dinner. Still, the Aussies were favourites. Especially when the next morning

Willis was out with only 5 more runs added. Botham was left 149 not out.

Momentum is an extraordinary thing in cricket. It can turn on a few lusty blows from tailenders against tiring bowlers. Psychologically it inspires the team about to field and demoralizes the team about to bat. That is exactly what happened. The Aussies lost wickets regularly, and Willis, once he was given the wind and the slope and told not to worry about overstepping, bowled like a man possessed. Bryan's must have put something special in his fish. With pumping arms, bouncing afro and manic expression, he was, as sportsmen like to say, 'in the zone'.

Only Lillee, with some typically defiant shots, threatened to thwart England. When Gatting dived athletically to dismiss him and leave a small crater at mid-on, Australia were 110-9. Willis burst through Ray Bright's defences and ran straight off the field pursued by his ecstatic teammates. England had sensationally won by 18 runs, becoming the first team that century to win a Test after following on. Botham was a national hero, Willis offered the freedom of Birmingham (a dubious pleasure?), Gatting a lifetime's supply of battered haddock and Brearley renamed King Midas. Oh, and Marsh and Lillee were suddenly £7,500 better off, much to Botham's chagrin (he had been tempted to put some on himself). They had to send someone else to collect their winnings, though.

The series moved on to Edgbaston on a pitch which looked, to Kim Hughes, to be full of runs. In fact no one made a fifty in the entire match. Australia, having bowled better than England, again needed only a moderate score (150) to win. At 105-4, they were almost home. Botham, finding no swing, was strangely reluctant to bowl, but Brearley persuaded him to 'keep it tight for Emburey'. He did exactly that. After Emburey had dismissed Allan Border, Botham conceded only 1 run in 6 overs. Even handier, he took 5 wickets. Charging in with increasing zest, he clean bowled three, had one lbw and the other caught behind. He celebrated each wicket as if he were King Kong. England had won by 29 runs. Lightning had struck twice in the space of a fortnight.

Sandwiched between these two melodramas was Charles and Diana's wedding. The date was Wednesday, 29 July, declared a national holiday. I mainly remember it because Middlesex were playing Lancashire at Southport and the crowd at the little club ground were six deep behind the boundary, many in their Sunday best following the pageant on their transistors. And between the time Charles walked up the aisle as a bachelor and returned down it with his princess, Clive Lloyd larruped 91.

The decisive Test was at Old Trafford. The decisive moment was when Australia took the second new ball on Saturday afternoon. A bareheaded Botham erupted, flaying it to all corners of the ground in an innings of majestic dominance. Lillee was thumped back past him, nearly decapitating the umpire, and twice hooked for six off Botham's eyebrows, while not apparently looking at the ball. Alderman was creamed through the covers and pulled massively into the stand beyond mid-wicket.

He pillaged 66 runs off 8 overs, mainly with orthodox strokes of withering power. He brought up his century with a sweep for 6, and left Australia needing an impossible 506 to win. When Willis had the last man, Mike Whitney, caught at short leg, the Ashes were England's. And the world was Botham's. Through supreme talent, subtle goading from Brearley and innate desire, he had turned the series, and the Australians, upside down. Even worse, if you were an Australian, he had made their captain blub.

The final Test, at the Oval, was Brearley's last. He signed off with a fluent 51 and though he never made a Test century, he was a better batsman than he's given credit for. In county cricket he scored hundreds against Underwood on a dust bowl and against Willis on a green top when no one else could lay a bat on it. He was a deft player with natural timing who just lacked power. Botham still pokes fun at his inability to hit sixes.

Obviously it's as a leader that he is most admired. He had a deep fascination with cricket and studied it carefully. He weighed up a player's mental and physical strengths. Not only highly intelligent, but extremely sensitive, he seemed to quickly understand people. He would make a statement and gauge a reaction or ask a question and listen carefully to an answer. You always felt as if you were being subtly scrutinized.

He had a range of moods. Usually sympathetic, invariably sincere, sometimes angry, always aware. He loved the dressing room banter and had a bubbly, infectious laugh. But he was hard and ruthless too and occasionally scary. Botham said his main asset was that he listened, and I would agree. (Anyway, if you disagree with Botham you get serious earache.) Brearley canvassed opinion from the oldest pro to the youngest apprentice and took most of it on board. He was brilliant at making people feel important. When he asked you, a novice, who should bowl next, you felt ten feet tall. Even if the suggestion on one occasion (mine) resulted in the batsman making a double hundred . . .

Last word should go to a *Guardian* letter-writer. 'Sir,' he wrote, 'on Friday I watched J. M. Brearley directing his fieldsmen very carefully. He then looked up at the sun and made a gesture which seemed to indicate it should move a little squarer. Who is this man? Yours sincerely, S. A. Nicholas, Longlevens, Gloucester.'

The Essex gnome, Keith Fletcher, inherited the England captaincy and took England to India in the winter of 1981–2. The matches were pretty dull. It was what was going on off the field that was interesting. Geoff Boycott, who had business acquaintances in South Africa, was the prime mover in recruiting a 'rebel' team to tour there and play some unofficial Tests. The money was enticing (£50,000) and most, even Botham, were tempted.

Boycott didn't endear himself to many when he passed Garfield Sobers' aggregate of Test runs in Delhi, then left the field in the next Test complaining of fatigue only to be found that afternoon playing golf. However, he helped assemble a decent rebel team (minus Botham, Gower, Willis and Gatting, who rejected the offer). Soon after England had beaten newly initiated

Sri Lanka in their inaugural Test, half the side, led by Graham Gooch, headed off to South Africa for a month of one-dayers and 'Tests'. They were all subsequently banned from playing for England for three years, which produced the extraordinary paradox of Allan Lamb, born and raised in Langebaanweg, Western Province, playing for England, while Graham Gooch, born and raised in Leytonstone, was not allowed to. At least they could all still turn out for their counties.

Most of the rebel participants were doubling their money and, as a professional cricketer, I could understand why they went. I would have been tempted myself if asked. The rewards, the standard of the opposition and the impression that you were helping the rehabilitation of an ostracized Test-playing country would have been persuasive. I was playing in South Africa the following winter (encouraged by Brearley to experience the place for myself) when the rebel West Indies toured and felt then that their presence might encourage South African blacks to take up cricket. It might have helped if a few had been allowed in to watch, and if Colin Croft hadn't been banished to third class on a train. I can see now that the rebel tours were mainly a favour to the white supremacists.

India, meanwhile, were taking their first steps into ultimately seizing control of the cricket world. It was 1983 and it was the third Prudential World Cup in England. Captained by the 24-year-old Kapil Dev, India were unfancied at 66-1 at the start. But the omens for an upset were established on the opening day when Australia were beaten by Zimbabwe (man of the match,

Duncan Fletcher). Strangely for a country famous for wristy batsmen and wizardly spinners, it was India's little medium pacers Madan Lal, Mohinder Armanath and Roger Binny (nicknamed 'Rubbish' by most of his opponents) who were their trump card. They contained England to 213 in the semi-final and bowled out the West Indies, chasing 184, for just 140 in the final. Southall became a no-go zone as the entire Indian population of west London had an all-night party. Lord alone knows what it must have been like in Bombay. The victorious players were all lavished with goods and never had to pay that annoying £1.50 charge for popadoms and chutney ever again.

Early in the tournament the Indian board president, N. K. P. Salve (nicknamed 'Lip'), had been given two tickets for the final. When India unexpectedly qualified for it, he requested two more for colleagues who had just arrived from India. The request was refused by the MCC. Well, you couldn't expect Colonel Ponsonby-Smythe and his snooty son to budge up a bit could you? Much miffed, Salve orchestrated a campaign to get the next World Cup staged elsewhere.

The upshot of all this was that, against their will, the ICC invited tenders for the next tournament from other countries. India and Pakistan entered a joint bid and got the nod ahead of England. A pledge of £75,000 to each participating country probably swayed it. At last, fifty-odd years after its inception as a serious cricket nation, the game's most populous country had got its foot in the door.

The Real Invincibles

India's playing success was shortlived and for the rest of the decade the West Indies were totally dominant. After 1980 they didn't lose a series for fifteen years. It's not surprising really if you look at their team. The 1984 side that toured England included not three, not four, but *seven* all-time greats of the game: Greenidge, Haynes, Richards, Lloyd, Marshall, Garner and Holding. You wouldn't fancy Bradman's 1948 Invincibles against them. They won the Test series 5–0 to inflict England's first-ever 'blackwash', and but for an early one-day international loss remained unbeaten for the entire four-month tour.

They had numerous match-winners. Richards had been the man in '76, but in '84 he was upstaged by Greenidge, who made two double-centuries in the series. His 214 not out at Lord's, as West Indies successfully pursued 341 in less than a day to win by 9 wickets, was one of the most devastating innings of all time. Marshall and Garner took a stack of wickets at under 20 apiece.

Their hidden secret was fitness. From the advent of World Series Cricket, they had always had the services of Dennis Waite, the ebullient Australian physio with a voice like a blunt razor, at their side, organizing their limbering up and attending to their aches and pains. He became an honorary West Indian and had them doing proper stretching every day, morning and evening. To the rest of us stretching was regarded as totally girly, and something that just happened to the waistbands of elasticated trousers after a curry banquet.

Look at the respective injury lists. Bowlers like Marshall, Garner and later Walsh rarely missed a match. Whereas poor preparation, constant cricket, bad diet and chilly weather meant a catalogue of injured England bowlers. The line outside the England physio's room was longer than a dole queue. Marshall was incredible. Small and whippet-like, he sprinted in on the balls of his feet off a long, curving run, maintaining his energy and appetite for wickets when everyone else was flagging (he was impossible to get the ball off playing for Hampshire, getting through 822 overs in 1982, almost double the overs of any other quick bowler).

He talked as fast as he bowled (colleagues nodded and chuckled at his banter but it's not certain even they always knew what he was on about). His speed, from a perfectly balanced, if slightly open-chested, position at the crease, was staggering. His sting, achieved by precise control of the wrist in release, was lethal. He could swing the ball either way at will. His bouncer skidded at you, rarely going over your head. He exuded menace. When he bowled round the wicket, the angled run and his small stature meant he was practically invisible behind the umpire until the last four strides. He was like a sniper jumping out from his hiding place to put you away. And he took no prisoners. If no.11 hung around he'd be roughed up like anybody else.

Clive Lloyd earnt a reputation as a great captain, and he certainly was proficient at getting a team of discordant origins and attitudes to play in harmony. But captaining a bowling attack like that was a cinch. Basically Lloyd captained by numbers. This is how it usually went.

'OK, Macco, give me six!' Marshall would bowl half a dozen rapid overs. Regardless of whether he'd taken 4-10 or 0-30, he'd then hear: 'OK, thanks, Macco. Mikey! Gimme six . . .' So Holding would get his regulation six overs. Then: 'OK, thanks, Mikey, take a blow. Bird!? OK, man. Gimme six!' And Garner would come striding up and make the batsmen hop about. Perhaps Lloyd did it in the interests of fairness, to avoid accusations of favouritism. Anyway, it worked, and invariably the opposition were rolled over.

Of course, they took their time. The over rates were appalling, which put official backs up. They failed to notice that England's were as bad if not worse. And, as Desmond Haynes pointed out, 'If we speeded up between overs we'd beat you in three days instead of four!' To rub it all in, at Headingley Marshall hit a boundary, grabbed a caught and bowled, and took 7 wickets, all with a broken left hand. He missed the next Test but England were still thumped by an innings.

The great thing about the 1980s West Indies was they had so much in reserve. Apart from the immense fast bowlers in the 1984 squad there were a legion of them bouncing around the county circuit. Glamorgan had Winston Davis, Gloucestershire Franklyn Stephenson, Lancashire had first Colin Croft then Patrick Paterson, Leicestershire had George Ferris. Wayne Daniel was at Middlesex, Tony Merrick at Warwickshire, Hartley Alleyne at Worcestershire and Sylvester Clarke at Surrey.

County cricket sustained West Indies fast bowling stocks.

All these guys were seriously fast. Clarke, whom his Surrey teammates nicknamed 'Silly', was the most feared (though also lazy, which is why he only played a handful of Tests). A roly-poly man who rumbled to the wicket in mincing little steps, he generated fearsome pace from his barrel chest and whirling arms, and made the ball leap and jackknife off the pitch so that batsmen were in as much danger of suffering from whiplash as broken bones. His deliveries were notoriously hard to pick up and he clanged more helmets than anyone.

Including mine. Well, actually not mine, but Paul Downton's. It was plonked on my head by Graham Barlow before I went out to bat at the Oval and it probably saved my life. Clarke's third ball was just a blur and crashed into the side of my head as I vainly fenced at it. It left a telling little red mark on the plastic sidepiece protecting my temple as a permanent reminder of how close you are to death facing 90mph bowling.

Most players, with the exception of a young Botham and Viv Richards, were now wearing helmets (Richards never wore one throughout his career). Purists and Flat-Earthers moaned about them, saying that (1) they bred a tendency for batsmen to take their eye off the ball, (2) they provoked more short-pitched bowling and (3) they made it harder to recognize which batsman was which. You *what*? So spectators would rather see a batsman writhing in agony than not be able to *identify* him. Tell that to Roland Butcher, whose unprotected jaw was literally shattered by a ball from George Ferris. He *was* pretty unrecognizable after that.

All-Round Expertise

When Bob Willis retired with an English record of 325 Test wickets, England were left fighting a raging furnace with, well, a few water pistols. It was argued that the presence of so many overseas pacemen was holding the locally born ones back, and it was probably true. It was a particular problem at Sussex and Notts, where *both* opening bowlers were foreign. Imran Khan and Garth le Roux terrorized batsmen at Hove (the speed and bounce looked even worse for the next man in sitting side-on in the Hove pavilion) and Notts had Hadlee and Rice.

Imran at least tried to help the English cause by practising on his own at Lord's and showing any interested wannabes how to prise up the quarter-seam of an old, dog-eared ball and make it (reverse) swing. But we lacked either gumption, courage or fingernails to actually try it out in a match. A while later, he admitted roughing up one side of a ball with a bottle top in a county match, though he declared this was a one-off. Whether by fair means or foul, there was no doubt about his ability to utilize late movement with the old ball. Having learnt the technique from Dennis Lillee in Australia and then fine-tuned it on the parched, unforgiving surfaces of Pakistan, he began making a habit of suddenly wreaking havoc with wicked late swing when batting teams least expected it.

The image of Imran haring down the hill at Hove, dark mane flapping, tight shirt clinging to his sculpted torso, will be embedded in the memory of anyone who saw it, especially from 22 yards away. A Pathan – proud, fearless nomads from northern Pakistan – he charged to the wicket as a warrior would into battle, legs and arms pumping, features clenched, brandishing 5½oz of leather with which he intended to instantly take the life of his opponent. The cacophony of sounds when he was bowling, the thump of the ball into the pitch followed by a yelp of anguish from the batsman and the exultant appeals from the slip cordon became a more familiar sound than the incessant squealing of Brighton's seagulls.

He was stirred by duelling with immortals, and often became distracted against mediocrity – he actually refused to play against New Zealand when their ace all-rounder Richard Hadlee wasn't on the tour. County cricket largely bored him and he chose his games for Sussex and was intolerant of his colleagues if they didn't come up to scratch. When one younger teammate pronounced proudly that he had made a double century for the second team, Imran retorted, 'Two hundred . . . by you . . . in one innings?! But that's impossible.' He had a reputation for being aloof. He was certainly often distracted by the charms of a bevy of Sloanes.

If Imran would have taken his conquest to bed, Hadlee would have given her a blow-by-blow account of his wickets. A meticulous man, he actually planned his double of 1,000 runs and 100 wickets in 1984 (a feat which hadn't been performed since 1967 and has been done only once since). He carried a file around with him specifying how many runs and wickets he expected to achieve at each venue. He recorded his stats at the end of the day's play, and made extensive collections of bats, balls and scorecards associated with distinguished performances.

There were plenty of those. The son of New Zealand's former captain Walter Hadlee and initially a tearaway, he cut his run-up in 1980 and became a ruthless exterminator of batsmen. 'Theoretically every ball is a wicket-taker,' he explained to me, 'but I relate bowling an over to having six shells in a gun. I use each one to manipulate the enemy into some sort of position where he's not sure, and I can exploit him.'

An innings against him was like an interrogation. 'Here,' his bowling seemed to say, 'try a slippery outswinger on off stump . . . mmm you didn't play that too well. Try another . . . dear, dear, you're groping at it! Right, here's a fuller one angled in . . . all right, you didn't handle that too badly. OK, let's see how tough you are. Here's a short one into your ribs . . . Hah! Flinching now then? OK, time to finish you off . . .' (sound of stump cartwheeling out of ground). Hadlee was relentless. His main disadvantage, internationally, was a lack of bowling support. As Gooch pointed out, batting against New Zealand was 'like facing the world at one end and Ilford 2nd XI at the other'.

Like Imran, Hadlee could bat too (though he was not as technically proficient) and for a few years the subplot to an English summer involved the world's four great all-rounders – Imran, Hadlee, Botham and Kapil – each trying to establish himself as the best. In the end it's all pretty subjective. Imran was the fastest bowler, Hadlee the most consistent, Botham was the most destructive batsman, Kapil the most unpredictable. But, for his superior record against the premier team of the eighties, the West Indies (775 runs at 28 and 80 wickets at 21) – and his trophy girlfriends – Imran just shades it.

FIFTEEN

Pass the Parcel

Between 1984 and 1989 the England captaincy resembled a kid's new toy. Unwrapped and enjoyed for a little while, before the batteries run out and it becomes unloved and shoved to the back of the cupboard. The sequence went Willis, Gower, Gatting, Emburey, Cowdrey, Gooch, Gower, Gooch. Not a lot of planning or vision evident there really. More desperation. It was partly a result of lousy performances. After beating an insipid Australian team in 1985, England didn't win another home Test series for five years. They lost to India, Pakistan and New Zealand and were annihilated home and away by the West Indies.

One-day cricket – the microwave oven of the game – was blamed for batsmen not wanting to properly 'cook' an innings any more. Quick TV dinners from M&S (i.e. a tasty 40-odd) were all the rage. In fact it was the bowling that was the problem. County quicks were footsore from their endless travails (frequently in July or August you'd be playing twenty-eight days out of thirty-one),

Botham was either crocked, indoctrinated by mad entrepreneurs with designs on Hollywood or banned for possession of illicit substances, and England hardly ever fielded the same seam attack for two successive Tests. In one series eleven different pacemen were picked. It was the selectors who should have been smoking dope.

Viv Richards put the England attack into perspective in Antigua, blitzing the fastest century in Test history off just 56 balls. This was black power at its most audacious. And he didn't even bother with an arm guard, never mind a helmet. English bowling to him was brushed away like an annoying fly. His batting was a human aerosol. Trying to ape the power of the West Indies, England called up a sequence of bowlers of Caribbean origin. Reflecting Britain's growing multi-ethnicity, Norman Cowans, Gladstone Small, Philip DeFreitas and later Syd Lawrence, Devon Malcolm and Chris Lewis took the new ball for England with varying degrees of success. Small and DeFreitas both featured prominently on the 1986–7 tour of Australia, where first-class cricket was in an even worse state. There was an over-emphasis on one-day internationals and the domestic Sheffield Shield competition was decimated by a squad of players on a 'rebel' tour of South Africa.

In '86/7, Gatting's team's performances were initially woeful Down Under, prompting the journalist Martin Johnson's immortal line that 'England have only three problems: they can't bat, they can't bowl and they can't field.' Chris Broad then proved otherwise with a prolific Test series, Gower prospered and Botham spanked an authoritative 138 to set up victory in the first Test in

Brisbane after Allan Border had politely put England in.

The key Test was the fourth, in Melbourne. Australia, disconcerted by a short, stout chap with no neck shuffling in to bowl, batted recklessly and Small took 5-48. Largely through Broad's third century of the series, England were more resourceful and took a substantial lead, to eventually win in three days by an innings. They had an unassailable 2–0 lead in the series. This was on 28 December 1986. Gatting is pictured on the front page of the next day's *Daily Telegraph* being doused with champagne.

The Australian press were full of 'Can Pat Cash bat or bowl?' and 'the Australian selectors couldn't even pick Bill Lawry's nose.' But it all went a bit pear-shaped for Gatting afterwards, and that's not just a reference to his gradually expanding frame. In twenty-three attempts, those were the only two Test victories of his captaincy tenure. And it's still the last time England won the Ashes in Australia.

It was a huge turning point in Anglo-Australian encounters. From then on Australia adopted an entirely different attitude. They appointed a full-time coach, Bobby Simpson, to knock their team into shape. They vowed never to be pleasant on the field to anyone ever again (the nice Allan Border turned into Captain Grumpy, with the taciturn Steve Waugh at his side).

Most decisively they incorporated cricket into the government-funded Australian Institute of Sport, creating the Australian Cricket Academy in Adelaide, with the aim of grooming young talent for the international arena. One of the first batch was a tubby bleached-blond leggie from Melbourne who stuffed his face with pizzas and smoked like a chimney. Yes, you know who I mean. He arrived at the academy and . . . ate pizzas and smoked like a chimney. But my, could he spin a ball. It was mainly a case of getting him to eat less and bowl more. More of him later.

England, in spite of deep-rooted problems, did nothing more than tinker at the surface. Four-day county cricket was recommended by a TCCB working party, and was later introduced, but only half-heartedly. Each team would play eighteen three-day games and just six four-dayers. Micky Stewart, part of the reason for England's Ashes success, was appointed as the country's first full-time cricket manager. But he had few resources other than an office phone and a bag of balls. Apart from that nothing happened, except the usual dithering about slow over-rates and adjusting the qualification rules so that the dazzling Zimbabwe batsman Graeme Hick could eventually play for England. There was no appetite for radical change because the county game was in profit even if, in terms of locally bred talent, it was virtually bankrupt.

In a piece looking back at the 1986 county season I noted the dominance of overseas players. Greenidge and Marshall topped the batting and bowling averages (seven foreign players in the top eight of the bowling), Terry Alderman's excellence at Kent marginalized Richard Ellison, who subsequently lost his Test place, and Glamorgan relied on all manner of imports. They still came bottom. Attitudes were becoming more cut-throat. A long-time devoted servant of Lancashire, Jackie

Bond, was unceremoniously sacked as manager along-side Peter Lever, the coach, and Botham walked out of Somerset in sympathy at the release of Richards and Garner. Even Derbyshire's Geoff Miller, who, I wrote, 'is one of the only remaining players who shakes every-body's hand at the end of the match thanking them for the game', requested a football-style transfer. The impact of football – whose season now began in early August and ended in mid-May (three weeks longer than in the 1970s) – was becoming overbearing.

In 1987, Gatting's team lost a home series to Pakistan. They had players to die for. Apart from Imran, there was also the inimitable Javed Miandad, a brilliant batsman who made it his business to be a total pain in the neck with provocative comments and actions. He was so good he sometimes deliberately prodded catches to non-existent short legs so that one would be re-instated, creating a useful gap in the outfield; and he was famous for strolling an easy single to long leg, then, when the fielder was lobbing the ball back having assumed he was satisfied with one, he would hare back for a cheeky second. That was all very well, but he also frequently stretched the patience of umpires and opponents. Apart from Pakistan's strong batting line-up, Imran had excellent bowling support from the wizardly leg-spinner Abdul Qadir, who looked as if he'd come straight from Aladdin's cave, and Wasim Akram, a raw left-arm quickie Imran had seen in the nets and invited on tour.

Later that year England did at least get to the final of the fourth World Cup – staged for the first time outside

England – though it was largely by virtue of Graham Gooch sweeping the Indian spinners off the planet in the semi-final. The final itself was there for the taking until Gatting attempted a sweep himself, of the reverse variety and off Allan Border's first ball. He was bowled and England fell irreversibly behind the required rate. Australia had won their first World Cup.

In everyone's opinion 1987 was Gatting's *annus horribilis*. Although his able lieutenant John Emburey put it another way. 'Gatt's always had a horrible arse!' he said. Three weeks after the World Cup England toured Pakistan, a country where they hadn't won since 1962. The sequence looked likely to continue when they were routed by Qadir in the first Test, though he was assisted by some dubious umpiring which Gatting, a man of strong principle, took exception to.

Continually irked by the local officials' habit of yelling 'owzatt' almost before a Pakistani bowler had released the ball, Gatting totally lost it on the second day of the second Test in Faisalabad. Half an hour before the end of play, he beckoned for the square-leg fielder, David Capel, to come closer to save the single. Capel was late responding and Gatting was still indicating where he should stand as the bowler, Eddie Hemmings, was running in.

The square-leg umpire, Shakoor Rana, an officious type who liked throwing his not inconsiderable weight about, stepped in, claiming that Gatting was moving fielders behind the batsman's back. In other words he accused him of cheating. Gatting blew a gasket and a war of words ensued. The match was suspended for almost a whole day as both men refused to back down and at one point it looked like the tour would be abandoned till everyone came to their senses.

The incident had three effects. It soured relations between Pakistan and England and England didn't tour there again for fourteen years. It hastened the advent of neutral umpires, which was long overdue anyway (they were eventually brought in during 1992 but Imran had been campaigning for them for years). And it initiated a joke that did the rounds the following summer.

A history teacher is quoting great speeches and testing his class on them.

Teacher: 'We shall fight on the beaches, we shall fight on the landing grounds, we shall fight in the fields and in the streets, we shall fight in the hills.' Who said that?

Taquil (pupil): Winston Churchill, London, 1940, sir.

Teacher: Very good, Taquil. How about this one: 'I have a dream that one day on the red hills of Georgia the sons of former slaves and the sons of former slave owners will be able to sit down together.'

Taquil: Martin Luther King, Washington, 1963, sir.

Teacher: Excellent, Taq—

Dwayne: Sir, sir, Taquil's looking them up in a book hidden under the table, sir.

Alfie: Cheating Pakistani bastard!

Teacher: Who said that?!

Taquil: Mike Gatting, Faisalabad, 1987.

The press were all over it. 'Conduct Unbecoming!' yelled *The Times*, adding that there would be questions in the house. 'The Series Hits a Sticky Wicket', declared the *Daily Mirror* and the usual 'not cricket' allegations were bandied around.

Gatting survived the rest of the winter as captain, but was sacked following the first Test of the summer against the West Indies, after apparently taking a barmaid to his hotel room. This constituted bizarre logic. It was deemed worse to take a woman upstairs – which was a private matter in any case – than to make racist comments. The West Indies captain would more likely have been sacked if he *hadn't* taken a barmaid to his room.

Plumbing the Depths

The last two years of the decade were the nadir of English cricket. In an attempt to improve standards, some four-day championship matches had been introduced. The idea was immediately panned by myopic county officials for its potential impact on revenue. This was a bit like a kid complaining about getting only £1 from the tooth fairy. The counties only generated enough money to buy themselves a second-hand sofa for the club office anyway. To commemorate its bi-centenary, the MCC did open a fantastic new Mound stand at Lord's, a throwback to the Victorian era with its tented roof and lawyers bunking off work. But that was paid for by John Paul Getty.

The West Indies came in 1988 and inevitably conquered. After Gatting's dismissal, Emburey, whose own position in the team was far from secure, took over the captaincy. Two heavy defeats later he was omitted from the squad for the Headingley Test, and Chris Cowdrey, who hadn't played a Test for more than three years, was put in charge. He had led Kent to the top of the championship table.

Cowdrey, eldest son of Colin, was well known to the chairman of the selectors, Peter May, being his godson. It prompted some touching exchanges during team selection. You can hear it now:

'We're thinking of recalling Bill Athey and Derek Pringle . . .'

'OK, Uncle Peter.'

'. . . And we thought you could bat at no.7.'

'Thank you, Uncle Peter.'

'How's dad?'

'Fine, Uncle Peter!'

'Say hello to him, won't you?'

'I will, Uncle Peter.'

Cowdrey junior wasn't so well known to the Headingley gateman. The day before the match he didn't recognize him and wouldn't let him in.

Cowdrey tells an amusing story about the events leading up to the toss in this Test. He got to the middle smartly, ready to exchange teams with Viv Richards, who eventually deigned to stroll over, chewing incessantly. Richards made an extravagant play of listing his players, with heavy accentuation on the vowels . . . 'Well, who we got? There's Haaaynes, Duuuujon, Riiiichaaards, Riiiichaaaardsooon, Loowwwgie . . .' Then, as Cowdrey was about to run through his team, Richards waved a hand airily and said, 'Man, you can play who you like.' When the coin went up and Richards called correctly, he said, 'OK, man, what d'you wanna do?' Slightly taken aback, Cowdrey said, 'Well, thank you, er, well, seeing as it's a bit muggy I think we'll have a bowl.' 'OK,' said Richards, 'you can bat!'

The match is mainly memorable for the antics of Dickie Bird. The game began in sunny weather, but after two overs, as the West Indies' new pace discovery 6ft 8in Curtly Ambrose was about to run in, Bird was conscious of squelching sounds and Ambrose saying in his deep basso profundo, 'Mr Dickie, Mr Dickie, we got a problem.' Bird went to investigate and found water seeping out of a drain that had been deliberately blocked to keep the moisture in the pitch. It was overflowing from recent rain and pouring over his boots. Viv Richards intimated they would have to go off. 'It's best day of summer, they'll lynch me!' Bird said, but despite cloudless skies he had no alternative but to suspend play. An umpire forever associated with bad light and rain delays, he received the usual antagonism from aggrieved spectators, including, 'Well, Mr Bird, I suppose you're off to get your light meter to see how strong t'sun is!' 'We don't need a light meter,' Bird retorted, 'we need a bloody ploomber.'

The interruption only delayed the inevitable English defeat, during which Cowdrey was hit on the toe by a yorker and was thus ruled out of the final Test. A reluctant Gooch was pressed into service as captain, but England lost that game as well. The use of twenty-three different players in the five Tests emphasized England's paucity of talent and lack of selectorial vision.

Yet that was nothing compared with the twenty-nine that tried and failed to distract the Aussies the following summer. The new chairman of selectors, Ted Dexter, had them reciting verse when he wasn't introducing new recruits who hadn't met each other before. You think premiership football teams have trouble remembering and pronouncing each other's names early season? At least they've spent the previous week training together.

England began on the wrong foot and never recovered. Dexter's wish to recall Gatting as captain was vetoed by the TCCB chairman, Ossie Wheatley, who obviously subscribed to the old principle that England captains should be paragons of virtue (e.g. W. G. Grace, Douglas Jardine, Wally Hammond and Tony Greig, etc.). He chose the debonair, laid-back David Gower, when the ultra-determined, no-nonsense Gatting would have been preferable. Understandably, bearing in mind the sacrifices he'd made to English cricket, Gatting went off in a huff and recruited a rebel team to tour South Africa.

Other forces were at work to destroy England. One was a ruling to prepare pitches that were bland and devoid of grass. Under official instruction, Harry Brind, the former Oval groundsman, introduced Surrey loam (a type of clay) into all the Test pitches. It made them seam bowlers' graveyards, denying England the traditional advantage of movement off the pitch. (It wasn't just an expanding girth, for instance, that caused Botham to take only 13 wickets in his last twelve home Tests. In the years before he had taken 213 in forty-seven.)

Gower put Australia in at Headingley, historically a seamer's paradise, and Australia scored 600. Their *lowest* first-innings score of the series was 424. Steve Waugh wasn't dismissed until the third Test, by which time he'd contributed 393 runs. The increasing uniformity of English pitches has cost the first-class game much of its intrigue and variety.

The (English) umpires also couldn't stop giving the home batsmen lbw, perhaps favouring the visiting side to emphasize their impartiality. It was as if a Terry Alderman appeal had a magnetic power over their index fingers. He got nineteen lbws in the series, and when political graffiti appeared from disgruntled Tories demanding 'Thatcher Out' someone had added 'lbw Alderman'. By contrast, débutant Devon Malcolm's first ball to Mark Taylor at Trent Bridge had him plumb in front and wasn't given. England didn't take a wicket until after midday on the second day. Where were Hawkeye and umpire referrals when you needed them?

England were injury-jinxed, constantly losing a player from the twelve on the morning of the match. And the Australians had been to angry school. Border wore a permanent scowl and when Robin Smith asked for a drink during a superb 100, Border retorted, 'No, you can't have a fucking drink. What d'you think this is, a fucking tea party?' Merv Hughes, he of the fat belly and the mincing run and the absurd walrus moustache, turned from a comic figure supping beers into a galumphing villain grunting 'Arsewipe!' The wicket-keeper, Ian Healy, sent dismissed English batsmen off with 'Back to nets, idiot!'

After two years of tough drills there was a new hardness about the Australian team, especially the batsmen. Under the guidance of Bobby Simpson, who, it might be recalled, was one of the original grinders, they had acquired the art of staying put. Not much of it was pretty – a batting order comprising Mark Taylor, Geoff Marsh, David Boon, Allan Border and Steve Waugh was a bar-filler, although the abrasive Dean Jones was quite entertaining, especially if he got a dodgy decision. His bat then entered the dressing room horizontally some time before its owner. But in the main the Aussie batting mantra was 'It's not how, it's how many.' Ugly runs were as good as stylish ones. Runs were runs. Where did they get this staying power from? From tough, two-day club cricket back home, giving players the scope to bat all day, that's where.

The *shortest* Australian first innings lasted 132 overs that series. The red-faced English seamers had a summer of hard labour, with little reward. And the advent of two fifteen-year-old Indians – V. Kambli and S. Tendulkar – putting together an unbroken world record stand of 664 for their school, Sharadashram Vidyamandir, suggested it was liable to get even harder. In the late twentieth century, it was better to be born with a bat, or a microphone, in your hand rather than a ball.

SIXTEEN

All Change, Please

The Berlin Wall came down, South Africa abolished apartheid, Nelson Mandela was released, there were anti-communism demonstrations everywhere, Saddam Hussain invaded Kuwait, Ayatollah Khomeini issued a Fatwa against Salman Rushdie, Maggie Thatcher resigned as British prime minister, McDonald's opened in Moscow, Sky TV began transmitting in England, *The Simpsons* made its début on American TV and George Bush senior became president of the United States. Nothing much happened as the eighties departed and the nineties arrived.

In the US presidential race of 1989, Bush's opponent for a time was the Democrat Gary Hart, until he was discovered to be having an extramarital affair. His mistress was later interviewed and asked who she thought would win the election. 'Well,' she said, 'in my heart it will be Bush, but in my bush it is Hart.'

In keeping with the general mood of reconciliation, the ICC changed its name to the International Cricket

Council (from the old Empire-flavoured 'Conference') and allowed a chairman (Colin Cowdrey) to be properly elected rather than just automatically installing the president of the MCC. He was still English (and his initials were MCC), but it was progress. And by 1993 the ICC would have its first non-white, non-MCC chairman, Clyde Walcott. In England, Oxford and Cambridge had lost their divine right to make up the Combined Universities team in the Benson & Hedges Cup, and players from other seats of lounging were allowed in too.

England went to the West Indies under Graham Gooch, Sky covering a winter tour for the first time. They thought they were on to something when a multi-ethnic England side (including two South Africans, two of Caribbean origin and an Anglo-Asian, Nasser Hussain) improbably seized the first Test by 9 wickets, to much 'Goodnight Charlie!' exclamation from Tony Greig. But after that the West Indies, occasionally demonstrating an unsavoury side, with deliberate delaying tactics and provocation of umpires, regained control.

An alternative England XI, led by Gatting, headed to South Africa. The tour was orchestrated by Dr Ali Bacher, South Africa's last official captain before isolation and now the head of their cricket union. A Lithuanian Jew whose parents had emigrated to South Africa before the war, he knew a thing or two about racial discrimination, and his motives seemed honourable. He was passionate about developing and integrating non-white cricket. The politicians and the press didn't see it that way and gave Gatting's men a rough ride. There were demonstrations everywhere.

The team manager, David Graveney, desperate to forge a more coherent relationship with the media after a spate of inaccuracies and misquotes, asked for questions to be put in writing, and they would be similarly answered. He was slightly taken aback when a group of journalists approached him at a practice day brandishing a sheet of paper. On it was scribbled: 'Please can we borrow your football?' All the players involved, including 1986–7 Ashes winners Gatting, Emburey, Broad, Dilley and Athey, were banned from Test cricket for three years.

England finally got back on the winning trail in the summer of 1990, largely by virtue of Gooch's insatiability against India. His colossal 333 at Lord's, the highest-ever innings at the ground, followed by another century in the second innings, set up a resounding victory there, which India, despite Mohammad Azharuddin's wristy brilliance and a first Test century for the teenage Tendulkar in the third Test at Old Trafford, couldn't avenge.

Margaret Thatcher, fighting, like England, for her waning credibility as Prime Minister, made a defiant speech at the Lord Mayor's Banquet in the autumn of 1990, using cricket as a metaphor for her life. 'Since I first went in to bat eleven years ago,' she said to the newly elected mayor, 'the score at your end has ticked over nicely. You are now the 663rd Lord Mayor. At the Prime Minister's end, we are stuck on 49. I am still at the crease, though the bowling has been pretty hostile of late. And in case anyone doubted it, can I assure you there will be no ducking the bouncers, no stonewalling, no playing for time. The bowling's going to get hit all round the ground. That is my style.'

She was deluding herself and was obliged to resign as Prime Minister two weeks later. The same week an England side ravaged by bans and injury capitulated to Australia by 10 wickets in Brisbane. There was a chasm between the teams and after England's heavy defeat in the second Test as well, Gooch's speech was rather more prosaic. 'It's like farting against thunder,' he said. Thereafter the tour was chiefly remembered for David Gower's exploits in a Tiger Moth (such antics are invariably gratifying if you're winning and gratuitous if you're not). In any case, the real cricketing headlines were being made elsewhere.

In the summer of 1991, South Africa were readmitted to the international fold by the ICC and in November flew to India for a hastily arranged series of one-day internationals. The tourists' plane was the first from South Africa ever to land in India, and they were welcomed as heroes. A crowd of 90,000 in Calcutta watched their first day of readmission, which in spite of Allan Donald's 5-29 ended in defeat.

Despite their isolation, South Africa had a pretty potent attack. But they were having to play catch-up in the rapidly evolving skills department. In fact every country was, because Pakistan had something lethal that no one else had: 90mph reverse swing.

Alongside the whippy, wailing-for-lbw Wasim Akram, they had unearthed a bowler who was a sort of cross between Malcolm Marshall and Jeff Thomson: Waqar Younis. I'm not exaggerating. The young Waqar pushed off almost from the sightscreen and, with arms swinging and cheeks quivering, tore to the wicket before unleashing deliveries of blistering pace with a catapulting action that looked as if it would wrench him apart every ball.

Exceptionally fast, Waqar was oddly ineffective with the new ball. It was when it got old and scuffed that he seemed to be in his element. Suddenly, a ball that was heading outside off would bend back wickedly in the air and uproot the leg stump. The state of the pitch was largely unimportant to him since many of his victims were bowled or lbw with swinging half-volleys or yorkers. Recommended to Surrey by Imran, who had originally spotted him bowling in a local game on telly, he detonated stumps with such regularity in 1991 that a new phrase, 'You've been Waqared!', was coined.

As time went by, suspicion mounted as to how he, and Wasim, achieved their late swing. Even today nobody's quite sure. But in the trade bowlers were becoming aware that scuffing up one side of a ball, as opposed to the traditional act of *polishing* one side, could aid swing. Allegations of ball tampering, which they denied, were made against them during the acrimonious 1992 series in England, and in a one-day international at Lord's the ball the Pakistanis were using was confiscated and put under lock and key, like some miscreant who had stolen the England batsmen's credit cards. (To avoid its creating another political incident, the issue was shrouded in secrecy, and the ball was never put on public view, although it now resides on umpire Don Oslear's mantelpiece in Cleethorpes.)

But however they achieved their vicious swing, Wasim and Waqar were brilliant at utilizing it. Having learnt the game on the dusty concrete paddocks of the Punjab, bowling with a tennis ball wrapped in tape, they knew all about the aerodynamics of a scuffed sphere and how to bowl with it. Wasim gave a classic exhibition of polishing off a tail at the Oval, racing in round the wicket to bend balls improbably past groping bats.

His defining moment had been in the World Cup final a few months earlier. The tournament, staged in Australia and New Zealand, was a ground-breaking one in many ways. South Africa made their World Cup début, reaching the semis, and Jonty Rhodes set astonishing new standards of agility in the field. It was the first series to use coloured clothing, white balls and floodlights, and 'neutral' umpires. New Zealand, the joint hosts, best exploited the new fielding restrictions (only two boundary fielders allowed in the first 15 overs), opening the batting with a pinch-hitter – Mark Greatbatch – and the bowling with an off-spinner – Dipak Patel.

England made it to the final rather fortuitously, having been beaten in the group stages by the newest Test nation, Zimbabwe, then been saved by a rain inter-ruption in the semi. When play had resumed, South Africa's target had been 'adjusted' to 22 runs off one ball. Even the Herculean all-rounder Brian McMillan couldn't hit it that far. Pakistan, manhandled to the final by the power of Inzamam-ul-Haq, cobbled together 249 in the final which they then feistily defended.

England had been cruising at 141-4 with Neil Fairbrother and Allan Lamb in control, but two balls from Wasim abruptly changed that. Lamb was bamboozled by a wicked delivery that was angled in from round the wicket and then bent away at the last second to trim his off stump. Even if he'd known it was coming he wouldn't have been able to play it. With a bat twice as wide. The next ball swung the other way and castled Chris Lewis. Nobly as Fairbrother hung on, ingenuity had swung it, and England lost by 22 runs. Imran held the glass trophy aloft into the Melbourne night, thanked his team for responding like 'cornered tigers' and said goodbye to cricket and hello to politics, for which, as a rambling speaker rather fond of his own voice, he was perfectly cut out.

New Kids on the Block

The events of 18 April 1992 were even more momentous, and I'm not referring to Durham's baptism as the eighteenth first-class county with a Botham-inspired one-day win against Lancashire. It was South Africa's inaugural Test in the West Indies, a match laden with symbolism. Here were descendants of the old white masters paying homage to the great stronghold of black cricket, Barbados, where the West Indies hadn't been beaten for fifty-seven years.

Only a couple of years before it would have seemed unthinkable that a South African team would include one non-white player, never mind that they would be playing a Test in Bridgetown. But only a couple of years before it had seemed unthinkable that East Germans would be free to cross to the 'other side' unaccompanied by the Stasi. Yet looking back now, it seems amazing that, just twenty years ago, parts of the Western world were so starkly divided. We could orbit the earth and create a baby in a test-tube and make mobile phone calls on a gadget the size of a brick, but in certain places a black couldn't fraternize with a white or a commie talk to a capitalist.

So Test match number 1,188 was the first to feature South Africa against a non-white nation. It was a cracker of a game too, which South Africa, undaunted by their twenty-three years of Test isolation, could have won at 122-2 chasing just 201. Spurred on by the misery of their forefathers – no, actually just galvanized by the prospect of defeat – Ambrose and Walsh raised their games and demolished the South Africans on the fifth day for 148. But the event was more important than the result.

India's first-ever visit to South Africa, in late 1992, heralded another revolution: the third umpire. An increasing number of cameras were picking up things the field umpires couldn't (run-outs, fielders stepping on the boundary, spectators with pert breasts), so it was decided to try using the TV replay to adjudicate on certain matters, including run-outs, stumpings and whether said spectator was a C or D cup. In the first Test in Durban, when South Africa's first official non-white cricketer, Omar Henry, also made his début, an appeal for a run-out of Sachin Tendulkar was upheld by the man with the monitor, Karl Liebenberg. At times in the succeeding years it seemed to be the only way to get the little man out.

Tendulkar had himself broken an even more intransigent racial code. That year he became Yorkshire's first-ever overseas player. The fact that they had fielded only Yorkshire-born players up to that point was up there with other urban myths such as that Panama hats come from Panama (they come from Ecuador) and that Gordon Ramsay played for Glasgow Rangers (he didn't). In fact there had been at least twenty Yorkshire players born elsewhere, including the pompous ex-captain Lord Hawke himself (born in Lincolnshire). But Tendulkar was the first real 'foreigner' as they might have put it. Or worse. They had originally chosen the Australian fast bowler Craig McDermott, but he broke down during the winter so at the last minute they hired the Indian teenager instead.

The summer was relatively damp and he had a difficult time, scoring only one century. Unfortunately that was at Durham and mostly off my bowling, as he exacted revenge for his first-innings dismissal, nicking a delivery from me that hit a dead slug and jagged sideways like a leg break. No other player would have got near it. His match-winning second-innings century, studded with elegantly precise strokes on a tricky pitch, advertised his stunning talent and his disarmingly squeaky voice when he called for a single.

Tendulkar's arrival at Headingley could have been a panacea for the racial divisions in English cricket, but he wasn't yet quite established and anyway the appetite wasn't there amongst the county administrators. There were only ten Anglo-Asian professional cricketers by the mid-nineties, despite there being 1.5 million British Asians, the majority of whom loved cricket. Most of the eleven-year-old Pakistanis and Bangladeshis I chatted to in a Bradford school failed the Tebbit test. Many said they would cheer for Australia against England and all, of course, supported their parents' country.

The trouble was that Asian cricketers were, and to an extent still are, living in a parallel universe. There are numerous Asian leagues, like the famous Quaid-i-Azam in Yorkshire, mainly played on Sundays so that shopkeepers and restaurant owners can participate, that are barely acknowledged in 'official' circles. (The winners of the Quaid-i-Azam were finally credited in the 2007 *Wisden*. Before that the league didn't even get a mention.) There is a 'them and us' nature to these competitions. Both sides of the divide are to blame. The white clubs are regarded as inflexible (demanding annual subs, attendance at social functions, etc.), the Asian players as uncooperative. There is no doubt that many of them have oodles of talent. Following the prolific Tendulkar into the Yorkshire team was never going to be easy, of course. 'Whoever he is they'll have to call him Fivedulkar,' Graham Gooch observed.

Gooch was the non-striker when another great cricketer of the century really came to prominence. Shane Warne was one of the first intake of the Australian Cricket Academy, identified as having the subtle skills that could undermine the all-conquering West Indies. Instead of fighting fire with fire they'd use smoke and mirrors. Jack Potter, the former state player in charge of the academy, recalled Warne's arrival:

He was chubby, bright blond. Great personality, adman's dream. I'd got a call from Jim Higgs, one of the national selectors. 'Spins the ball like no one I've ever seen,' he says, 'but he has a problem with discipline – it'll do him good to come to you.'

Warney was in London and when he called I said, 'Right, these are the rules: no smoking. Athletes don't smoke. Make up your own mind about alcohol but if I know you've been on the turps you'll work harder than anyone the next day.'

'All right, mate,' he replied. Such a good kid. Knew straight away he had something. Ruins every other leg-spinner because he's got that strength in his shoulders. 'Right,' I said, 'I've seen your leggie – how do you get people out?' 'Well,' he said, 'that's why I'm here. I can bowl that and a bit of a googly but nothing else.' So I told him how Benaud used to bowl, showed him the flipper, the toppie. Two weeks later he asked me up to the indoor centre – he had it all.

We had a good understanding. I sent him home from a tour for some prank and he accepted it. He had trouble giving up smoking amid all that peer pressure – I told him to do it round the back so no one saw. Even after I left, I still wasn't sure he had the discipline, but in 1992 he came to my place and he was slim and fit. Somebody had had a word.

Warne made his Test début after just four matches for Victoria. Australia like chucking their players in at the deep end, where they'll either sink or swim. Warne sank initially. Two Tests against India brought him figures of 1-228. His body was out of condition too. He went back to the academy and got fit. He was picked to tour Sri Lanka and Allan Border bravely threw him the ball in Colombo when Sri Lanka were 147-6 needing 181 to win, Warne took 3 for nought in 13 balls and a star was born.

Still he was a relative unknown beyond his home beach as, in the first Test of 1993 at Old Trafford, he was summoned by Border, now himself the leading Test run-scorer, for the 28th over of England's innings. Facing Warne was Mike Gatting, back in the England fold after his ban, and a well-known destroyer of spinners. Warne had been expensive in the county match at Worcester. Gatting was salivating at the opportunity to devour a few juicy offerings almost as much as he was thinking about Old Trafford's hearty baps for tea.

Warne shut his ears to Merv Hughes's ramblings at mid-off and ran a final hand through his gelled hair. He settled himself and sidled up to bowl his first Ashes delivery. He sent down a hard-spun exploratory first ball aimed at middle and leg. It dipped in the air, pitched outside leg stump on the perfect length so the batsman could neither smother it on the front foot, nor go back to it, then spun viciously across Gatting's cautious prod and clipped the top of the off stump. If he'd tried 1,000 times he couldn't have bowled That Ball again. Gatting looked bemused, thinking initially that Ian Healy's gloves might have dislodged the bails. But Dickie Bird's forboding expression told him the reality and off he trudged. A startled Gooch was looking on. Hence the famous cheese roll line (see p. 152).

Warne finished with 8 wickets in the match and his final figures were a portent of things to come: 73-36-137-8. Not only did he twice steal the heart of England's batting but he also conceded fewer than 2 runs an over throughout the match, and indeed the series. Impressive for any bowler. Remarkable for a leg-spinner. Australia won the Ashes 4–1. And Glenn McGrath wasn't even in the squad.

Not a Larra Laughs If You're a Bowler

Another Ashes loss led to another change of captain and another batch of selectors. Mike Atherton, aged twenty-five, was handed the chalice, and Ray Illingworth (61), Brian Bolus (60) and Fred Titmus (61) had the job of finding something nutritious to pour in it. That was the problem. Resources were scarce, or exhausted. The County Championship now consisted exclusively of four-day matches, finishing on a Monday (instead of Tuesday), giving England players an extra day to prepare.

But the system was yet to bear fruit, and, with a 40-over Sunday League match sandwiched in the middle of a four-dayer, the top players were more knackered than ever. In two years, sixteen different pacemen played for

England. Atherton was opening the batting and captaining in six Tests and three one-day internationals and still turning out for Lancashire for ten championship games and eighteen one-dayers. It was claimed he had put dirt in his pocket against South Africa in order to keep the ball dry. In reality it was there because he hadn't had time to launder his trousers.

England kept losing. They were ignominiously dismissed for 46 by the West Indies in Trinidad and Brian Lara dispatched them for a world record 375 in Antigua. The batsmen, Atherton and Alec Stewart apart, looked like startled rabbits and the bowlers, the honourable Angus Fraser excepted, cowered like nervous kittens. So much for the Three Lions.

Phil Tufnell, a talented spinner who lacked ruthlessness and freaked out at the sight of an ample bicep, encapsulated the problem. He coasted along and was often more concerned how his own performance looked than about the health of the team. He had some inspired days, and was an excellent reader of the game, but he could be flaky. His chaotic private life didn't help, though he usually saw the lighter side, which has provided good material for the after-dinner circuit. He came in one day looking a bit rough and muttering that his wife had gone out to get some milk three weeks ago and hadn't returned. 'Christ, are you managing OK?' he was asked. 'Yeah, I'm using the powdered version for the moment.'

The fingers for England's general inadequacies were pointed, rightly, at county cricket. There were too many teams and too many games and the standard was too low. The editor of *Wisden*, Graeme Wright, wrote, 'Eighteen counties will attempt to keep the show on the road and off the breadline. Why? Because it has always been thus? Because it is part of the fabric of British life? Or because no-one will stand back and say the time has come to overhaul the professional game?'

The County Championship was (is) actually a bit like London Underground. Created in a previous century when requirements and attitudes were different (and people were smaller and less in a flap), it is an unwieldy, inefficient network which keeps malfunctioning. But it is too late to abandon it and start again. There are too many associations and vested interests and to dig it up would cause insurmountable upheaval. It's bad enough just replacing a few Victorian sewers. So you have to work with what you've got and make the best of it.

In the end the only thing about county cricket that everyone is agreed on is that no one can agree about it. Some think its sole purpose should be to produce England players, others believe it is there to serve the local community, a third group see it as a plateau upon which fairly good cricketers thrive, a fourth regard it as a cosy and exclusive little club. That, of course, is how it began, as a rather whimsical notion of the aristocrats who cobbled together some mates and a few local pros and called it Sussex. Anything for a bet.

Brian Lara wasn't complaining about it, of course. Well, not playing for Warwickshire in 1994 anyway. After stroking the England bowling all round the Antiguan Recreation Ground in an innings that looked destined to never end, he arrived in Birmingham and did the same thing to everyone else he came across. The sequence went 147 (v Glamorgan), 106 and 120 not out (v Leics), 136 (v Somerset), 26 and 140 (v Middlesex) and then his extraordinary 501 not out (v Durham). And this was all before the second week of June. If English bowlers were pie throwers then Brian Lara loved stodge.

Naturally his innings were anything but stodgy. The 501, for instance, was scored off only 427 balls. Lara wielded his bat like a scimitar. If he had been an Oriental warrior he'd have sliced his opponents to shreds. Like his childhood idol, Roy Fredericks, the backlift was baseball-high, pointing straight upwards like a periscope. The knees flexed slightly as the bowler bowled, the body crouched ready to pounce. The balance shifted according to the length and direction of the ball. Leg-stump deliveries were whipped away with a flamboyant flick of the wrists. Width on the offside was catapulted to the boundary in a blur of willow. The shot finished with the bat wrapped round his back. The ball scorched the earth. His footwork to the spinners was balletic. He could execute the finest sweep or the deftest glide. His range was fully 360 degrees, and without a reverse sweep or a switch hit in sight. Only the most perfect ball on middle and off stumps was resolutely defended, always with the bat out in front of the pad.

'You never see him use the pad,' said Garfield Sobers, who was present the day Lara overhauled his 36-year-old Test record and walked out to congratulate him when he did so. 'He hits the ball with the bat and that's the way the game should be played.' I met one of Lara's old schoolmates at the back of the stand later and he gave some insight into how he'd developed his technique. 'Sometime we used a scrunched-up evaporated milk can for a ball,' he said. 'If you miss it, it cut your leg.'

Lara was touched with genius. His match-winning 153 not out against Australia in Bridgetown, getting the West Indies home by 1 wicket against McGrath and Warne in their pomp, and his 221 and 130 against Muralitharan in Colombo, were innings belonging to another galaxy. The touch, the reflex, the speed, the focus were devastating. Twenty-two fielders wouldn't have stemmed the flow.

There is one small caveat. Unusually for a West Indian he never looked entirely happy against the fast, short-pitched stuff. He flailed a bit. He took a few glancing blows. It's fair to speculate that without helmets he might have been less prolific. Because of that you can't say he was better than Sobers, even though he eventually passed his run aggregate by some distance. But he was definitely just as good. And just as mercenary. He would have been thankful, then, that he helped Dermot Reeve's Warwickshire to an unprecedented three trophies in 1994, making off with a bonus of £10,000.

The Bouncer Waugh's Over

Lara's flowering, Warne's emergence and the arrival of McGrath culminated, in the spring of 1995, in the Clash of Titans. Australia were on a roll, having comfortably retained the Ashes at home; and, to add insult to injury, they included alongside the Australia XI their 'A' team in a quadrangular one-day tournament, that still proved too good for England and Zimbabwe. Now they were touring the unconquered West Indies, who hadn't been beaten at home since 1973, or anywhere in a Test series for fifteen years.

This was expected to be the series of the Blue Touch Paper, and so it proved. It was explosive from the start, when West Indies were reduced to 6-3 on the first morning; through the middle, when Curtly Ambrose warned that 'Slater is going to have nineteen ambulances waiting for him when he goes out to bat in this match' and had to be restrained from laying a hand on Steve Waugh; to the end, when the Waugh twins stood up to the bouncer barrage and earnt the Australians an innings win and a series victory.

There were signs early in the first Test that the West Indians' aura of invincibility was about to crack. McGrath was at his most virile, unhesitatingly sticking it up the West Indies batsmen, and bowlers (who didn't appreciate such a lack of respect), and the West Indies captain, Richie Richardson, wore a helmet for the first time. The Australians, who pay great heed to body language, saw this as a backward step. After the opening salvoes they ground out a valuable lead through the doughty Ian Healy, and then McGrath bowled a limp West Indies out for 189. It was their first three-day defeat for thirty years.

The second Test, in Antigua, was ruined by rain. Lara, threatening to run amok as he had a year earlier against

England, was brilliantly caught by Boon for 88. In the third, on a verdant-green pitch in Trinidad, the great West Indies pair of Walsh and Ambrose held sway, leaving the series poised at 1–1 for the fourth and final Test in Jamaica.

The match was a triumph for the Waughs, especially Steve, who withstood everything the West Indies threw at him, including at least 150 bouncers, insults and a thief in his hotel bedroom. He batted for ten hours, often leaping off the ground to fend the ball off his chest, to record his first double century, and put on 231 with his twin, Mark, who also made a hundred. Leading by 266, the astute Mark Taylor set his seamers on the West Indies, and their meticulous plans – to deny Richardson width, to tempt Lara with wide full deliveries, to contain Carl Hooper to make him do something silly – paid off. This was a victory of pragmatism over passion. They barely needed Warne. At 5pm on 3 May 1995 the Great Wall had crashed to the ground and the Frank Worrell trophy was Australia's.

Although Ambrose and Walsh held their side together for a while longer, they lacked the support of old, and this was the beginning of the end for West Indies cricket. They never beat Australia again, and by the late 1990s were losing to everyone, even, eventually, god help them, England. They had just returned from a 5–0 thumping in South Africa – the first whitewash in their history – when I arrived in the Caribbean to see what had gone wrong.

The answer was a lot and the people were angry about it. They grumbled and ranted and bickered. Their shook their fists at the way team spirit had been ravaged by consistent defeat, irresponsibility, and player power. Lara was now captain but his record of lateness and disappearance and disrespect was exacerbating the situation. 'De horse is out of de cart and dey can't get de horse back,' said one disgruntled Bajan.

In fact, curing their list of ills would have tested a United Nations taskforce:

No money
No discipline
No leadership
No promotion
No ideas
No coherence
No competitive structure
No TV or radio coverage
No facilities
No opening pairs

The stoop of the West Indies team manager, Clive Lloyd, was getting more pronounced by the day. 'We've lost the cricket ethic,' Lloyd said, squashed at the back of a tiny plane flying out of Antigua. 'There's a lack of professionalism, of passion, of pride. We worked very hard for our success when I was captain but you don't see that sort of discipline now. Not many of our boys play in county cricket these days and that was a very good place to learn it.

'We've got very complacent,' he went on, 'and, unfortunately, there are too many people involved in the management of the game who don't have any real knowledge of cricket.'

The administration of cricket in the Caribbean was, and still is, hopeless. With no forward thinking or unity in the islands, cricket had been left drifting. There was no investment in facilities or coaching and there was zero marketing. It was a blueprint for self-destruction. So where once you saw kids playing cricket on rough recreation areas, they were now playing football, hockey or basketball: the sports they saw on American satellite TV. Caribbean-made television was fuzzy and amateurish, and, anyway, islands hosting Test matches were not allowed to broadcast them.

The consequence was a declining standard of cricket all round. First-class cricket, renamed the Busta Cup, consisted of only five matches for each of Barbados, Guyana, Trinidad, Jamaica, the Leewards and the Windwards, and was universally regarded as poor. The only place you found nets in the Caribbean was on fishing boats. 'I warned them that others would start to catch us, but they didn't listen,' said Desmond Haynes. 'They just said "lack of funds". How could the best team in the world have the poorest board?'

The amazing success of West Indies cricket was *in spite of* their system, as Viv Richards pointed out with his story about unearthing Ambrose. 'I happened to see him bowling on a bit of ground near his village one day. I was impressed and I made some inquiries. No one really rated him. I got him into the Leeward Islands team before he'd even played for Antigua. It was a chance discovery.' Great ex-players were now deterring their sons from playing because of the cricket board's attitude.

Hubris. That's what the West Indies were suffering from. Prompt action was needed, to address the lack of coaches and facilities and self-belief, though, in a region where the fire engines travel at 20mph, that was unlikely. But, somehow, West Indies cricket, the only thing that bonded that archipelago of islands together, needed to rediscover its riches. Without it, world cricket was a poorer place.

SEVENTEEN

New Religion

In a way Sri Lanka was the new West Indies. A palm-fringed, cricket-mad isle, it boasted uninhibited batsmen who charged down the wicket first ball, mercurial bowlers with gangly actions and wild eyes who hustled the ball through (or spun it viciously), and beach dudes trying to sell you anything from coral necklaces to ganja. In 1996 they came of age in identical fashion to the West Indies twenty-one years earlier. They won the World Cup.

It was no fluke. They played to their strengths, basically dashing batsmen and a host of diddy spinners. The latter was particularly sensible because the pitches of the subcontinent were flat and the tournament was interminable, lasting over a month and consisting of thirty-eight matches (the first World Cup was done and dusted in a fortnight), and endless rides in cramped taxis and internal flights on poky Indian planes are no fun for 6ft 4in pacemen.

Sri Lanka did have an initial advantage. Two of their

group games were cancelled because the opposition, Australia and the West Indies, were nervous of bomb threats after a terrorist attack in Colombo killed ninety people. West Indies created a shock of their own soon afterwards. They lost to Kenya. If they hadn't been aware of their decline before, they were then. England didn't fare much better. Utterly confused by the advent of fielding circles and pinch-hitting, they tried four different opening pairs and only managed to beat Holland and the United Arab Emirates in the group stages before being put out of their misery by the Sri Lankans in the quarter-finals.

The Calcutta crowd threw bottles and set fire to the stand when Indic collapsed to 120-8 against the spin of Muralitharan, Jayasuriya, Dharmasena and de Silva in the semi final. The match was abandoned and awarded to Sri Lanka, who faced Australia in the final.

The same four innocuous-looking bowlers applied the squeeze on the dominating Australians in Lahore. A target of 241 was comfortably overhauled by the compact Aravinda de Silva, a right-handed Lara, whose funny bow-legged walk belied fleet footwork and an unerring eye enabling him to cut, pull and flick at will. The rotund captain, Arjuna Ranatunga, a left-handed Gatting, kept him company to seal a comprehensive 7-wicket victory. Ranatunga brandished the trophy, the fifth time out of six tournaments that a 'non-white' nation had won it. The front page of the *Ceylon Daily News* declared 'Lanka Conquer Cricket's Mount Everest'.

The 1996 World Cup shaped the future of Indian

cricket. Before it Test match crowds had been large. The Calcutta and Madras grounds had been packed for every day of the England Tests in 1993. They were covered by the state broadcaster Doordarshan. A court ruling in 1994 allowed satellite stations to bid for cricket, co-inciding with a vast expansion in the number of one-day matches. In the 1970s, India played thirteen one-dayers. In the 1980s that figure was 158, and in the 1990s it was 256. (No wonder they are so unmemorable.)

The TV coverage got slicker and American drinks companies like Coca-Cola and Pepsi vied for sponsor-ship. Players advertised mainstream goods like chocolate, ice cream and motor bikes. Cricket and cricketers had become cool. A one-day match, which had all the melodrama and escapism of a Bollywood movie, was the thing to go to. You could see your heroes bat and bowl without having to take much time off work. Even less if it was a day–night game. In cities and villages people all gathered round the TV set – the community's new temple – to watch the conclusion of a one-day match. Indian Test match crowds began to dwindle.

There's another reason why the Indians are mad for cricket. It's the one sport they can properly compete at internationally. They are not into contact sports and hockey has declined. Cricket is one arena in which they have a serious world ranking. It gives them a global presence. Their quest for international supremacy bonds the nation. Oh, look, they just like the slow evolution of a cricketing contest, the way its flavours develop. Watching a cricket match is like cooking a curry . . .

You Have Been Warned

Shane Warne was now the dominant force in Test cricket. Warne had confounded the image of the archetypal Aussie – in the previous generation it was a strapping sheep shearer quaffing lager round the barbie and telling crude jokes: 'What's a Queenslander's idea of foreplay?' 'Brace yourself, Sheila!' Their patron saint was the marauding fast bowler Dennis Lillee, he of the bristling moustache and throbbing temples and bouncing medallion.

With Warne's arrival, sexist macho had been eclipsed by cool grunge. He was a beachboy leg-spinner with two earrings and a leisurely stroll to the stumps. He was a modern, accessible sporting hero symbolizing skill and success and vitality. He didn't burst blood vessels to achieve his goals, but tormented opponents with a flick of the wrist and a flashing smile. He could make five apparently identical deliveries all do different things. One was the leggie, another the slider which went straight on, then there was the googly of course, and a favourite, the pickpocket delivery which sneaked behind the batsman's body and bowled him round his legs.

Deadliest of all was the backspinning flipper, desperately difficult to master, bowled underhand like scooping ice cream. It floated through the air in smiling innocence, luring the batsman into attack mode, skidded wickedly on pitching, skating along the ground and crashing into the stumps. He was that good he even had a ball that nicked the off bail, whistled 'Waltzing Matilda' and nipped off to put some snags on the barbie.

But the art of Warne wasn't just his different deliveries. It was so much more about how he used them. Within a blanket of suffocating accuracy, he was able to systematically and psychologically lure the batsman to his doom. It might be a change of angle, an adjustment in the field or a provocative word. He loved baiting batsmen with 'Jeez, is that the best you can do?' when an opponent hit one over the top, or 'Go on, Ramps, you know you want to!' when he sensed a batsman like Mark Ramprakash wanted to charge him. (Two balls later he did, and was stumped by a mile.)

Central to his prowess was Terry Jenner, the former Australian leg-spinner. After retiring, he had gone into business, fallen on hard times and actually been jailed for embezzlement. Ian Chappell helped throw him a lifeline by recommending him to the Australian Cricket Academy, which is where he met Warne. Jenner was part of a long line of Aussie leg-spinners, from Arthur Mailey and Clarrie Grimmett, inventor of the flipper, through Bill O'Reilly and Bruce Dooland, who befriended the young Richie Benaud and taught him the skills (Benaud said the flipper took him four years to perfect). They were like members of a magic circle, passing on conjurers' secrets.

Jenner and Warne bonded immediately and worked on techniques and tactics together. Often Jenner, the teacher, would demonstrate something in the nets and then Warne, the pupil, would try it out. Most of the strategies were based round the leg break itself, which, with Warne's strong forearms and wrist, he could spin sharply. They worked on subtle changes of wrist position, varying angles, different grips. Jenner became known as the 'Spin Doctor' and Warne learnt to steal dismissals from under batsmen's noses. He was a brilliant wicket thief.

The dismissal of the Pakistani Basit Ali in Sydney was a classic example of his art. Basit was looking composed as the light faded, and was batting for the close. But Warne knew he was temperamentally flawed. Before the last ball of the day he made a big play of discussing with Ian Healy what he was going to bowl. They stood in the middle chatting for some time (actually they were debating whether to go for a Mexican or an Italian later). At last Warne wandered back to his mark. He went round the wicket and bowled one into the rough. Utterly confused, Basit made a hash of kicking it away, the ball went between his legs and bowled him. It wasn't the first, or last, time someone had been nut-megged by Warne.

Warne's impact was massive. A gift pack of specially designed Warne balls outsold everything at Christmas, and kids on the outfield at Australian grounds were all experimenting with leggies rather than trying to bowl fast. He was a one-man travelling circus, and everyone was captivated by his show. Tom Cruise, filming a movie in Australia, hired a corporate box at the SCG and asked to meet him. Batsmen pored over videos attempting to unravel his mysteries. Other countries tried to develop their own leg-spinners to counter his threat. England eventually gave up and instead constructed Merlyn, an elaborate machine that could replicate all his deliveries so the batsmen could prepare for facing him. Nothing could stop him siphoning wickets. He was cricket's greatest conman.

Skirting the Issue

English cricket watched all these developments like a car weaving along a B road not knowing whether to turn right or left. Players and coaches came and went, competitions were tinkered with, sponsors tapped up, working parties assembled. But the game seemed to be heading down a cul-de-sac. Michael Atherton was the right driver, and steered England out of a big pothole with his remarkable undefeated 185 in Johannesburg, defying the hostile South African pair of Donald and Pollock for almost eleven hours to save the match and keep England in the series. But they lost it in the end. And just about everything else.

After a calamitous tour of Zimbabwe, the *Sun* proposed sending the whole team to the moon in a rocket, and when they failed to dismiss the New Zealand no.11 for three hours, sheep heads were superimposed on their bodies under the headline: 'EWE'LL NEVER GET 'EM OUT'. They were even beaten by Sri Lanka at home. England's only response was to accuse the man they had been routed by, Muttiah Muralitharan, of being a chucker (he had already been called for throwing in Australia).

It wasn't as if they were particularly bad players. But they were tired and overworked and underprepared. They hardly ever had their first-choice bowling attack on the field. The trusty seamer Angus Fraser missed fifty-seven tests through injury and fatigue. It was calculated he only bowled 18 per cent of his balls for England. The Australian fast bowler Craig McDermott, by contrast, bowled 52 per cent of his balls for his country.

Atherton had too much on his plate, not just marshalling the batting and changing the bowling and setting the field, but accommodating a complex range of personalities from diverse backgrounds: outspoken northerners (Gough), sensitive Zimbabweans (Hick), tactless Kiwis (Caddick), feisty Anglo-Asians (Hussain and Ramprakash), enigmatic Afro-Caribbeans (numerous), self-deprecating South Africans (Smith) and neurotic Londoners (Tufnell). The social services should have been called, and occasionally were. Jack Russell, the wicketkeeper, who wore the same battered sunhat throughout his career (even after it caught fire while drying in an oven) and erected a no-go zone around his kit with yellow masking tape, would have taxed a sports shrink all on his own.

Until David Lloyd arrived as coach, Atherton had to organize practice as well, while the supremo Ray Illingworth, with whom he had a difficult relationship, played golf. Atherton pleaded for the main players to be put on central contracts, to allow more time for practice and recuperation (and counselling), but no one listened.

Lord Ian McLaurin of Tesco fame arrived in 1997 as chairman of the newly created England and Wales Cricket Board and announced a ten-year plan of action entitled Raising the Standard. With a perma-tan and shiny shoes he had a reputation for disingenuousness, but his heart seemed to be in the right place. He wanted to make England the best team in the world in both forms of the game by 2007. Central to his plan was a pyramid structure, with school and club cricket feeding into a host of two-day (club) premier leagues (like Australian grade cricket), and further up the ladder dividing county cricket into three conferences. Though it was complicated, it did seem to be more dynamic. And therefore unlikely to be introduced.

It aroused debate though, and eventually there were changes. In 2000 there were two divisions in the championship with promotion and relegation (though no relegation from the second division which seemed to defeat the overall object) and a new one-day 45-over league. The two-day (all-day) club cricket idea never caught on. We are just not like Australians. We English men have other things to do on Saturday mornings like go to B&Q for a new rechargeable drill or mow the lawn in neat stripes.

McLaurin also thought he was doing the game a favour by encouraging the government to take Test cricket off the protected list of televised events. He secured a gentleman's agreement that not all Tests had to be on terrestrial TV. He imagined it would encourage competition to bid for Test match rights, which would bring in more money, and he was right. In 1998,

Channel 4 and Sky ended BBC's monopoly of Test match coverage, paying £100m for the (dubious) pleasure, almost double the previous deal. What he didn't imagine was that the 'gentleman's agreement' would be ridden over roughshod six years later, and *all* cricket sold out exclusively to the highest bidder. The 'gentlemen' were up to their tricks again.

There was real progress in one direction: women. On 29 September 1998, just 211 years after their formation, the MCC finally admitted women members. It had not looked likely six months earlier when the motion was defeated. Then a real cross-section of types – from forensic scientists and literary agents to Tube employees and printers – had exhibited attitudes that were not just Victorian but positively prehistoric. 'The Long Room will resound to the clattering of teacups!' declared one man. Another said, 'In twenty years' time, the Lord's shop might be full of twin sets and lingerie in MCC colours!' 'I'd feel uncomfortable with women in the pavilion, my behaviour would change,' declared one individual. 'Well, I don't know what your behaviour is towards women but I'd be most interested to see it,' the MCC president, Colin Ingleby-Mackenzie, the former Hampshire captain, retorted to gales of laughter. One chap claimed that he would vote against the motion whether it was the introduction of fruit machines or women, an interesting juxtaposition, on a par with a sign at Royal St. George's Golf Club in Sandwich which said, 'No women or dogs.'

The motion did not get the two thirds of votes it needed and thus was defeated, to much derision in the press. But after six months of campaigning, the MCC committee, who in general were a good deal more enlightened than the membership, got it through. I often wondered why women wanted to gain entry to a place of halitosis and hard seats and lukewarm pies (the Lord's pavilion), but you couldn't deny them the opportunity, and anyway women's involvement and participation in cricket were becoming more and more significant.

With cricket's popularity in decline through competition from football and other leisure activities and its absence in comprehensives, the emphasis was on the primary schools (and clubs) to entice kids to play. Most primary school teachers are women. The more well-versed in the rudiments of the game they were, the more chance there was of them teaching it in Games or PE. Surely a game of indoor cricket had to be more fun than backward somersaults or vaulting over a horse? And now we're world champions!

The Women's Cricket Association was actually formed in 1926, and they staged their first World Cup two years before the men, in 1973. And England won it. Test matches had been played since the 1930s and there was a thriving county championship. They have their own Ashes. Skills levels were high, and some players, like Brighton's Clare Connor, were infiltrating men's teams. Most importantly, in 1998, they had abandoned their pleated skirts in favour of trousers, thereby saving their bare legs from the unbearable sensation of hard leather on cold skin. Men don't play in shorts for the same, very sound, reason.

There was one very sad occurrence in 1998. The Yorkshire and England wicketkeeper David Bairstow committed suicide. He was forty-six. Such deaths are always a shock, but even more so when the person in question was such an ebullient character. Stocky of body and ruddy of face, the ginger-haired Bluey, as he was known, was an instantly recognizable, and audible, figure on a cricket field. My abiding memory was setting a field to him at Headingley, and, respecting his penchant for the pull shot, asking Brearley, the Middlesex captain, if I could have square leg slightly deeper. Bluey, overhearing, barked, 'If I git 'old of it you'll need 'im a lot fookin deeper!'

He was absolutely central to everything at Yorkshire – making light of being captain, keeper, pugnacious batsman and lead vocalist. He flung his keeping gloves in the air with unbridled joy when Yorkshire won a big cup game. It all meant so much to him. But that was the problem. As with all these other cricket suicides – and there were three others in the 1990s – he was so completely immersed in the game that he had lost the sense of who he was. Retirement led to a feeling of worthlessness. We all feel it when we leave the enveloping cricket family. Some obviously more profoundly than others.

RIP English Cricket

We are at the end of the century, one which began with gas lamps and steam engines and concerns about a Briton's lack of physical activity, and ended with solar power and 'leaves on the line' and rising levels of obesity. *Plus ça change*, eh? Tongue sandwich did have a slightly different connotation in 1999 than it had a hundred years earlier, as, for cricket fans, did wagon wheel and nightwatchman. But Australia were in charge then, winning the first Ashes series of the century 4–1, and they were still in charge 99 years on, winning the seventh World Cup.

The tournament, in England, was a damp squib. The MCC had built the swanky new Lord's media centre to coincide with the 1999 World Cup and it won architectural awards. But there've been more exciting openings of crisp packets than the ceremony which launched the competition, with a lame parade, cheap fireworks which filled the arena with smoke rather than light, and mist-hampered skydivers. The World Cup song, recorded by the Eurythmics' Dave Stewart, was only released halfway through the tournament. It didn't mention cricket. Sorry if English cricket administration is being depicted as a total shambles but that's the way it is. Even the lousy weather was their fault. Why hold a major tournament in May and early June?

The England players were no better. Captained now by Alec Stewart after Atherton had resigned in the West Indies, they were sidetracked by arguments about contracts and performed abysmally. In fact, after losing to India, they didn't even make it into the second (supersix) stage, being eliminated by Zimbabwe on run-rate. By *Zimbabwe*. Who only had about six bats and four pairs of pads between them (though they did have Andy Flower, who was rather good). 'There are honourable defeats, unfortunate defeats and ignominious defeats. The manner by which England's interest in the cricket world cup ended yesterday, rests, unfortunately, in the final category,' said *The Times* pompously. The *Sun* was more succinct. 'Flippin' useless!' it wailed.

Why were (are) England so bad at one-day cricket? Two reasons. One, the fact that it has always been regarded as inferior to Test cricket in England; therefore the intensity, focus and resources are never properly channelled into it. One-day internationals are an after-thought. Basically a bit of exhibitionism. Two, England have tended to lack explosive or mercurial cricketers who can, with a blistering fifty or, more importantly, a couple of vital wickets, turn a one-day game in a few overs.

Here's an example. The highlight of the five-week World Cup competition – apart from the end – was the semi-final between Australia and South Africa. There was feeling between the teams after a needle match in the super-six stage at Headingley which Australia won. South Africa were out for revenge. They were looking a good bet at 48-0 chasing only 213. Warne came on and produced a classic repeat of That Ball to get rid of Gibbs, bowled Kirsten and had Cronje caught behind for 0. Suddenly it was 61-4. The South Africans recovered, but then Warne returned to snare Kallis.

Wickets fell but Lance Klusener, the star of the tour-nament, butchered 31 off 14 balls to make the match all but South Africa's. One was needed off the last 4 balls. There was only 1 wicket left but Klusener was on strike. Then his brain seized up. He kept biffing the ball to the close-set field. With 1 to win off the last, he drilled it back straight and set off. Mark Waugh flicked the ball back to the bowler, Damien Fleming; Donald, the non-striker, regained his ground but dropped his bat; Klusener was already at his end and the run-out was a formality.

The match was tied, but Australia were through because, unbeknown to almost everyone except them, their run-rate was superior in the super-six table. Another triumph for the cock-eyed organizers. But not for South Africa. They had started the competition as innovators – Cronje wearing an earpiece to be connected with the coach Bob Woolmer in the stand (an arrangement that was immediately outlawed) – but, after their third semi-final failure, they finished it as chokers.

Australia coasted past Pakistan in the final to win a competition that was significant because, during it, the total number of one-day internationals played overtook the number of Tests (1,454) despite the longer form having a ninety-four-year head start.

If that was a defining moment for the game, there was also one for English cricket with the appointment of Nasser Hussain as captain – England's first Anglo-Asian leader. He began with a win against New Zealand, though few people saw it as it was the first Test match shown *exclusively live!* on satellite TV. But two defeats followed as a tired, dispirited, poorly selected England slumped in the face of enthusiastic Kiwi bowling and determined batting. The abiding image was of Tufnell ducking apprehensively as the muscular Chris Cairns advanced up the pitch and smote him into the stands.

Hussain was booed as he collected the losers' cheque at the Oval, England were officially bottom of the world – the outcome having cast them to ninth out of nine in the Wisden World Championship (there was still no official ICC version). The *Sun*, delighting in the moment, commemorated it with a mock obituary under a picture of burning bails.

Newspapers and ex-players had a field day, as they always do when England lose. It's a sad but inevitable aspect of English society that people rather enjoy others' misfortune, especially if they remember being there themselves. Botham, for once talking complete sense, said 'the complacency, self-interest and indolence of some of the men running English cricket in the past decade meant that such an outcome was merely a matter of time.' Bob Willis, a clear thinker and someone who had campaigned for reform for years, called for control of the game to be wrested from 'a self-interested and parochial county-led administration'.

Outside the corridors of power there was a universal belief that the county game was three quarters rotten but still gobbled up most of the money. If you had told a visitor, let's say an American, that there is this competition, the County Championship, which goes on all summer in front of no one, and knackers the best players who are then needed by England to perform and bail those very same counties out of their financial crises, they'd have looked at you askance and said, 'Gee, don't make no sense to me. Can't you just identify the best players and keep them together and throw the counties out with the trash?'

Sometimes there's merit in being a country with no history. It means you're not imprisoned by it.

EIGHTEEN

Fix 'Em Up

Remember the Millennium Bug, that disease that was going to make every computer go up in smoke and all our modern, luxurious lives with it as Big Ben struck twelve on 31 December 1999? Never happened, did it? Was that because of the reputed £400bn spent to protect us from it? Like wondering whether the light goes off when you shut the fridge door, we shall never know.

There was a bug in the cricket world though, and it reared its head soon afterwards. An Indian detective heard a tape recording of South Africa's Hansie Cronje offering to fix some one-day internationals. Within weeks Cronje had admitted colluding with a book-maker to set up England's last-day run chase in the rain-ruined fifth test at Centurion, which they un-expectedly won. He, and others, confessed that the manipulation of games involving top Asian and South African players had been going on for a decade. The truth was out. Match fixing was rife.

Though the news was shocking, it was not wholly

surprising. There'd been rumblings for a while of huge betting syndicates in the Middle East and India that focused on cricket. The increase in the number of one-day internationals, many involving Asian countries and some staged in Sharjah, was the reason. At the outset of one-day cricket in the 1970s India and Pakistan had played a total of just thirty-three one-dayers between them, i.e. about four a year. By the 1990s that figure had mushroomed to 518. That's one a week.

The one-day international had become the cash cow of the cricket boards. They guaranteed sustenance. But the number of games, their general superficiality and forgettability, make them easier to manipulate. Betting can be on anything, from the winning margin to a batsman's score to the number of lbw appeals. I once saw a gaggle of men at an inconsequential club match in Lahore betting on potential maiden overs. Gamblers are desperate for inside information, and the first trickle of stories involving players – Shane Warne and Mark Waugh receiving $5,000 for pitch and weather details before a one-day international in Pakistan – had, by 2000, become a flood.

Though it sounds like sacrilege, you couldn't totally blame the players. They were still being exploited. The cricket boards were hawking their teams around like prize cattle and making a handsome profit. It wasn't being passed on. Still earnings were not high, especially in Pakistan and South Africa, whose squads shared less than £100,000 for getting to the semi-finals of the 1999 World Cup (the profit from the tournament was £31m). A pre-agreed innocuous over costing 10 or a tame dismissal for under 20 in an anonymous one-dayer was an easy way to make a five-figure sum.

The upshot of all this was a huge investigation, the banning and fining of several players, including Cronje and Mohammad Azharuddin for life, and Pakistan's Salim Malik, and the setting up of the ICC's anti-corruption unit headed by Sir Paul Condon, which after several years of probing came up with lots of suspicions but very few facts. Worst of all, international players had to sacrifice their mobile phones during matches, which meant they were now denied a little flutter on the 4.20 from Catterick if they'd had a tip.

The issue shook cricket badly (forcing a few journalists and commentators to be a bit more discreet about their betting habits) and elicited a lot of ill-informed criticism of the sport, suggesting that it had finally sacrificed the moral high ground now that it was knee-deep in match fixing. This conveniently ignored the regular existence of such activity in the cricket of the early nineteenth century, perpetrated by, among others, one of the original MCC presidents, the arch-swindler Lord Frederick Beauclerk. It always has existed in moderation, and probably always will.

The match-fixing story had a tragic sequel. Almost two years after admitting his guilt, Cronje died in a plane crash returning to his home in South Africa. At first sabotage was suspected – after all, he had got involved with some seriously vicious members of the Asian mafia, and had given the police a lot of valuable leads. In the end it was declared an accident as his light plane, manned by experienced pilots, lost its way in bad weather and struck a mountain. His death at thirty-two was mourned by many current South African players, notably Allan Donald and Gary Kirsten, who'd remained loyal to their old captain throughout. Elsewhere, people were less sympathetic to the man who, it was thought, had besmirched the game. Clearly he was a weak and duplicitous character. Ultimately, however, he was a victim of an unstoppable greed, a greed that every cricket administrator who had scheduled a one-day international in the 1990s had helped to sustain.

Generally Above Average

England were playing so badly they couldn't have fixed a match even if they'd tried. Nasser Hussain had predicted that things might get worse before they got better, and he was right. Duncan Fletcher had become the new coach, and in his first Test in charge England declined to 2-4 in Johannesburg. The first thing a modern captain and coach do, however, is emphasize the 'positives' and there was one, the arrival of Michael Vaughan, who made his début in that match.

There was another the following summer: Marcus Trescothick, who made his début with a fifty against the West Indies at Old Trafford. It was also Atherton and Stewart's 100th Test match (and the Queen Mother's 100th birthday). Stewart, one of those batsmen who tends to know his average to the fourth decimal point, celebrated it with a hundred. Atherton, who was always more concerned about the bigger picture, didn't.

Averages were an interesting aspect of Fletcher's approach – or rather his lack of faith in them. Ramprakash and Hick, who had scored mountains of runs in county cricket (Hick already had a hundred hundreds) were discarded, and Vaughan and Trescothick, whose county averages were modest (in the mid-30s), were picked. Fletcher had seen something in their make-up, their character, that he'd liked, and he valued that more highly than an ability to churn out scores in low-intensity county games. Having being fully immersed in the domestic game as coach of Glamorgan, he realized the system would never change. So he overrode it.

He had one big advantage. Central contracts for England players had finally been agreed thirteen years after they'd been first proposed, and he had the chosen men under his jurisdiction. The best fast bowlers, Caddick and Gough, were virtually denied to their counties and stayed fit all summer. Both were responsible for the West Indies' two dramatic collapses – 54 all out at Lord's and 61 at Headingley, in a dramatic match that was all over in two days, before the weekend had even begun.

In front of an enormous, euphoric last-day crowd at the Oval – who had also come to see Ambrose and Walsh's last Test – England clinched the series, the first time they'd beaten the West Indies for twenty-seven years. Hussain sank to his knees in relief and satisfaction. It had made for real-life melodrama on

Channel 4, rather than the contrived stuff featuring a lesbian nurse, a transvestite lawyer, a gay trucker and a chaste lap dancer that everyone was addicted to on the new phenomenon, *Big Brother*.

England's improvement continued in the sub-continent. Hussain instilled greater commitment and responsibility in the team, and Fletcher was meticulous, subtly improving batsmen's technique against spin, introducing a short first movement he called the forward press. He fashioned good team plans, stressing patience, enabling England to hang in the game longer against the wily off spin of Pakistan's Saqlain Mushtaq and Sri Lanka's Muralitharan. Pakistan were defeated in the dark in Karachi, and Sri Lanka in the sultry heat of Kandy and Colombo.

The 2001 Australians gave England a reality check. They arrived having previously won sixteen Tests in a row and were a supreme outfit. There was a dynamic opening pair – Slater and Hayden – a remorseless middle order of Ponting, the Waugh twins and Damien Martyn, and Adam Gilchrist, whose bat flashed and scythed like a samurai sword. Brett Lee's pace and Jason Gillespie's skiddy outswing augmented the relentless-ness of McGrath and the ingeniousness of Warne. If you were creating a blueprint for the ideal team, you couldn't do much better. They employed an American baseball coach to fine-tune their brilliant fielding and had perfected the art of sledging too, with pointed remarks as hapless batsmen played and missed, en-couraging the bowlers with 'Don't worry, Dodgy Technique will nick one in a minute!' They clapped and yapped and urged their quickies to 'Give him a Kuala!' ('Bumper', after Kuala Lumpur.)

McGrath, originally an up-country tearaway, had been refined into a beautifully oiled bowling machine. With a robotically straight approach, he ran rhythmically to the wicket and, with arm bolt upright, fizzed the ball down on a tight off-stump line. He was metronomically accurate, even more so than Hawkeye, the computerized ball-tracking device first introduced on Channel 4, and with his height and long levers was able to make the ball bounce disconcertingly. Despite a spare frame that earnt him the nickname Pigeon for his spindly legs, he had deceptive speed.

More than that though, he had an unshakeable desire to uproot the batsmen, the more accomplished the better, and made them well aware of that with menacing stares and comments. He always made it his business to target the key member of the opposition, as Atherton, whom he dismissed nineteen times, would testify. A quietly spoken, practical joker off the field, he was a ruthless exterminator on it, and feared nothing and nobody. He was the dalek of bowling.

McGrath and Warne enabled Australia to boss the game from any situation. If there was help in the pitch, they would utilize it. If there wasn't, they'd impose a sort of hypnosis on the batsmen, drying up the runs with monotonous accuracy or balls you couldn't hit – over the head from McGrath, or into the rough from Warne. Australia had won the Ashes for the seventh successive time, and there were calls for the famous urn to be relocated in Australia. England weren't the only sufferers. The only series Australia lost between October 1999 and July 2005 was the sensational one in India, when the Indians, following on in Calcutta having already lost the first Test, posted 657-7 and won by 171 runs. V. V. S. Laxman's irrepressible 281 was positively Bothamesque.

Steve Waugh was their MC. Mortally wounded by Ashes defeat in 1986–7, he had vowed to never experience it again as long as his old baggy green cap stayed intact. It was partly his idea to visit Gallipoli on the way to England, as further motivation. For him, the Ashes *was* Waugh minus the shooting. Uncompromising and gimlet-eyed, he was hewn from the same lump of granite as Ian Chappell. He would not budge an inch. Even for his twin brother Mark. Mark, a batsman of silky touch, was more of a gambler and they were not bosom pals. Which is why the following retort from England débutant Jimmy Ormond will have hurt more than ever. When Steve Waugh saw him walk out to bat, he gave him the usual Aussie welcome: 'Fuck me, look who it is. Mate, what are you doing out here? There's no way you're good enough to play for England.' 'Maybe not,' Ormond replied, 'but at least I'm the best player in my family.'

Festival of Speed

The Indian batsmen ground England down as well in the summer of 2002. Sachin Tendulkar, now the prince of runs, made two hundreds and Rahul Dravid, the original immoveable obstacle, contributed three.

Duncan Fletcher, like his opposite number at Arsenal, Arsène Wenger, was a disciple of pace, and two young quicks made their début – Simon Jones, son of Jeff, England's tailend saviour in the West Indies, and Steve Harmison, son of Jimmy, centre back at Ashington FC, the club that produced the Charlton brothers. After his four years in and out of the team, Andrew Flintoff's bowling was also beginning to look as impressive as his ability to open bottles of lager with his teeth and swig from three simultaneously.

Michael Vaughan replied with two big centuries of his own, and was not inconvenienced by the new delivery from India's off-spinner Harbhajan Singh, which was originally christened the mystery ball but was now known as the *doosra*. This was Hindi for 'the other one' and was basically a ball released from the back of the hand which spun in the opposite direction to a normal off break (i.e. away from the right-hander). It was the off-spinner's googly.

The conventional off break had actually become increasingly redundant, owing to one-day cricket and batsmen's expanding repertoire of slog sweeps, reverse sweeps, deft paddles and huge larrups over mid-wicket. Confronted with big, light bats, shorter boundaries and shirt-front pitches, it was too plain a delivery to be a threat and specialist, old-fashioned off-spinners were being marginalized. The *doosra*, pioneered by Saqlain Mushtaq, had given them a new lease of life, and other off-spinners were following Saqlain's lead, though no English ones. They seemed to lack the flexibility to bowl it.

It was one-day cricket that had brought about a much more dramatic development: intimidatory batting. Not content with just beating everybody in Test cricket, the Australians were now battering teams into submission with scoring of unprecedented rapidity. It was their view that imposing yourself on the opposition bowlers was the best way of wearing them down.

Viv Richards used to do this, almost subconsciously, playing outrageous shots when he first arrived, then, once the field had been pushed back and the bowlers' optimism banished, he'd rather theatrically play himself in. Led by the pectoral-flexing, chest-thrusting Matthew Hayden – Australia's incredible hulk – the Aussies had the personnel to do it. The caution and circumspection of traditional opening pairs to 'see the shine off' the new ball had had a dramatic makeover. Hayden and his nimble opening partner Justin Langer saw the shine off all right. They flogged the new ball into the boundary pickets.

Australia's opening partnership would fly along at four an over, posting the 100 well before lunch, Ponting and the rest would maintain the tempo, then Gilchrist would arrive to really put the boot in. Bowlers of a fragile disposition were quickly found out. It was the batting equivalent of the West Indies' four-pronged pace attack ofthe 1980s. And it was just as effective. Their average run-rate of 4.08 an over was the highest in Test history.

The England bowling soon wilted in the heat of the Australian bat when they arrived for the Ashes of 2002–3. With the Aussies 364-2 after the first day in

Brisbane, having been put in by a misguided Hussain, the series was over almost before it had started. England contributed to their own demise by taking unfit bowlers on tour. Gough failed to recover from knee surgery in time, and Flintoff from a hernia operation, and Harmison had sore shins. Maybe they had read the race beforehand. But the horrible injury to Simon Jones, rupturing his knee attempting a slide-stop in the outfield on that first day, was genuinely unlucky. Then again, luck usually favours the brave, and England, apart from the majestic Vaughan, were chickenfeed. They surrendered the Ashes by 1 December 2002 after just eleven days' cricket. 'IS THERE ANYONE THERE WHO CAN PLAY CRICKET?' yelled the Sydney *Daily Telegraph* smugly.

The Australians' impetus was important. They were rejuvenating Test cricket at a time when the one-day version – in fact all cricket – was becoming repetitive and boring. There was just too much of it. We were approaching the 2,000th one-day international, each country staging its own triangular tournaments: the Standard Bank Trophy in South Africa, the VB Series in Australia, the NatWest series in England, the LG Albans in Sri Lanka, the 'I'm a Richer Industrialist Than You' Trophy in India. Even the Morocco Cup. Actually in Morocco. The manufacturers of the trophies themselves, and of all the players', umpires', match referees' and scorers' medals, given away at yet another of those interminable 'presentation ceremonies', must have been coining it. As for the cricket boards and their one-day competitions, well, they were like dogs: they didn't know when to stop eating. And no one had the gumption or wherewithal to make them stop.

Tests, too, were everywhere, one a week on average, the accounts of various three-match series around the world taking up 200 pages of *Wisden* (three times the space of ten years before). The public were being short-changed by a lot of one-sided matches and the players were being flogged to death. Or, as Brett Lee put it, 'I'm running on a sniff at the moment.'

It didn't prevent Lee from unleashing the second 100mph delivery in cricket history at the 2003 World Cup in South Africa. Pakistan's Shoaib Akhtar had produced the first. But, proving that speed was not everything, Shoaib was spanked for 7 an over and England won that match with the dramatic late swing of the newcomer James Anderson. (A rarity in the modern English game in that he had acquired his skills mainly in Lancashire League cricket. Echoes of S. F. Barnes? And he was from the same club, Burnley.)

A potentially vibrant World Cup was marred by the ICC's hopeless handling of the Zimbabwe issue. The political situation had drastically deteriorated there, but the ICC stuck their heads in the sand and tried to consider only 'cricketing' matters. After much procrastination from the ECB, mainly over lost revenue, England refused to play there. Mourning 'the death of democracy in our beloved Zimbabwe', Andy Flower and Henry Olonga wore black armbands when playing for the country, whose cricket administration was as corrupt as its government. New Zealand also refused to play their match in Kenya over safety concerns, which was a bit feeble. Having said that, it was a bit absurd scheduling matches there, given the tournament was based in South Africa. You might as well have a couple in Cairo while you're at it.

The forfeited matches catapulted Zimbabwe and Kenya into the second stage at the expense of England, who lost a critical group match to . . . you've guessed it . . . Australia, and South Africa, who got their run-rate calculations wrong in a rain-affected match with Sri Lanka. Kenya even made it to the semi-final. Shane Warne was in the sin bin for taking a banned drug, but Australia still trounced all-comers with their aggressive approach, reducing some of the Indian bowlers to jelly in the final as they rattled up 359-2 to win by 125 runs. 'It was the most compelling, destructive cricket performance I have ever seen,' said the former Australian captain Greg Chappell, who was shortly to become India's coach. 'The Australian team cannot be faulted for its brilliance,' wrote Greg Baum in the *Age*, 'but it would be to cricket's benefit if the rest of the world provided some competition.' We all said yea to that.

Perfect Vision

England weren't able, yet, to produce a new team. But they did come up with a new ground: the Riverside in County Durham became England's first new Test venue for 101 years when it staged the second Test against Zimbabwe in 2003. The cosy, six-ground cartel had finally been broken. And there was no finer welcome in Britain than from the weather-beaten but eternally cheery locals who said everything was 'proper champion!', despite their team finishing mainly bottom for a decade.

Even more significantly England came up with a new game. After extensive market research, which suggested that two thirds of the English population couldn't give a hoot about cricket, they had introduced 'short form' 20-over cricket into the summer schedule. It took the place of the Benson & Hedges Cup, which after thirty years of service had, like its patrons, been forced outside.

Twenty20 hadn't been universally approved – nothing ever is when you've got about twenty-five people voting – but at least it had got the green light for a three-year trial. Stuart Robinson, the ECB marketing manager, got the credit for creating it, to much chuckling in Durham, and Yorkshire, and any other club environment that had been playing 20-over cricket for most of the last century. But fair's fair, the Australian Cricket Board hadn't thought of it.

Of course, despite the competition being launched on Friday the 13th, it was an instant success. Well, why wouldn't it be? It was cricket without the boring bits and on at a time when normal, sane, employed people could actually come and watch. Grounds were packed. Some ran out of beer. Most ran out of toilet paper. It was like the M25, suddenly creating twice as much traffic as anyone was expecting. And despite exceptional scores, including some over 200, it wasn't *all* slogging, although, with shorter boundaries than ever and a licence to swing from the hip, it wasn't much of a bowler's game.

There were inevitable reservations from the purists, a euphemism for the short-sighted and the hard of hearing, suggesting that Twenty20 cricket wasn't a *proper* contest between bat and ball (actually, I might have said that). But the compensations were huge. The 5.30pm start time benefited everyone. You could see all the skills of the game – even the forward defensive and the shouldering of arms, occasionally – compressed into 2½ hours, supping wine and sitting next to Julia from accounts, and still be able to go out for dinner/get home in time for supper afterwards. The players, ground down by their monotonous routine, revelled in the concept and the public response, and in only having to report for 'work' at 4pm – and knock off at 8.30 – and their enjoyment was infectious. Twenty20 made cricket fun again. And almost cool. I said almost.

Eventually, *eureka!*, the all-new, succulently tasty England team arrived. It all began with the 2003 series against South Africa, which England came back from 2–1 down to level at the Oval with a performance of great character and resilience, after conceding 484 in the first innings. For just about the first time in living memory, England posted 600. After that, they won nearly every Test series going.

There were two catalysts for this turnaround. Michael Vaughan's touchy-feely leadership, and the transformation of Andrew Flintoff from hefty biffer to hardened bully. Hussain had resigned as captain, having injected new steel and togetherness into England (symbolized by the daily pre-match huddle) and won some important battles with weak administrators. He had created a good template, which the less abrasive Vaughan inherited and built on with more sympathetic handling of the bowlers and a less intolerant demeanour. He began calling players by their nicknames rather than barking, 'OK, Caddick, have a blow!' as Hussain had tended to. But he also instituted a much more rigorous approach to fitness.

Flintoff, previously overweight and underwhelming, bought into the Vaughan mantra and got fit. The unlikely figure of Richie Benaud had given him vital self-belief. In a quiet ceremony before the third Test at Trent Bridge, Benaud had been invited to present personal trophies to those who'd excelled in the previous match. Flintoff had made a spectacular but fruitless century in a losing cause. He strode forward to receive his award, but took a reverential step back when Benaud raised his hand. Benaud complimented him on his performance, but then set him a task. 'What I want you to do now, Freddie, is be there at the end of the innings. That way you can have the most influence on it,' he said. Two Tests on at the Oval, Flintoff followed the advice to the letter, contributing a mature, muscular 95 to give England an unexpected lead, and eventually an unlikely victory.

From then on Flintoff cultivated a path of calculated violence with the bat, and bone-shaking vehemence with the ball. He seemed, subconsciously, to raise his game against the best players, an alpha male marking out his territory. He cranked up his pace and his intensity against the likes of Lara and Ponting and Graeme Smith and took the big wickets. There was no more hostile adversary in the game. There was only one problem. Every time he released the ball his left ankle was forced to absorb the force of a rhino landing on concrete. This led to severe pain and the dreaded scan – the four-letter word for our times. In the era of the nanny state and medical people behaving like jobsworths, everything must be scanned, even broken fingernails. And once a crack is detected, no matter how hairline, a lay-off is inevitable. If they'd had scans in Brian Close's day he'd never have been allowed out of intensive care.

Overrated and Over Here

Sussex, one of the cradles of cricket, won the County Championship for the first time in their history in 2003. It was not what you could call a home-bred success. The captain was the forthright Chris Adams, recruited from Derbyshire, the leading batsman was the Zimbabwean Murray Goodwin, and the really decisive factor the leg spin of the Pakistani Mushtaq Ahmed, who took 103 wickets. At least the coach, Peter Moores, was a Sussex man – as a player anyway. His mix of straight talking and science – making astute use of newfangled computer analysis of every shot and delivery – was hugely influential.

County cricket itself, however, was in flux. Yes, *again*.

384

Three teams out of nine were relegated from division one each year. It was too many, consigning most teams to looking over the shoulder for much of the season, promoting defensive cricket. Not that many people were actually watching it. Attendances were lower than ever. Also there was much disgruntlement in the shires that Duncan Fletcher was denying them their England players for most of, if not all, the summer.

Maroš Kolpak, a Slovakian handball player, offered a solution. No, he didn't invent the switch hit or the chinaman *doosra*. He was the guy that attempted to play for a German league team (*what*, you didn't know there was a German handball league – are you not glued to Eurosport at 5am on Tuesday mornings in March?) but was prevented from doing so because he was foreign. He went to the European Court of Justice in Strasbourg and had this obstacle overthrown, as his country was a member of the EU. It was like the Bosman ruling in football and paved the way for any Tomas, Dik or Hari, either a European citizen or someone from a country with an 'Association Agreement' with the European Union (places like South Africa, Zimbabwe and some in the Caribbean), to play for an English team and not be considered an overseas player.

Leicestershire prised open the sluice gates. Early in 2004 they hired the South African left-arm spinner Claude Henderson, despite already having two Australians as their overseas players. Henderson hadn't played for South Africa for over a year so was allowed in. There were wails of complaint from other counties, but soon the gamekeepers were turning poachers and a torrent of Kolpak players arrived. Even Yorkshire succumbed.

Kolpak players were often ex-internationals representing a quick and relatively inexpensive fix for a county team, instead of investing time and money in a promising youngster and hoping he would develop. Players were being regarded as commodities – white goods I suppose you'd call them – and buying a cheap and reliable foreign make was preferable to going British and taking pot luck. That's fair enough if it's a washing machine you're purchasing. But if it's a cricketer, and, what's more, the money you're spending is mostly generated by the England team you're supposed to be supplying, then it's just not on.

Yet the Kolpak revolution continued unhindered. There were ninety-six non-England-qualified players in the County Championship in 2004. Of those thirty-seven were through the European or Kolpak route. That number had soon risen to over sixty (plus all the official overseas players, who changed counties on a whim, sometimes in the same season). In 2008 there was a match between Leicestershire and Northants featuring eleven players not qualified for England. This was in the realms of premiership football matches. The difference being that Chelsea, Arsenal and the rest are the ones who generate the income to spend on players, therefore they can do what they want. Financially, counties are just like children – forever hungry, always whining and leaving their room in a mess, all for little obvious return. Though at least children grow up. (And are forever hungry, always whining and leaving their room in a mess. But you still love 'em, doncha?)

Generally 2004 was a statistician's dream. Steve Waugh retired at the beginning of it with a world record 168 Test appearances, three times as many as Bradman, each one documented – down to the details of virtually every dressing room toilet he'd known – in a world-record-sized 800-page autobiography resulting in another swathe of Amazonian forest destroyed.

Brian Lara reclaimed the record Test score from Matthew Hayden with 400 not out against England, during an ordeal that Andrew Flintoff, who bowled 35 overs in the innings, said, 'I never want to experience again.' Lara's feat, achieved ten years after his world record 375, on the same ground, in the same month and against the same side, took just twelve minutes longer than his previous effort, such was the consistent rhythm of his scoring. The *Daily Mirror*'s Mike Walters called it 'the equivalent of Neil Armstrong walking on the moon then going back 10 years later to set foot on Mars'. It was too late to stop England, galvanized by as good a quartet of fast bowlers as they'd ever had – Harmison, Flintoff, Hoggard and Jones – winning a series in the West Indies for the first time in thirty-six years.

A rehabilitated Shane Warne and Muttiah Muralitharan both overtook Courtney Walsh's world record wickets tally of 519, and then vied with each other to be considered the leader of the pack. Murali was there for a while, till forensic surveys of his action pronounced that his new-found *doosra* was a chuck and he had to stop bowling it. Subsequent analysis revealed that almost every bowler, fast or slow, bent his arm to some degree, so he was let off with a caution. A 15-degree flex in the bowling arm was now permitted. Moderate 'chucking' was now legal, though umpires would have to add a protractor to all the other paraphernalia in their pockets.

With 561 Test wickets, Warne ended the year on top, so to speak. He had been captaining Hampshire and allegedly propositioning local girls with messages, so that he became known as the greatest text cricketer of all time. One girl had sold her story, proclaiming that he had fallen asleep on the job. It led to a tale doing the rounds that there'd been a poll of 500 Southampton women asking if they would ever sleep with Shane Warne: 493 had replied, 'Never again.'

Meanwhile Sachin Tendulkar drew level with his idol Sunil Gavaskar's tally of thirty-four Test hundreds. Add to that his thirty-seven one-day hundreds and he was already comfortably the most prolific international batsman of all time. Idol to a billion people, Tendulkar had continued to churn out runs in his own methodical way. He didn't have Lara's spark, but he was meticulous in everything he did, from deliberately roughing up net pitches to prepare for facing Warne, to rearranging his gear between deliveries, to his calculated shot selection. Before batting on a slow pitch in Sydney, he had decided the cover drive was a risky shot. In his epic innings of 241, he never ever attempted to play even one.

Continuing on the landmark theme, Richie Benaud commemorated his 500th Test as either player or commentator. That's more than 2,000 days playing or watching Test cricket, or about five and a half years back to back, and way more than anyone else, be it Swanton or Woodcock or the beloved CMJ. So when someone of that experience says it's the best thing he's ever seen, you betta believe it.

That was the amazing thing about him. Richie often thought it was the best thing he'd ever seen. To him the world kept on improving. He was the antidote to all those septuagenarian nostalgists. He never had an in-my-day thought in his body. He was Mr Magnanimity, finding a smile and something gently encouraging to say about everything, from streaky shots to dodgy commentary. The only time he was stuck for words was when Dermot Reeve showed him his nipple ring.

His 500 Tests were broken down thus: 63 on the field, 5 off the field when he was still a player; as a commentator 231 in England, 182 in Australia (oddly, he started working in TV here in 1963 but wasn't accommodated in the commentary box back home till 1977) and 19 elsewhere. Occasionally you're reminded of his longevity. 'Amazing bowling by Jim Laker at Old Trafford,' he said, talking over some old Pathé footage of the 1956 Ashes Test. 'Nineteen wickets in the match . . . and I was one of them.'

And his first Test? '1952–3, Sydney,' he said. 'My first Test wicket was Alf Valentine. I noticed he died recently. I don't think he ever got over it.' With not a hint of self-satisfaction or vanity, he had no idea his 500th Test was approaching until someone told him. Then, the man who still arrived earlier than anyone else to set up his little nest in the corner of the commentary box, with his laptop and his Laws of Cricket and his racing selections, went beavering away to tot it up for himself. His enthusiasm, his energy and his optimism had him closing on 600 by the time he announced his impending retirement in 2009. Quite remarkable that.

Benaud's 500th Test was also Andrew Strauss's first (he made a hundred) and Nasser Hussain's last (so did he) and the start of England's winning streak. With a sound captain, a settled side and a sizzling attack, they won all seven summer Tests in 2004, equalling England's best-ever run. They even beat the Aussies in the semi-final of the ICC Champions trophy – the most superfluous tournament in history – before losing a pulsating final to the West Indies. England still hadn't ever won a serious one-day trophy. But with Sky TV signing up all English cricket *exclusively live!* from 2006 for a cool £200m, the coffers were bursting. So everything was rosy in the English garden.

NINETEEN

Cometh the Hour, Cometh the Man (or Two)

All roads led to the 2005 Ashes. Benaud and Hussain
would be commentating, Warne, Flintoff and Strauss
would be playing, Murali bowling for Lancashire, Lara
and Tendulkar would be watching, and Steve Waugh
would be adding another chapter to his book about
clipping his toenails. Sorry, 'Tugga', you were a fine
player and a stunning captain but why always so stern?
Don't you want to sometimes get out and have some
fun?

'Eighteen years' was the phrase on everybody's lips.
The longest continuous sequence that England had
been denied the Ashes. It was a colossal burden to
carry. But England could look at it another way. It was
an ignominious record for the Aussies to lose. And
England had a team capable at least of competing.
Didn't they? The same squad had been doing the
business for twelve months now, while the Aussies were
obviously stuttering. There was one more ingredient to
blend into the mix.

Having been lured to Notts by their director of cricket, Clive Rice, in 2001, Kevin Pietersen had done his four years' residential qualification in county cricket and taken international cricket by storm. After a low-key entry in Zimbabwe, he strode on stage in his former South African homeland, making three centuries in seven one-day internationals. It was an astonishing arrival.

The man with the dead skunk for a hairstyle inflicted the same damage on the Australians in June during a series of one-day internationals, and the first ever Twenty20 international, which England won at a canter. His innings of 91 not out at Bristol, to haul England to victory from the parlous position of 160-6, was breath-taking in its audacity, as were the tabloid stories about his love life.

It was all the more bewildering then when he was not an automatic selection for the first Ashes Test. Graham Thorpe, a distinguished servant, clinging on with runs against Bangladesh, on their first tour of England, was expected to hold his place. But the selectors got it right. For the Lord's Test they ditched Thorpe and promoted Pietersen. The force was with him.

The first Test was electric. The teams were like dogs who'd been cooped up for days with their teeth bared being let out to tear at each other's flesh. Harmison smashed Langer on the arm and cut Ponting's face, Hoggard ripped through Hayden, Flintoff bounced out Langer, Jones cleaned up the middle order. England were in Australia's faces. Glenn McGrath retaliated with a ruthless masterclass in how to use the Lord's slope.

England conceded a lead of 35 and eventually capitulated but Pietersen's input was vital. In the first innings he started cautiously, but then, as wickets fell, he took the attack to McGrath, hammering him through the covers and launching him memorably into the old Lord's pavilion. The members spluttered into their Chablis. In the second innings he creamed Warne gloriously through the covers, and slog swept him for six. Although England were defeated, Pietersen had shown them the way forward and that was not to sit back and be trodden on.

Australian complacency contributed to the turn-around. Ponting put England in at Edgbaston, almost out of pure conceit, especially since McGrath, his principal bowler, had just trodden on a ball and was out of the match. England were far more forthright from the word go. Trescothick crunched the ball through the covers, Strauss, his dapper partner, advanced up the pitch and plonked Warne over the top as he had in the nets against England's special Merlyn spin-bowling machine, a large ball-firing contraption with flashing lights which looked like something off *Doctor Who*. You half expected it to say, 'Exterminate!' Pietersen, undaunted by the Australians declaring 'The Ego has landed!' when he walked in, unveiled his one-legged whip through mid-wicket, christened the 'flamingo shot' by David Hopps in the *Guardian*. Flintoff swatted them for six off his nose. Spared the law and order of McGrath, England batted as if on speed. They were 407 all out in a day.

The match carried on at that tempo. Vaughan

out-thought the Australian batsmen, tempering their aggression with boundary sweepers, Warne outsmarted the English. Flintoff frollicked alone on the burning deck. Then, with the Australians 47-0 chasing 282 to win, he bowled an over that will rank with anything unleashed by Holding, Marshall, Wasim and the rest. He was still on a high from his batting; his second ball hurried Langer and ricocheted into his stumps. The third and fifth (a no ball) whistled past Ponting's edge at 90mph. The fourth and sixth rapped him on the pad. The seventh left him late, took the edge and he was gone. Flintoff's primeval reaction roared England on. This was the moment they began to believe.

The final morning, at which point Australia needed 107 with 2 wickets remaining, was agonizing. Warne kept flaying wide balls through the covers or waltzing across his stumps to flick through mid-wicket, Harmison seemed unable to find his rhythm, edges flew between Vaughan's carefully staggered slips. Warne finally trod on his wicket, but Flintoff bowled a way-ward yorker that went for 4 byes, and Harmison did the same. Simon Jones dropped a difficult chance at third man.

Then it was 1 wicket left, 4 to win. At that precise moment the match, the Ashes and English cricket, that struggling sideshow pottering along in the shadows, seemed dead. Gone up in smoke. Puff! The urn was heading for Australia, probably for ever, and, with the Premiership due to begin the following weekend, it would be an endless diet of Wayne Rooney and José Mourinho and three-in-a-bed 'roastings' from then on.

Harmison overpitched, Lee square-drove and that, everyone assumed, was that. Yet, somehow Vaughan had managed to leave a man out for the shot and the ball went straight to him. Five yards either way and the series was over. Then Harmison gloved Kasprowicz, Geraint Jones sprawled and caught and the celebrations began. England had won one of the most incredible Test matches by 2 runs, and anyone watching needed a stiff drink. Luckily it was past noon. Flintoff and Lee lingered in the middle, victor and vanquished in manly embrace, a classic vision of sporting solidarity.

England had many heroes from then on. Vaughan for his spirited batting and enterprising leadership. Trescothick for his booming strokes. Strauss for his calm reconnaissance. Pietersen for his swashbuckling attack, especially that inspired 158 at the Oval after Vaughan had implored him to 'go for it'. (It was the same score as D'Oliveira's in that infamous Oval Test thirty-seven years earlier.) Giles for his safe catching and nerveless runs. Hoggard for his trusty bowling and That Cover Drive at Trent Bridge, with England faltering at the penultimate hurdle (they finally got home by a knuckle-chewing three wickets to go 2–1 up). Jones for his express pace and wicked stare. The People for flogging halfway across the country to get a seat and clapping and cheering till they were hoarse. All the players for dealing with the general hysteria. God for allowing every game to go tantalizingly to the wire.

And of course Flintoff. Belligerent batsman, buccaneering bowler and bucket-handed fielder. He really was a team in one. He had begun the series as the most capped

Englishman (45) never to play a Test against Australia. He ended it as a colossus who was, on that final Sunday morning at the Oval, systematically cutting Australia down on his own. Ball after ball was rammed in short of a length at a challenging pace and on a testing line. There was no let-up. He had out-Glenned McGrath. His 5-78 was a triumph of fitness and skill and willpower, accompanied by an impassioned wicket-taking holler that belonged more to a New Zealand *haka*. He was becoming the bowler batsmen least liked to face. He was England's relentless enforcer.

And he could drink them all under the table too. As he proved after the umpires had ostentatiously lifted the bails to declare the match a draw, and the urn had been presented to Michael Vaughan in an emotional ceremony and the lap of honour had been done to roars of 'Land of Hope and Glory' from the ecstatic flag-waving supporters. England had won the Ashes at last, their most distinguished sporting achievement for thirty-nine years. It definitely entitled someone to piss in the prime minister's garden.

In the sober light of the next day, or it may have been the day after that, it was worth considering how they had done it. Central contracts ensured consistency of selection. That was vital. Only twelve players were used, and England was *their* team (not Hampshire or Kent or Gloucestershire). Under Vaughan's calm, calculated leadership they had experienced a sort of catharsis, rather like England's world-conquering rugby team in 2003. It was an almost orgasmic coming-together. There was a real sense of unity and belonging and enjoyment.

The turning point was the nerve-jangling draw at Old Trafford which Australia transparently celebrated as if it were a victory.

After that, England, personified by the sharp penetration of Simon Jones, had more energy. The Australian fast bowlers showed their age. The England bowlers' command of reverse swing, especially from round the wicket to the Australian left-handers, was hugely influential. Flintoff more or less wiped the dangerous Adam Gilchrist out of the equation with that method. They had an Australian, Troy Cooley, to thank for it (and when he returned to coach Australia, the tables were dramatically turned). And ultimately cricket is about match winners. England had two – the freak show Pietersen and the man-mountain Flintoff. Australia had only one – the virtuoso Warne. And 2–1 was the final score. In the end it was all about hunger. And England, for once, were the more ravenous.

Where Do You Go To, My Lovely?

The impact of the 2005 Ashes was huge. It reinvigorated the parts of English cricket that no buy-two-get-one-free, or naked-player calendars, or Kwik Cricket sets to schools could reach. The six-week drama drew in people normally not remotely interested in the game. Kids abandoned their footballs in neighbours' gardens and got out their stumps and bats. The sales of Woodworm, the company that sponsored Pietersen and Flintoff's bats, outstripped supply. England players advertised posh four-wheel drives and designer gear and cosmetics. They were invited on talk shows. They were followed by paparazzi. They won *Strictly Come Dancing*. They were national property. Cricket *was* the new football.

And then everything fell apart. English cricket has an uncanny knack of shooting itself in the foot. In particular Flintoff's foot. He played a full part in England's subsequent winter but hardly at all thereafter. Test matches and one-day internationals came thick and fast – roughly fourteen Tests and thirty one-dayers a year – and his body couldn't take it. One ankle operation followed another. The Ashes-winning bowling quartet – Harmison, Hoggard, Jones and Flintoff – never played together again. By 2007, they were all injured. Michael Vaughan's suspect knee gave way, and Marcus Trescothick's mind couldn't handle the constant pressure of international travel and performance. Player turnover returned and with it inconsistency. Only two of the next eight series were won.

Perhaps, then, it was a good thing that not many people could see them. The transfer of all cricket *exclusively live!* to Sky meant a reduction in the viewing audience of a peak of 9.5 million during the Ashes to an average of around 300,000 on Sky. Suddenly the game was being denied the oxygen of exposure. Sky might get decent audiences for the odd game (600,000 if they were lucky, and only if it was presented by a naked bimbo), but a Test match had ceased to be a *national* event as people happened across it because they could all get it and word seeped across garden fences that the Aussies were getting a pummelling.

Of course Sky's money was valuable, to sustain the central contracts and the counties – an average county pro was now on £60,000 a year, and an England player might earn £400,000 – and the swelling ECB staff. But it was a contract with an insatiable beast. Because the more you get, the more they want. They've paid top dollar. So extra matches are crammed into the schedule to satisfy a satellite broadcaster's gluttonous appetite for something to show, the players are worn out and the product's just skin and bone. The exclusive deal with Sky is in danger of administering the last rites to English cricket as a major sporting influence. Cricket became the only major sport with no live terrestrial presence. It could relegate it to the status of rugby league or snooker. God help us all then.

PR own goals – like the abandoning of a Test because an umpire has confiscated the ball and the team won't come out to play – don't help. Exactly twelve months after the epic Ashes series, the cricket on Sky was invisible not just to two thirds of the population but to everyone. An umpire on his high horse about ball tampering had got a Test match abandoned. It was Darrell Hair, a strong official who occasionally got an over-inflated sense of his own importance, who slapped a 5-run penalty on the Pakistanis for supposedly scratching the ball at the Oval.

When the penalty was issued the Pakistan captain Inzamam-ul-Haq played dumb for a while. But, after apparently being influenced by one or two more re-actionary types in the dressing room, he refused to bring his players out after tea unless the implied accusation of cheating had been withdrawn. So Hair and his rather more benign colleague, Billy Doctrove, emerged in front of a Sunday afternoon full house, removed the bails and called off the match.

The umpires had applied the letter of the law and the Pakistanis had reacted with impassioned obstinacy. There were lots of emotions flying around. The umpires were intransigent, the Pakistanis petulant, the ICC incompetent. The one commodity lacking amongst all the involved parties was common sense. And the chief sufferers were the paying public as usual.

As a 'witness' in the subsequent inquest, I inspected the offending ball some time later, presented to me in a lawyer's office wrapped in cling film. There were some scratches on it which *probably* were imparted by finger-nails. But you couldn't be sure. Balls get naturally scratched and scuffed on dry, bare pitches, and bowlers have become very adept at mimicking the typical abrasions a ball might suffer being banged into the pitch and/or whacked to the boundary, to help it swing. They are, after all, cricket's burglars and will use every-thing in their power to steal a wicket while leaving little or no evidence at the crime scene.

After the inquest, Hair was suspended from the inter-national umpires' panel, while Inzamam, who displayed a poor understanding of English, was initially banned from a few one-day internationals for bringing the game into disrepute. England were awarded the match, though some time later it was declared a draw, and then later still granted to England again, a decision which took a number of high-level ICC meetings to achieve. *Haven't these people got anything better to do?*

In the final equation, it was patently ludicrous that a Test match had been abandoned for a few fingernail excursions on a ball, which, incidentally, had had no influence on its behaviour. But cricket's superiority complex and labyrinthine cultural landscape often produce bizarre outcomes, perpetuating the game in people's minds as the theatre of the absurd.

That's Another Fine Mess You've Gotten Me Into

While English cricket spent the year after the 2005 Ashes unravelling, the Australians spent it reconstructing. The loss of the urn had sent shockwaves through their egos, and they installed a sixteen-month campaign to reclaim it and their arrogant beach-strut. There were soul-searching weekends, boot camps in Queensland and assiduous recruitment. The prime target, the Tasmanian bowling coach Troy Cooley, who had so successfully orchestrated the destruction of his compatriots, was quickly secured.

His absence was immediately felt by England. Entrusted with the opening over of the 2006–7 Ashes, Steve Harmison, the bowler Cooley had for five years cleverly distracted from thoughts of his Ashington hearth, produced the second most famous Ashes delivery with his first effort. It was the diametric opposite of That Warne Ball, barely landing on the cut strip and finishing up in the hands of the stand-in captain, Andrew Flintoff, at second slip. Wide? It wasn't as good as that. Geoff Boycott reckoned you would have needed his moom's clothes prop to reach it. It was a delivery born of apprehension and lack of preparation and symbolized the mess England were in.

Arriving without their injured captain (Vaughan), they soon lost their senior opening batsman (Trescothick) to mental fatigue, had only two warm-up matches before the first two Tests, the shortest build-up ever, and two of the bowlers (Giles and Anderson) hadn't bowled in anger for six months. Compounding all that, half the team had never played an Ashes Test in Australia before, including Flintoff, chosen as captain ahead of Strauss because it was felt he would be more 'up and at 'em'. England's fragile mental state, poor levels of fitness, inexperience and general inadequacy left them hardly able to take on Cleethorpes 2nd XI, never mind the undisputed world champions, and they were soon down and out.

Echoing their previous tour, England conceded 346-3 on that first day in Brisbane to the run-hungry, merciless Australians. They showed the virtue of having had most of the previous seven months off, during which England had laboured through seven Tests and twenty one-day internationals. Harmison, whose bowling had been out of sync for a while, revealed himself as a fragile ornament. The Australians smashed him to pieces. In spite of valiant bowling from Flintoff England were soon looking at 403 just to save the follow-on. They fell 246 short and subsided to a massive defeat.

To their credit England staged a temporary fightback in Adelaide, four days later, posting 551-6 dec in the first innings. Paul Collingwood made a doughty double century, and 'The Ego', Kevin Pietersen, made light of the Aussies now deridingly calling him 'Figjam' ('Fuck I'm Good, Just Ask Me') to cream a big hundred. But England's resilience deserted them on the fifth morning after Australia had all but drawn level. On a blisteringly hot day the second-wicket pair of Strauss and Bell was becalmed, having sailed along merrily the night before, as Warne produced one of his mesmerizing spells. Hapless batsmen panicked, wickets crashed and suddenly the Aussies only needed 168 in a session and a half to win. They breezed home at 5 an over and were soon 2–0 up. England's timid mentality – selecting the half-fit Giles ahead of the impressive Panesar, batting their best player, Pietersen, at no.5 to 'protect' him – had been brutally exposed. England were still stuck in 2005 as the world moved on.

Panesar finally got the call for the third Test in Perth and took a wicket in his first over. But England's first innings was tame, the Australian batting ran amok in the second innings, with Gilchrist racking up a hundred in 57 balls with an orgy of sixes, and at lunch on the fifth day only Panesar's rickety defence stood between Australia and the Reclamation. Two balls after the interval Panesar was bowled by Warne to give him 699 Test wickets. The Ashes were Australia's. After a small blip, normal service had been resumed.

The unedifying sight of the Aussies celebrating with each other and the crowd before even shaking the England players' hands was an extension of their ruth-less campaign. They had vowed not to fraternize with England players until the series was secured, or even acknowledge them in some cases. It revealed how much they had wanted this outcome and how poor their sense of sportsmanship was. The two are unhappy bedfellows, which is where English cricket has always had a big problem. In the modern game wanting to win *and* being nice are rarely reconcilable.

The cold draught of reality had struck England long before they arrived to unseasonally icy temperatures in Melbourne for the Shane Warne show. He had announced before the fourth Test that he would be retiring after the series, so this was his own public's chance to pay final homage. On an improbably chilly day that had the British hordes wondering why they hadn't stayed at home, and on a pitch described in *Wisden* as a 'shitheap', the master leg-spinner still conjured 5 wickets.

The first, Strauss bowled through the gate, was his triumphant 700th. That it was a regulation leg break rather than anything more mysterious was entirely appropriate. Forget the theatre of Warne for a moment. In essence what he had really done over the course of fourteen years was perfect the art of the hard-spun leg break in all its manifestations. The rest was all just bright lights and make-up.

The contest, if you could call it that, lasted not quite three days, giving all the players a little breathing space before the final curtain call of Warne, McGrath and, as it turned out, Langer, in Sydney. The day before the game Langer gave an emotional press conference shot through with Aussie fervour. He clasped his baggy green cap in his hand throughout. He had the luxury of hitting the winning runs, after a masterclass of seam bowling from McGrath, every ball landing on an area the size of a large sirloin steak, had cut England's second innings to a sad 147 all out. England had not only been whitewashed but painted totally out of the picture.

Many excuses were tossed out for their lamentable display. Some believed the coachload of players' partners and children, resembling a Thomson Holidays trip to Lanzarote, was an onerous burden (and you do wonder when you see an England fast bowler struggling to feed a two-year-old his Ricicles an hour or so before he was due to open the attack in an Ashes Test). Fingers were pointed at the absurdly short build-up and the ridiculously inexperienced captain, who was barely on speaking terms with the coach by the end.

In fact they were simply overcome by a level of intensity they could never match. In 2005, with a decent side at the top of their form, England had won the series. But it was by the skin of their teeth against a complacent Australian side. Hell hath no fury like an Aussie scorned. This time they were armed to the nines. They had their hands round their victim's throat from the first day and never let go until it had totally expired.

They had one whopping advantage: the most successful pair of bowlers in Test history: Glenn McGrath, the relentless predator equipped with precision engineering, and Shane Warne, full of spite and variation within a suffocating blanket of accuracy. By the end of their Test careers they had taken 1,001 wickets in partnership, or 9.63 per Test, about half the number required to win a match. Of the 104 Tests they played together, Australia won seventy-one. They made their team practically invincible.

To draw parallels with tennis, McGrath was Björn Borg, ice-cool and unyielding, the man who never gave in. With a robust physique and a wristy flick, he sent deliveries flying down, one angled to the right, the next to left, always to an awkward length. He was impossible to dominate. I once asked him what he focused on when he was bowling. 'Nothing,' he said. 'I run in with a completely clear head.'

Warne was John McEnroe, outrageously gifted and ultra-competitive, a natural entertainer with an equal abhorrence of cocky batsmen and stubborn umpires. More than once his expression at a denied lbw said, 'You can't be serious!' Intuitively he understood an opponent's weaknesses, always worked to expose them and invariably succeeded. Imagine five sets against Borg and McEnroe. That's what it was like for batsmen all those years.

A Fistful of Rupees

The retirement of Warne and McGrath – from Test cricket at any rate – coincided with the end of an era. It was the culmination of a 130-year sequence when England v Australia was the biggest event in world cricket. History gave it the meaning, the quality of play gave it the depth, the Ashes urn gave it the X-factor that no other cricketing contest could match. The score in Test wins from the inception of the encounter in 1877 to 2007 was England

97, Australia 131 (draws 88). From 1989 to 2007 it was 34–9 to the Aussies. By rights the urn should at that point have been exported to Australia (it did do a brief tour Down Under during that last series, in its own box together with its own security guard) and left there as a memento of past superiorities.

The 2007 World Cup in the Caribbean just underlined the disintegration of cricket's old order. It was a chaos of planning and execution in hastily built, sparsely populated stadiums featuring exhausted players and bungling umpires and numerous one-sided matches. The ICC burdened it with petty guidelines like only allowing 'official' sponsors' products to be consumed, and paying security men to tell spectators to sit still and be quiet, and inviting useless cricketing countries like Bermuda and Holland. The tournament lasted an interminable six weeks, and from the early point when England lost to New Zealand and Australia walloped South Africa for 377, it was obvious who was going to be eliminated early and who was going to win.

The cricket was soon overshadowed by events off the field. First Andrew Flintoff was found drunk in charge of a pedalo at 4am, a fairly inconsequential event in the normal sequence of things. Lads will be lads. But it was bound to cause uproar after England had just lost to New Zealand and with another game to come thirty-six hours later, especially as he hadn't paid the $2.50 hire charge. Subconsciously Flintoff was challenging the coach Duncan Fletcher's authority, as a growing lad might his father. He picked the wrong moment, and was sent to his room with no supper.

A day later Bob Woolmer, Pakistan's highly respected coach, was found dead in his hotel room. The investigation was as badly botched as the rest of the event. First it was assumed he'd died of natural causes. Then the Jamaican police claimed he'd been strangled. Links with the match-fixing mafia were alleged, and Pakistan's loss to Ireland was regarded as suspicious. Some of the Pakistan team were even implicated in his death. It was suggested he'd been poisoned.

None of it added up. Woolmer was a decent, law-abiding citizen passionate about his job. His *raison d'être* had always been to find ways of improving individual players. He didn't have a Machiavellian bone in his body. In fact that was more likely to have been the problem. He had hardly any bone in his body and a little too much fat. Not ideal for such a demanding task anyway. But after weeks of intense speculation, an open verdict was recorded. His tragic end certainly added to the feeling that coaching a national cricket team was not a job for the faint-hearted. Eight coaches, including England's Duncan Fletcher, who had become bitter and forlorn, were replaced after the World Cup. The tournament ended in total farce when Australia had to bowl three pointless overs in the dark to complete a match they had already won. There've been better organized pub crawls.

The World Cup's global audience died once India were eliminated from the tournament. Suddenly 400 million viewers had become a few lads in a sports bar in Brisbane. The Indian administrators probably didn't care. They had already pocketed $400m for the TV rights to the World Cup, as well as $612m for four years of India's domestic cricket. The Indian Cricket Board had been flexing their corporate muscle for some time, refusing to co-operate with the ICC or other countries on fixtures or finance. They were becoming increasingly independent and occasionally stroppy.

But no one was quite prepared for the announcement in September 2007 of the Indian Premier League, a revolutionary Twenty20 competition – a sort of Champions League of cricket – which would attract players from all over the world and catapult their earnings into the stratosphere. Cricket's sleeping giant had finally roused itself to push the small fry out of the way with a sweep of its big fat cheque book. The landscape of the game would be utterly changed, probably for ever. Unless the ICC eventually came round from its hundred-year coma.

TWENTY

Indian the Conqueror

This story has gone on longer than it was supposed to. There wasn't meant to be a chapter 20. But Twenty20 – or 'twennee twennee' in common Americanized parlance – is all the rage now so it makes sense to have one. There's even been the Twenty20 for 20 million. The only event with more twenties in the title would be an opticians' conference on perfect vision in the year 2020.

As the first decade of the twenty-first century elapses it has become clear that the 2007 World Cup was a sort of death. A final nail in the coffin of cricket's Imperial masters. Since then the game has leapt over obstacles and jumped through hoops and fallen down holes and crashed into trees and emerged a rather different animal. It is an animal that has suddenly escaped from its enclosure but now isn't sure whether to stay close to home or career on into the unknown. It will have to make its own decision because its ageing keeper is lying infirm and helpless in a dark corner and the beast has grown too big to get it back in.

Subhash Chandra, an Indian media baron, let it loose. One of the founders of India's satellite TV revolution and owner of Zee TV, Chandra attempted three times in the 2000s to buy the telecast rights to Indian cricket and three times he was scuppered. So in July 2007 he set up a Twenty20 tournament for the benefit of his own channel featuring six teams of internationals playing for a $1m first prize. He called it the Indian Cricket League (ICL), though a more appropriate title would have been the Fit of Pique. In an eerie parallel with the Packer enterprise, he recruited Tony Greig as an adviser and announced Brian Lara, who now held the record for most runs in Tests, as a major signing. Other, rather less celebrated names, mostly coming to the end of their international careers, joined up.

The move was a huge pinprick to the ego of the Indian board's marketing whiz, Lalit Modi, the man behind the BCCI's lucrative TV deals. He was stung into action. Within a month he had declared the ICL unauthorized and announced a grander, officially sanctioned version, the Indian Premier League (IPL), to be launched in April 2008. Having graduated in the US, his designs, which had been on the backburner for some time, were influenced by American sports with team franchises, salary caps, player auctions and so on.

The response was cautious at first, but once an Indian team with a phalanx of young stars had won the inaugural ICC World Twenty20 tournament in South Africa, watched by about 400 million on TV, Modi was deluged with would-be owners and sponsors. As soon as the players heard about a prize fund of $2.5m they too were quick to present their noses to the trough.

The ECB, miffed that some trumped-up Indian had muscled in on a format they believed they had invented, tried to spike Modi's guns by declaring that centrally contracted players would not be available owing to England's tight summer schedule. It didn't work. It put the players' backs up and their performances continued to be mediocre. In fact it just re-emphasized the feeling that India, the country that now generated 80 per cent of the game's global income, were progressive and that England had feet of clay.

For over a decade, TV executives had sought a viable alternative to football as the perfectly packaged sporting entertainment. The IPL had the potential to be it, as Sony obviously believed, paying an astonishing $1bn for the TV rights. As well as attracting all the best players in the world, just as football's Champions League had done, it was offering top-class cricket at a time when people could actually watch it (i.e. in the evening). After 150 years of the first-class game in England this was only just beginning to dawn on the cricket authorities. Despite being vastly richer, the English game's rulers were still mainly shuffling about pecking at scraps like farmyard hens.

Many counties were still run by unwieldy amateur committees, and at one typical meeting I attended in early 2008, more time was spent debating how many visiting officials from other counties should be allowed into the dining room for lunch on match days, and how much they should be charged, than in discussing the way forward for a struggling team. I kid you not.

The announcement of the IPL was a timely initiative for Indian cricket. Several years of underwhelming performance by the world's richest and most populous cricketing nation had resulted in the sport stagnating and being eclipsed in the television ratings by reality programmes. There were still legions of kids playing cricket on the streets and maidans of the subcontinent, but they craved appearing on *Deal or No Deal* rather than opening the batting for India. Indian cricket badly needed an injection of foreign expertise and sophistication.

It soon had that. A list of ninety top foreign players was drawn up and made available to the eight teams, who had been bought by a collection of Indian super rich and Bollywood stars. So it now had glamour as well. The city-based teams all had iconic stars – Tendulkar at Mumbai, Dravid at Bangalore, Ganguly at Kolkata – and now the owners could play their very own game of Fantasy Cricket, as they perused a mouth-watering array of talent, each with a reserve price, to select and purchase at a special player auction. They could even give their teams silly names: Bangalore Royal Chargers, Kolkata Night Riders, Chennai Super Kings, which sounded more like a cigarette brand.

The auction idea was an interesting spin on an Indian covered market. The players were the glistening trinkets, the owners the intrigued purchasers haggling for their goods. You could almost hear a vendor saying, 'Adam Gilchrist special price $400,000!' In the end India's charismatic wicketkeeper Mahendra Singh Dhoni attracted the highest bid – $1.5m – with Australia's

Andrew Symonds next at $1.3m. Shane Warne was bought for a bargain $450,000 by Rajasthan Royals, part owned by the English entrepreneur Manoj Badale.

The players, virtually to a man, were ecstatic, since they were about to earn in five weeks what it normally took them three years to make. The only people salivating more were their agents. Two unheralded New Zealanders, Brendon McCullum and Jacob Oram – one-day specialists – would rake in enough to buy a small Pacific island. Hyderabad's line-up of Symonds, Gilchrist, Shahid Afridi and Herschelle Gibbs represented a hard-hat zone for bowlers. And probably spectators. It was all set to be a carnival of cricket.

Perhaps the most amazing thing about the IPL was that it more than lived up to its hype. After six months of sustained build-up with television ads and celebrity press conferences and 50ft advertising hoardings from which players glared down with Tarantino expressions proclaiming, 'Be scared, be sh*t scared', it was destined to fall as flat as a dead skate. And reek of disappointment.

But the opening night in Bangalore exploded on to the sporting globe like a giant Catherine wheel. Thumping dance music, American cheerleaders and a spectacular laser show whipped 40,000 T-shirt-wearing, chip-eating, beer-supping Indians into a frenzy, after which McCullum carved, crashed and creamed his way to a pyrotechnic 158 not out including thirteen sixes. It was where cricket and mass entertainment finally met. The soporific atmosphere of the St Lawrence Ground, Canterbury, where Kent at that moment were pottering along at 2 an over against Notts in front of a handful of arthritic pensioners, seemed light years away.

The IPL's pulsating rhythm continued right through to the final more than a month later. That match, between Chennai Super Kings and Warne's unfancied Rajasthan Royals, went right to the wire. With the scores level the last delivery, bowled by Chennai's Lakshmipathy Balaji to Rajasthan's Sohail Tanvir, was the richest ball in cricket history. It was worth a cool $1m. Tanvir inside-edged it past mid-wicket to clinch the Royals' win and the $2m prize. Warne, of course, was in at the end. Even in semi-retirement he was the decisive influence.

The tournament had been a stunning success. Every one of the fifty-odd matches was played out to packed houses who were richly entertained by music and dance and acrobatics as well as the cricket. Each IPL match had the sense of a must-see-and-be-seen-at event the like of which the booming Indian middle classes had never experienced before. It was a huge boon to the players' talents too. Young Indians were rubbing shoulders with the greats of the international game – Warne, Gilchrist, McGrath, Sangakkara – and acquiring new skills. Deceptive back-of-the-hand slower balls had been in evidence, clever use of bouncers, delicate paddle shots against attempted yorkers and a flip over the wicket-keeper's head called the 'frying pan'. The IPL was a hotbed of physical exploration. It was a sporting brainstorm.

After one floodlit match in Delhi, I mingled with the happy throng of baseball-capped, replica-shirted supporters – not a sari or a sarong in sight – and headed out into the street. Four lanes of bumper-to-bumper traffic inched along the dual carriageway in both directions, their occupants blaring horns and waving flags. Along the road was a doleful looking little donkey trapped in the central reservation resigned to watching the traffic pass. It ought to have had 'English Cricket' painted on its tummy.

All the other Test-playing countries immediately began planning and scheduling their own 20-over premier leagues. The ICC were put under increasing pressure to make space for the IPL in the congested international calendar. They will be obliged to because players will always gravitate towards the money, and no one can compete with India's resources.

Inevitably flat-earthers all proclaimed that this was the end of cricket as we knew it. From here, the game would be boiled down more and more to a sequence of one-hour slogathons. Twenty20, Ten10 and Five5. The longer form would go the same way as the Dodo and the Sinclair C5. It was already an endangered species in some countries. How long till it was extinct? (These are the same types, by the way, who warned that disposable nappies and boil-in-the-bag rice signalled the end of civilization.)

Actually, Test cricket's future was fine if the IPL's opening ceremony was anything to go by. As the eight tournament captains were introduced – Warne, Tendulkar, Dravid and the others – heavy emphasis was placed on their Test match statistics. 'Ladies and gentlemen – Shane Warne, taker of 708 Test wickets!!' Vast applause. 'Sachin Tendulkar, scorer of 11,000 Test runs and thirty-eight Test centuries!!!' Bedlam. (Mind you, there is hysteria for Sachin when he picks his nose, and a clamour for his bogies.) Test match success was, for the time being, the main barometer by which players were judged (and therefore priced) in the IPL. And, similarly to an athlete's perception of the Olympics, a cricketer appreciates that a Test match is the true measure of his ability.

For the spectator, Test cricket was a full and wholesome meal. It might take a bit of digesting sometimes, but you weren't generally feeling hungry half an hour later. Twenty20, on the other hand, ought to be accompanied by a government health warning. For all its novelty and tastiness, it was about as nutritious and fulfilling as a 7-day a week diet of McDonald's, and dangerously addictive. It had rejuvenated an ailing game, but if spectators were allowed to overdose on it, they would soon become like Morgan Spurlock, of *Super Size Me* fame. You can see the banners now: 'Wanna suffer mood swings, sexual dysfunction and liver damage? Then consume three Twenty20 matches a day for a month . . .'

As cricket's marketers attempt to stuff the schedules with Twenty20 tournaments, they should reflect on that. Too much Twenty20 cricket will make a lot of people quite sick.

Lost Soul(s)

One trusts, of course, that the people who run the game are sane. But that is a huge assumption. The evidence of

417

the last year suggests that English cricket administrators are a bunch of dosh-seeking, ego-driven lunatics. And the year before that, and . . . The instant success of the IPL set them off on an orgy of prospecting, trying to find their own goldmine. So far it has resulted only in a humiliating fall down a number of black holes. The deepest is the one left by Sir Allen Stanford.

The digging began in the summer of 2008. Anxious to re-establish their hegemony, the ECB, under the chairmanship of a master of the universe, Giles Clarke, announced various initiatives, notably the establishment of an English Premier League, a lavishly sponsored Twenty20 tournament featuring the eighteeen counties, and including overseas players and foreign teams. Despite counter-proposals of a city-franchise-based competition, they remained wedded to the county framework. Well, *of course* they did. The ECB *are* the counties.

Rumours of an English-run champions league, bankrolled to the tune of $750m by an Abu Dhabi businessman, surfaced. This alienated the Indians, the Australians and the South Africans, who were already structuring a tournament, incorporating the English, with the same man. A Texan sugar daddy – Stanford, so self-satisfied you could see he wanted to lick himself – landed on the Nursery ground at Lord's in a company-branded helicopter (later revealed to have been hired for the day from Battersea) to announce his Twenty20 for $20m. This alienated everyone from the Lord's groundsman with his 'Keep off the grass' sign to normal, decent sports lovers (the rest of us) with a distaste for anything tacky and superficial. The concept of one match played for $20m between England and the 'Stanford All Stars' was exactly that.

The result was meaningless to everyone except the twenty-two participants (and their families and agents), it was not part of anything, or involving two official sides, and the individual performances wouldn't be registered in the annals. It wasn't a cricket match – it was a reality TV show with bats and balls and some big lolly on offer. Basically it was a sweetener to aggrieved England players eyeing up the Indian pudding. Crucially, it allowed the ECB to keep control. It was a giant raspberry to the Indian board. But individual egos got in the way of common sense and integrity. And when the whole Stanford empire was declared bogus, it was the English who ended up with pips on their faces.

To be fair to the beleaguered administrators, change was happening so fast it was almost impossible to keep abreast of it. They needed to install speed cameras and traffic-calming humps and get everyone to slow down a bit. On the field too. Runs were coming in torrents. Previously unimaginable targets were being attained (South Africa successfully chased 435 to win against Australia in a one-day international in Joahnnesburg), totals were exploding (Surrey made 496 in a 50-over match, Worcestershire 227 in 20), Yuvraj Singh hit six sixes in an over, and Kevin Pietersen hit two maximums batting left-handed. One went over a right-hander's extra cover, the other, to a deliberate slower ball, sailed over long-off like a Phil Mickelson five iron. They were two of the most amazing shots ever played. 'I couldn't hit my sweeps that far, and I *am* left-handed,' said David Gower.

Pietersen had already demonstrated his exceptional combination of skill, power and outrageous intent by reverse-sweeping Muralitharan for six in a Test match at Edgbaston. But these huge switch hits were charting new territory, primarily because he was actually changing the order of his hands on the bat at the moment of release, to hold it like a true left-hander. That and his quick two-step to reverse his body position enabled him to hit the ball phenomenal distances. It made the original reverse sweep – such an outrageous innovation at the time – resemble a mere toe in the ocean.

As with anything revolutionary, it immediately raised hackles, with suggestions that the shot be outlawed because he was temporarily turning himself into a left-hander, therefore messing up field settings and denying lbw chances. Others countered that the risk of such a premeditated shot outweighed the gain. It was left to that august body the MCC to arbitrate. We all held our breath. Knowing them, Pietersen might have his hands tied, his qualification rescinded and be sent back to Pietermaritzberg with his head shorn. But of course, he was a *batsman* and he played for *England*. So happily, this was their verdict:

M.C.C. believes that the 'switch-hit' stroke is exciting for the game of cricket. Indeed, the stroke conforms to the Laws of Cricket and will not be legislated against.

Instead of a rebuke it was a celebration of cricket's

first-ever truly ambidextrous batsman. The MCC were growing up.

England, although a team truly reflecting its multi-cultural society with a Yorkshireman as captain, a couple of Lancastrians, two Geordies, three public schoolboys, a Sikh, a Hindu, a South African and an Australian, remained stunted. Despite a change of coach (Peter Moores), post-Ashes performance remained woefully inconsistent. Taking this to heart, an exasperated Michael Vaughan resigned as captain once the Test series against South Africa had been surrendered to Graeme Smith's resilient side.

Now Pietersen was captain as well. Initially he seemed to refresh the parts other Boers could not reach. He scored centuries, his energy was infectious and England won five matches in a row. The two alpha males in the team – himself and Flintoff – were forging a productive partnership. But the final one-dayer of the summer – at Cardiff, the newly appointed Test match venue – was a washout. And so, it turned out, was the rest of England's year.

The first-class counties, it was revealed, received £30m a year from the ECB to keep them afloat. It promoted complacency in the shires which were supposed to be centres of excellence, but in many cases were actually loss-making little fiefdoms. The money to prop them up was generated by the England team, who were obliged to play all the time to satisfy their ravenous paymasters (Sky TV), resulting in injuries and tired performances. Basically English cricket was eating itself.

There was one uplifting tale at domestic level in 2008.

Durham won the County Championship for the first time. At the St Lawrence Ground, Canterbury, beneath the shadow of the little sapling (the great 180-year-old lime tree blew down in 2005 and had a forty-page booklet dedicated to it entitled 'A Legend Dies'), Durham's energetic mix of home-grown talent and shrewdly selected imports steamrollered Kent to clinch their prize. They piled ecstatically on top of each other at the final wicket, embodying their attitude. They played cricket the way it should be played: hard but fair and with a sense of enjoyment. They mirrored their supporters: tough as moorland thicket – you have to be to watch cricket in the north-east – yet full of bonhomie inside.

The newest first-class county, untrammelled by history, Durham had got their blueprint right. With a freshly built ground they had created a stable environment in which to grow their own. Academies will be the bedrock of counties from now on. The flow of decent, available foreign players is declining to a trickle, so nurturing your own is vital. A number of Durham's players – the Harmisons, Collingwood, Mustard, Onions, Davies – grew up together at the academy. Like the Manchester United of the 1990s they were a family presided over by a dedicated, uncompromising father-figure, Geoff Cook. Their eight-man reservoir of feisty seamers was entirely home-bred.

Kent, one of the cradles of the game, was, by comparison, looking as dilapidated as its old ground. The loss to Durham cast them adrift. In 2009, exactly 300 years after their inaugural match, they were playing second-division championship cricket for the first time. They had paid the price for a short-term approach, devoting their focus to winning one-day trophies with some beefy South African all-rounders, rather than properly investing in the future. Their four-man seam attack was entirely imported.

Short-term borrowing or long-term investment? I suppose that is the dilemma facing all of us.

Twilight of the Gods

While the Indians' Twenty20 bonanza unfolded, Test cricket was still proving its ability to make dramatic headlines. In early December 2007 in Kandy, just up the road from his father's biscuit factory, Muttiah Muralitharan became the world's leading Test wicket-taker, bowling Paul Collingwood with a *doosra* to overhaul Shane Warne's tally of 708 victims. *709 Test wickets?* How would that have made S. F. Barnes (189) or Clarrie Grimmett (216) feel? Well, probably the same as the Wright brothers if they'd seen Concorde take off.

The debate resurfaced as to which of Murali or Warne was the better bowler. The comparison was awkward because they were so different. Murali was born with extraordinary joints. Apart from the permanent kink in his right elbow, there was also a double-jointed wrist which could rotate through 360 degrees and allow him to bend his hand back so far his middle finger touched his forearm. He should have been a contortionist rather than a cricketer. It enabled him to impart exceptional, and deceptive, spin to the ball. Apart from the fact that Warne existed mainly on a diet of pizza, beer and fags, there was nothing unusual about his body except large hands and very strong fingers.

Warne was an orthodox spinner, utilizing the traditional tricks of the leggie – the leg break, the top spinner and the googly – which had been around for generations. Murali was entirely unorthodox. There had never been a bowler like him, whirring down befuddling off breaks and top spinners from out of the back of the hand and hunting you down with his crazy eyes. He was basically a freak. Two things united them. They both spun the ball miles and were deadly accurate.

Once Murali's quirky biomechanics enabled him to develop the *doosra* – the ball that spun the other way – he became doubly effective, though not in Australia, where his 12 wickets cost 75 apiece – and, for a time, doubly controversial. Age, however, withered Warne's physical attributes, but he managed to remain potent because of a mastery of his art, an astute cricket brain and a provocative nature. For his perennial ability to outwit a batsman, to con him out of his wicket with artful deception, even in totally unfavourable conditions, he got the vote. He was the ultimate confidence trickster.

And yet the miracle of Murali was that, in an age of widespread television coverage and microscopic analysis, he was still largely unfathomable to most top players. They confessed they would rather have faced any of the great fast bowlers than him. They feared the humiliation of spin torture more than the jab of physical pain. He's heading towards 800 Test wickets now. Who knows where it will end? But be assured, no one will ever catch him.

That is surely true too of Sachin Tendulkar. In mid-October 2008, at the Mohali stadium, he steered a ball through the slips to eclipse Brian Lara's record and soon became the first batsman to 12,000 Test runs. Ricky Ponting, who quickly went to congratulate him, is probably the only man with any chance of overtaking him. But there's something perennial about Tendulkar, a suggestion born of his boyish, imperturbable looks and his calm, inexorable acquisition of runs.

If there was any gradual decline of Tendulkar's motivation it was not evident, and after the Mumbai terrorist attacks of November 2008 – a shocking assault at the very hub of engaging, industrious, smiling India – it was immediately banished. Promoting the short Test series against England, a sombre Tendulkar was shown on television about every five minutes looking straight into the camera and pronouncing, 'I play for India . . . now, more than ever.'

Tendulkar is a man of his word. In Chennai (formerly Madras) in the Test match that almost wasn't, he honoured England's courage and commitment in returning to India with one of his greatest performances. From the first day of the game he seemed imbued with added determination. As the Indian bowlers warmed up on a side pitch before the toss, he emerged fully padded and helmeted, stood to the side of the stumps and shadow-batted a series of deliveries, rehearsing the leave, the drive and the back cut. Each morning afterwards he grooved his strokes in a practice net more meticulously than he'd ever done. He was back for more practice in the twilight at the end of the day.

In the field he acknowledged his idolizing fans more than ever before, as if appreciating his responsibility towards them. At the crease he seemed more deliberate than usual, taking extra time between balls to properly assemble his thoughts and channel his concentration. England were treated to an exquisite exhibition of nimble footwork and neat deflection. He wielded his chunky 2lb 12oz blade like a scalpel, cutting his innings to a precise pattern. He manipulated the field. When Panesar pitched up he swept. At first the shot was intercepted, but soon the fielder was pushed back and he could nurdle the ball for one into the resultant gap. He toyed with the bowling. He could angle balls to deep cover in his sleep. There were forty-five singles in his innings and maidens were scarcer than Indian frowns.

No one was going to deny the favourite son of Mumbai hitting the winning runs in a record-breaking run-chase and registering a hundred. Immediately he was overcome with emotion, embracing his Sikh partner Yuvraj Singh, the Muslim fast bowler Zaheer Khan, a sari-clad ground assistant, in a vivid, impassioned statement of Indian unity. You could feel how much he desired this victory, to soothe the fears of his devoted subjects.

Two days later we meet in the middle in Mohali. Tendulkar is an unlikely-looking god. He stands there by the wicket dwarfed by the gigantic Andrew Flintoff and the strapping Yuvraj Singh, a boyish figure with a cherubic face whose Michelin Man-style pads come halfway up his thigh. He shuffles away from the conversation and brushes the Mohali pitch affectionately with a bat that looks too big for him. It is quite a weapon, heavy with edges two inches thick and a pick-up like a magician's wand. It is curved like an oar. 'I like a bow in it,' he says, 'I can't bat with anything else.'

We chat in the middle for half an hour. He speaks softly, sincerely, self-effacingly. We talk about the unusual way he acknowledged the crowd at Chennai. 'Sometimes I do it,' he says, 'but it is not my way,' he adds sheepishly. He casts his eyes down; an essentially shy, private person. He is not stiff or awkward but he generally avoids engaging with his fans. He has to. As soon as he makes eye contact with one, they will all expect it. And he will be trapped in adulation.

The Indian poet C. P. Surendran captured superbly what it is like to be Sachin Tendulkar:

Batsmen walk out into the middle alone. Not Tendulkar. Every time Tendulkar walks to the crease a whole nation, tatters and all, march with him to the battle arena. A pauper people pleading for relief, remission from the lifelong anxiety of being Indian, by joining in spirit their visored saviour . . . The poor Indian lifts his hands to Sachin Tendulkar in supplication; Give us respite, a sense of liberation; lift us up from the dark pit of our lives to well-lit places of the imagination with your skill-wrought perfection. Give us an idea of what a light thing life ought to be. Take our blessings but give us a break. Please win. Win for us losers.

Tendulkar never shirks this enormous responsibility. He spends almost every waking hour seeking that perfection, practising, planning, preparing. He rings his brother, the man who knows his game best, daily, talking bowlers and bat angles and shot selection. He looks at the pitch and contemplates how he will make runs on it. He is thankful for his talent and dutifully delivers it to his public, the majority of whom have nothing.

He reflects quietly on the first Test, complimenting England on their batting, virtually overlooking India's win. I say the result was fated, it was meant to be, and that the way he manipulated the bowling was masterly and amazing to watch. He chuckles with a mixture of pleasure and embarrassment. He has not a scrap of ego.

And then he is gone from the centre, from the roped-off pitch, from the place where he is only truly at peace, there in the middle with a bat in his hand. He returns to the real world to be photographed and congratulated and bombarded with a million demands, all of which he handles with total equanimity. He is a gracious god. We will never see his like again. Or maybe we will. His nine-year-old son is just beginning to show signs of useful batting talent. All things considered it is not the time to be a bowler. Unless you have a double-jointed arm.

Coming Round Full Circle

Harold Pinter wrote: 'Cricket is the greatest thing that God ever created on earth.' He grew up watching in the 1950s when Compton was in his pomp, Sobers had arrived and Dexter was emerging. He liked the game played with style and panache. But with commitment and honour too. He would have regarded the Stanford challenge as sacrilege. It was a total abuse of the game for one man's own ends. It was the definition of 'not cricket'. The England players found it pretty gratuitous too, from the moment they arrived in Antigua and found Stanford hanging around the dressing room and perching their wives on his knee, as if by divine right. He strode about, shaking hands and patting heads, as if he owned the place. Which, of course, he did.

The match itself was a disgrace. Embarrassed England were rolled out for 99, which the West Indians knocked off with uncontained glee without losing a wicket. One or two of them earned $1m for 1½ hours' 'labour' during which they neither batted nor bowled. Nice work if you can get it. The England players were relieved when it was all over. Pinter died soon afterwards. He was dismissed in the nick of time, before he had to endure any more of this nonsense.

Early in the new year Pietersen emailed his blueprint for England's way forward, as he had been asked to by the ECB. It didn't include Peter Moores as coach. His views were leaked and within days they had both been sacked. It brought a smile to the faces of the Australians, who had just sacrificed their fifteen years of impregnability at home to South Africa. By the time they heard the scandalous truth about Stanford, they were laughing like hyenas.

England travelled to the Caribbean with a new captain, Andrew Strauss, in his rightful place after being badly messed about for two years. He had got the job by default, symptomatic of the woeful lack of vision in the English game. Pietersen, being originally South African, is not manacled to the cumbersome and often ludicrous expectations of English cricket. He alone consistently rises above a morass of mediocrity. He manufactured a brilliant 97 in the first Test in Jamaica before skying a catch trying for a big six over mid-wicket. 'Dumb Slog Millionaire' railed the *Sun*.

The new umpire referrals system was being trialled during the series. Several times an innings a batsman or a fielding captain could ask for a decision to be reviewed by the third umpire. Dickie Bird thought it was a rum business. 'It's a sad day, a sad day,' he said sounding sad. 'I used to train with Barnsley football club in the winter doing little sprints so I could be quicker at getting into position for judging run-outs. They don't need to bother any more. They can just stand at the stumps and refer the decision upstairs.'

Interviewing prospective umpires will soon resemble Woody Allen movie auditions. ('Can you do an American accent?' he said to the English actress Rebecca Hall as he assembled a cast for his movie *Vicky Cristina Barcelona*. 'Yes,' she replied. 'OK,' said Woody, 'you're in.') The umpire's equivalent will be: 'Can you count to six while holding a couple of sweaters, a pair of sunglasses and a walkie-talkie?' 'Yes!' 'Right, you'll do.'

The whole of the England batting order should have been certified, never mind referred, when they were shot out for 51 in the second innings of the Jamaica Test. At 26–7, they were in danger of their lowest total ever until Flintoff, the world's first million-pound cricketer, having just been sold in the second IPL auction for $1.55m, supplied some meaty blows. (Pietersen, who was bowled for nought, went for the same price.) But 51 was still a pitiful score – you don't see it all that often even in village cricket these days – and it consigned England to series defeat in the West Indies.

If that was a poor lead-up to England's chances in the 2009 Ashes series, the news from the IPL – relocated to South Africa after the terrorist attacks in India – was worse. Both Flintoff and Pietersen – the latter nursing a lingering Achilles injury – broke down and were sent home from South Africa, causing further trouble for the ECB, who were predictably lambasted for allowing them to go. In truth, the administrators had submitted to player-power long ago. In some ways the situation was not dissimilar to the habit of amateurs like Gubby Allen of disappearing off to hobnob in Hollywood after a tour of Australia in the 1930s, deigning to return to England in June for the summer's Test series. The only difference now was that Flintoff and Pietersen were centrally contracted to England and therefore supposedly under their jurisdiction. But no one had been big enough to stand up to them. Or more precisely, to their lawyers.

Both men were placed in cotton wool for the first part

of the summer, as England continued their five-month scrap with the West Indies. It didn't help particularly. In fact it didn't help at all. Pietersen, who was rested from the early-summer one-day series, was obviously incapacitated when he came to play in the Ashes, and a cortisone-loaded Flintoff was only declared fit a few days before the first ever Test match at the redeveloped Sophia Gardens stadium in Cardiff. The first Test between England and Australia in Wales? Gazongas! A bit like staging India versus Pakistan in Bhutan. But this ECB, who tried to justify it all by reminding everyone that they were called the England and *Wales* Cricket Board, knew no bounds when it came to maximizing revenue. They positively salivated over the £3m the Welsh Council guaranteed for the game, and to hell with the worthy campaigns Durham and Old Trafford had come up with. History, tradition and honest endeavour were, to them, totally irrelevant. Cash was King.

Welsh Rarebit

The build-up to the series was very different from the previous one in 2005. There had been no Twenty20 aperitifs or one-day internationals to whet the appetite and provide a guide to the two teams who were rebuilding and therefore of an unknown quantity. Predictions, therefore, varied wildly. Some believed Australia's rejuvenation had begun in South Africa, where they won a three-Test series to cling on to their spot as number one Test nation. A couple of new stars had emerged, notably the young blade Phillip Hughes, who treated Test cricket almost like a Twenty20 match, standing outside leg stump and carving anything within reach through the offside. Middlesex received a lot of stick for 'familiarizing him with English conditions' by hiring him for the first few weeks of the county season.

Others sensed England were experiencing a renaissance under Strauss – they had just defeated the West Indies at home in Test and one-day series – and felt they had the better bowling attack. Australia's spin reserves were clearly exhausted. The man picked to inherit Shane Warne's mantle was off-spinner Nathan Hauritz, who looked about twelve and had never even taken a five-wicket haul in first-class cricket. As a result there were calls to leave all the pitches as bare as Matt Prior's head.

In an attempt to avoid the hype and bond the team, the England squad travelled to the First World War battlefields of Ypres, in Belgium, the weekend before the series. Though regarded as copying the Australians' visits to Gallipoli, it was a good idea and some were clearly moved by the experience. It was humbling to visit the gravestone of 'Charlie' Blythe, the wonderful Kent and England left-arm spinner, killed in action in 1917. The main story to emerge from the trip, however, was that Flintoff, on his return from injury, had missed the team bus to the Menin Gate. At least he was discovered fast asleep in his room and not adrift on the Yperlee river in a paddleless canoe.

The outrage about the first Ashes Test being staged in Cardiff grew as the game approached. The ground was described as like a provincial rugby stadium in New Zealand, and Shane Warne himself described the decision as 'disgraceful'. He was in England at the time, playing a farewell match at Lord's for his Rajasthan Royals – inaugural winners of the IPL – against Middlesex. Remarkably the ground was full – 75 per cent of the crowd were Asian – confirming that the IPL's aims of achieving a global following are not totally far-fetched.

Actually, when it came to it, the Welsh put on a rather good show. The welcome was immensely warm, with 'G'Dai from Wales' signs everywhere, smiling faces and general bonhomie. The soprano Katherine Jenkins sang the Welsh national anthem and 'Jerusalem' rang round the ground as the England batsmen made their way to the middle. It has become very much England's theme tune.

Despite fears the pitch might not last, it was easy-paced and true. This didn't prevent England getting in an early bit of bother, but they didn't freeze with the bat as they had in the first Ashes Test four years earlier and were bailed out by Pietersen and Collingwood. An eventual first innings total of 435 seemed respectable. The only snag was that Australia, led by the redoubtable Ricky Ponting, replied with 674-6. England were given an object lesson in preserving your wicket, something the Aussies have been doing for decades. Australian batsmen invariably have to be winched from the pitch.

Their get-in-stay-in mentality stems from Australian club cricket – two-day affairs played over two Saturdays. One team bats one Saturday, the other the next weekend. You'd better make your innings count, because you might not get another bat for three weeks. Longevity at the crease is actually practised from a young age. Under-15 teams play two- and three-day matches, and the former Australian batsman Dean Jones recalls making a triple century as a fourteen-year-old. Fitness also plays a part. The outdoor life and the sport-for-all culture makes Australians generally hardier and able to maintain their energy levels for longer. It's probably also why they hold the record for in-flight beer consumption (fifty-three tinnies allegedly downed by David Boon on a flight to England in the 1980s).

The Australians had four sessions to bowl England out and go one up. Rain came to England's rescue on the fourth evening but not before they had declined to 17–2. With cloudless skies on the fifth day, the tourists smelt victory, especially when a confused-looking Pietersen left a straight one. England lunched nervously at 70–5. Collingwood remained defiant and, with first a watchful Flintoff and then Stuart Broad, nursed England to tea, 7 down. That still gave Australia 38 overs to get the last 3 wickets. Victory seemed a foregone conclusion.

With the ravenous monster of Twenty20 gobbling up interest in the longer game, the final session was a wonderful advertisement for Test cricket. England's lower order refused to come quietly, urged on by a rapt crowd, and Ponting was obliged to turn to part-time spinners to try and winkle them out. Graeme Swann finally succumbed at 5.30, giving the Australians over an hour to get the last two wickets. Collingwood denied them until at last, after nearly six hours of resistance, he was caught in the gully. He hung his head in despair. There were 11 overs left to get the last wicket, and at that point he must have thought, like everyone else, that all his endeavours would come to naught.

James Anderson, Monty Panesar and, it must be added, Ricky Ponting had other ideas. Anderson and Panesar, benefiting from the 'buddy' system decreeing that each England tailender would have a senior batsman as personal tutor, defended stubbornly. The pitch was helpfully benign. There were eight overs to go, then seven, then six. England did the usual thing in such situations and sent on the physio as a subtle delaying tactic. He just happened to be Australian and rather large. 'What are you doing out here, you fat cunt?' said Ponting gesticulating for him to get off. Ponting helped England's cause by bowling the occasional off spin of Marcus North in the critical final overs. Panesar was resolute, to increasing roars from the crowd. A couple of thick edges for four by Anderson gave England a crucial lead, eroding two overs from the final countdown because Australia would have to bat again. When Anderson negotiated Hauritz's 37th over, England, who had been completely outplayed for three days, had clung on. The first Test was drawn. To most in the ground it felt like a victory.

England, remembering the unbridled joy of the Australians when they had got out of jail at Old Trafford four years earlier, kept their celebrations muted. Relief was etched on Andrew Strauss's face. It had been an extraordinary escape, compelling to watch for Test match aficionados and virgins alike. It had had everything from desperate drama to absurd comedy, with the sight of Panesar, whose inept batting often induced people to call him Monty Python, surviving 35 deliveries. His name was regaled on a train all the way to Salisbury, according to one woman who, having witnessed the kind of gripping day-long struggle to a tense stalemate that Twenty20 could never deliver, had become an immediate convert to Test cricket. Well, until the mindless chanting continued past Warminster anyway.

And now, after each side had knocked pieces out of each other for five days, the battle moved straight on to Lord's. Five Tests in seven weeks. This was going to be the survival of the fittest.

They're Coming Home . . .

Ponting sacrificed the moral high ground in the aftermath. He drew attention to England's apparent sharp tactics (i.e. time-wasting), while completely overlooking his own conduct, which involved questioning a number of umpiring decisions, a far greater sin than waving the 12th man on to use up a couple of minutes. All it did was emphasize that the Australians were bad losers. Which, if you think about it, they have always been, from Bodyline onwards. It was they who invented whingeing, not the English.

Ponting also argued that, despite being robbed of victory, his team had vital 'momentum' in the series.

Added to that, Lord's, venue for the second Test, was England's bogey ground when it came to the Ashes. They hadn't beaten Australia there for seventy-five years. This was all proved to be utter hogwash. Within two hours of the start of the Test, England were 126–0. Mitchell Johnson, the tourists' much heralded new left-arm spearhead, had a horror morning, some of his wayward deliveries hinting that he was suffering a mild case of the yips. Andrew Strauss, whose beatific smile belied an unyielding determination, capitalized to record a big century, his eighteenth in Tests, giving him the best ratio of Test hundreds to fifties (18 to 15) of anyone who has ever played for England.

Strauss's innings laid the foundation for another decent first-innings score aided by a surprisingly mute Australian outfit. It was rumoured that Cricket Australia had asked its players not to indulge in sledging during the Tests. It seemed an absurd piece of political correctness (an Australian bowler without a sledge is like an arrow without a tip) and, although the players themselves denied this, their silence was deafening. It was a far cry from the 2005 series, during which the perennially provocative Shane Warne actually subjected the England *fielders* to verbal abuse while *batting*. Trying to put him off his game as Warne attempted a daring victory charge with the Australian tail at Edgbaston, Strauss made a couple of pointed remarks from silly point. Warne glared at him from under his helmet. 'Don't waste your breath, mate,' he retorted, 'you're fucking shit!' The England fielders were so astonished they remained speechless for the rest of the game.

Warne was now safely detained in the commentary box and, without McGrath as well, Australia's outcricket lacked a tangible aura. England's batsmen progressed relatively unencumbered past 400, and this time the bowlers didn't let their initiative slip. The ball swung and seamed, and Australia capitulated to Anderson, Broad and Onions, the introduction of the latter a headline writer's dream. All the obvious ones – 'Australia Fried by Onions', 'England Know Their Onions', 'Routed by a String of Onions', 'Onions Pickles Aussies' – were wheeled out. The Australians fell 10 short of avoiding the follow-on but, as had become the vogue, Strauss didn't enforce it. Instead England batted again to set the tourists an improbable 522 to win.

Flintoff, who had announced before the match his impending retirement from Test cricket, responded superbly to being given the new ball – an oversight in Cardiff – and quickly dismissed both openers. But, as always, the Australians had to be prised from the crease fingernail by fingernail, and progressed, with some style, to 313-5 by the close, giving England supporters (and players) of a nervous disposition a restless night.

Leading the team talk before play on the fifth day, Flintoff pronounced confidently about England's prospects, and once play started he was as good as his word, making a ball bounce up the famous slope to have the obdurate Brad Haddin caught at slip. He proceeded to deliver a spell of intense and sustained menace the like of which had rarely been seen at Lord's. For at least eight of his ten overs, his speed never dipped below 90mph, and he sent down at least a dozen deliveries nearing 93mph.

The pace was not the half of it, though. It was his control that was truly remarkable. There was nothing wide to either right- or left-hander, and only when he was trying for the toe-crushing yorker to the tail was there a ball down the leg side. Every delivery seemed laser-guided to its target, honing in on either off stump or the batsman's oesophagus. When a player of such nimble feet and quick reflexes as the Australian Michael Clarke is whacked on the helmet taking evasive action, you can deduce that the bowling is a bit serious. Some balls, leaping from the surface and soaring past the batsman's groping blade, made people flinch in the commentary box. This was on a manicured pitch with not a hint of unreliability or uneven bounce.

In spite of his gammy knee, Flintoff was in what sportsmen like to call the 'zone'. There was no let-up. The body was capable of unleashing a 50lb boulder; the arm, bolt upright and maximizing his height; the head, perfectly balanced and hell-bent on vaporizing an Australian batsman. It was an exploitation of the famous Lord's slope – some balls nipping down it, others holding their line but still demanding a shot – that has never been surpassed.

With the eye of a sniper, a Trojan's strength and the spirit of a warhorse, Flintoff that day was an irresistible force. The Australians fell like ninepins and he had his first five-wicket haul in Tests since 2005 (and only his third overall). He sank to his knees in gratitude when he took his fifth, as if thanking Lord's for its parting gift. He was now one of only eight cricketers to grace both batting (for Test hundreds) and bowling (for five-wicket hauls) honours boards at the ground. It was a glorious moment: it ended seventy-five years of hurt, and it put England 1–0 up in the series. The Ashes were England's to lose.

. . . Oh No They're Not

There was a ten-day gap before the Edgbaston Test. Despite the series being shown exclusively on satellite TV, the country was briefly gripped by Ashes fever, and there were daily bulletins on Flintoff's knee and Pietersen's Achilles and the Australians' state of mind. In the end Pietersen, who had been limping badly at Lord's, was sent off for an operation and ruled out of the rest of the series. Flintoff was declared fit, though he barely looked it.

The weather was as appalling as Edgbaston's drainage in the days leading up to the Test, and the start of play was delayed until 5pm on the first day despite glorious sunshine from lunchtime onwards. Cricket in England is still a prisoner to its fickle climate. You'd have thought by now someone would have invented an inflatable tarpaulin that covers the entire ground, allowing preparation to carry on underneath, and allow play to start immediately the rain has stopped. But no, we continue to stand by, mesmerized, watching it pour down, cursing the weathermen and saying, 'Ooo, isn't it a rubbish summer!' and then take an age to mop it up with giant sponges.

When play began, it was England's turn to sacrifice their moral advantage with some tense, loose bowling. They regained their composure within two balls of the second day beginning as Onions sent back the makeshift opener Shane Watson and Mike Hussey in successive deliveries on a lifeless pitch of compacted mud. With a positive approach, England took a lead of 114, Flintoff contributing a swashbuckling 75 on the ground where the boundaries just weren't big enough. But his bowling appeared spent, and neither he nor anyone else was able to intervene as Australia's nuggety middle order batted out for a draw.

So to Headingley, scene of so many famous Ashes incidents, for the fourth Test. Its reputation for unpredictable events was sustained even before the match began. England had decided to omit Flintoff the day before and he had departed in high dudgeon. England's spirits were already deflated by the time an alert went off in their hotel at 4.30am. At first the dazed players thought it was a terrorist attack and cowered in their rooms. Then when they realized it was a fire alarm they filed obediently into the street, spending half an hour there before going back to bed.

Twenty years before, this would have been an intriguing scenario revealing who was bedding which hospitality girl, with the added excitement of encountering the odd player just arriving back after a night out. But in the Noughties, it merely disrupted the team from its carefully crafted pre-match plans, in which eight hours' uninterrupted sleep after a day of carbo-loading, an ice bath and a power-point presentation on the

Australian batting would have been a key ingredient.

When England arrived at the ground the situation got worse. Indulging in their usual pre-match kickabout – an extraordinarily inappropriate activity: you don't see international rugby players tossing a cricket ball about before a match, or golfers playing tennis – caused Matt Prior to suffer a back spasm. His participation was suddenly in doubt, which meant a desperate search for a replacement wicketkeeper (evoking a bizarre occasion at Lord's in 1986 when, as a result of an injury to England's keeper, Bruce French, three men deputized, first Bill Athey, then the retired Bob Taylor, who had to be summoned from a hospitality box, and finally Bobby Parks).

Prior eventually played but the kerfuffle caused the toss to be delayed, and although Strauss won it, he had less than ten minutes to get himself mentally prepared. With all this fuss and a rejigged batting order, his mind was obviously scrambled; he played a sleep-deprived shot to the first ball of the match and should have been given out lbw, and was caught at slip driving loosely soon afterwards. By the time he had recovered his composure, England were 63–5 and soon after lunch a woeful 102 all out.

Trying too hard to strike back, England's bowling was, if anything, worse. Anderson's first two balls were slapped to the boundary, and the recalled Harmison's incessant habit of testing out the middle of the pitch had Geoff Boycott issuing his usual Headingley lament that you 'moost pitch eet oop!' Australia had almost doubled England's score by the end of the first day, and piled on the agony on the second to take a humiliating 343-run lead. Crucially, England missed the atmospheric lift Flintoff provided with the ball, both on the field and in the crowd.

Mitchell Johnson rediscovered his mojo to reduce England to 82–5 by stumps as England headed for one of their worst ever Ashes defeats. Some frisky hitting by Broad and Swann at least prolonged the match into the third afternoon and gave England's second innings score a modicum of respectability. But it couldn't camouflage the extraordinarily one-sided nature of the match or the fact that the Australians' performance curve was ascending while England's was plummeting. At the critical moment England's players had been found wanting and the series was now 1–1. The series was like a pantomime, with England after Lord's saying, 'We're going to reclaim the Ashes!' and Australia, at Headingley, retorting, 'Oh no you're not!' The tourists needed just a draw at the Oval to keep the urn.

The Final Act

Strauss's response to the Leeds debacle owed something to that quintessential English comedy series *Dad's Army*. 'Don't panic!' he repeated, though not quite in Corporal Jones's hysterical tone. The English media did anyway. After England's abject batting display, there were calls for the entire middle order of Bopara, Bell and Collingwood to be jettisoned, an SOS to the retired Marcus Trescothick to be issued and a clamour for the

Surrey run machine Mark Ramprakash, who had just recorded his 108th first-class century, to be recalled. Ramprakash admitted he was willing to help but he nursed a Test average of 27 (though admittedly it was 42 against Australia) and a reputation for mental fragility at Test level, where he had not appeared for seven years. The absurdity of the idea was emphasized when most of the pictures accompanying his claims were of him in a sequin top performing a Latin sequence on *Strictly Come Dancing*. England needed runs not rumbas.

The selectors saw sense. They realized they had to do something, dropped the obviously transfixed Ravi Bopara, and replaced him with the untried but recently prolific Warwickshire batsman Jonathan Trott. They also declared Flintoff fit for his Test swansong. But they wisely resisted the temptation to change anything else. Given that 1953 was the last time the Ashes were all square going to the final Test at the Oval, the hype was huge. A sense of stability was vital.

Much attention focused on the Oval pitch, which for most of the summer had resembled rolled Mogadon, leading to a series of bore-draws. England needed a result surface so it was left drier than usual. The England players, who had had a clear-the-air post-mortem straight after the Headingley Test, seemed relaxed in the build-up. Michael Vaughan had told Strauss the day before the game that he would see signs of the team's impending fate as the start of play approached. The first of these would be at 10.30am when the coin went up.

It fell in England's favour and Strauss had to contain his relief as England went in first and rattled up 108–1 in the morning session. Australia betrayed the paucity of their spin reserves and omitted their only specialist tweaker, Hauritz. It was a fatal oversight. The ball was breaking through the dusty surface from the first hour and the pitch was clearly going to spin. The sight of Warne turning the ball miles in a spin masterclass during one lunch interval underlined their folly.

Strauss fell after lunch, exposing England's soft underbelly. But Trott made a purposeful debut and Broad helped the score past 300. Still, the total of 332 seemed a little light, especially when the Australian openers replied strongly. That is until Broad was introduced into the attack after a rain break. He might have looked like an outcast from a boy band and tended to spend the minutes before taking the field doing his hair, but he had a keen bowling brain. Hustling in from the Vauxhall End and finding a hint of swing from a full length, he turned 66–0 into 111–7.

It was an extraordinary turnaround from which the Australians never recovered. They conceded a lead of 172, which Strauss, and later Trott, studiously built on. Strauss's unflappability was immensely reassuring, allowing Trott, who had been marginalized by the compulsory (non-white) quota system in his native South Africa, to demonstrate a decisive method which had brought him a stack of runs for Warwickshire. A hundred on Test debut in a match of this magnitude was some achievement.

There was a brief cameo from Flintoff, ended, as often with Flintoff's innings, by a catch at long on. He departed for a breezy 22, to the disappointment of the capacity crowd. It had been a typical Flintoff frolic. Forthright, uncomplicated, occasionally fortuitous and ultimately short-lived. Most of his innings have promised more than they have actually delivered.

Flintoff's statistics – five Test match centuries and just three five-wicket hauls – have never really told the story of him as a Test match all-rounder. It is much more his imposing presence both in the dressing room, where just the sight of him with his pads on is invigorating, and charging in with the ball or standing with his bucket-like hands at second slip that have made him such an important figure. The crowd buy in to his vigorous intent and his impassioned demeanour.

The sheer intensity of his bowling wore batsmen down, mentally and physically. There was tangible relief when he was removed from the attack, a relief that could translate into wickets for other bowlers. Spectators, many of whom play village cricket, identified with his lumbering running style between the wickets, his smiling demeanour, his rustic thumps over the infield, doubtless his glorious – and often futile – attempts to clear the rope.

It was not to be a fairytale Flintoff ending with the bat. And, after England declared, setting Australia an academic 546 to win, it was clear from his game but ungainly hobble to the wicket that it was unlikely to be a fairytale ending with the ball. He was due to have another knee operation straight after the match. He ought to consider having his crutches sponsored.

But Flintoff's monolithic presence still had a decisive influence. When the indefatigable Ricky Ponting and

Michael Hussey had put together a third-wicket stand of 127 that infected England with mid-afternoon doubt, Flintoff pounced on Hussey's quick single to mid-on and, with a powerful side-arm flick, flung down the stumps with Ponting a foot short. As the fateful third umpire's verdict was relayed to the ground, it must have dawned on the aghast Ponting that he was about to become the first Australian captain since the 1800s to twice lose the Ashes on English soil. Harmison and Swann administered the last rites. England won by 197 runs, took the series 2–1 and, amidst scenes of euphoria if not quite 2005 hysteria, recaptured the Ashes urn.

So, after being thrashed 5–0 in 2006–7, England, with a half-fit Flintoff and a half-available Pietersen, had won the Ashes back. How did they do that? Since Australia had eight individual centuries to England's two and the three leading wicket-takers in the series, it was a question that flummoxed many. In a fluctuating series between two moderate sides, Strauss's runs had been decisive and England's quintet of seamers had the greater penetration. The bowlers had contributed some tail-end capers too, beginning memorably and, as it turned out, critically with the heroic defiance of the last pair in Cardiff.

England had seized the key moments in the series, and in Strauss had a leader of calm assurance with the ability to absorb the heat from an awkward situation. He led unobtrusively but pragmatically and never looked flustered. He was very planned and deliberate in what he did, recommending patience, resourcefulness, opportunism. He created a structure in which everyone understood their collective responsibility. That was a major advance on the previous winter, when the England team resembled eleven individual PLCs. It helps to be a lucky captain, and Strauss won four out of five tosses.

The Ashes are as much about patriotism and national self-esteem as about sport, and therefore pose unique problems for a captain – handling all the external issues like public expectation and national fervour as well as managing the players. Strauss thrived on such demands. In fact his overriding dilemma was trophy etiquette: when you've finally overcome Australia do you, he wondered, parade the world's smallest sporting prize to the masses in one hand or two? Strauss, a diplomat at heart, went with a one-handed wave of the urn to start with, and then, after giving it a brief peck on the cheek, brandished it aloft in two. No one could complain.

And yet England winning the 2009 Ashes just papered over the widening cracks in the English game. It was still ravaged with an antiquated county structure and blatant self-interest. The national side, with double the number of professionals of any other country, were now languishing in fifth place in the ICC League of Test Nations, with Australia one place above having slipped to fourth. The leading team was now South Africa, with the Sri Lankans and Indians close behind. The world's leading Test runmaker (Tendulkar), the top-ranked batsman (Sangakkara) and the man with the most Test wickets (Muralitharan) all came from the Asian subcontinent. Indian cricket was generating the most revenue. The only thing England could boast was most support staff (thirteen). If you wanted to get on an England tour, become a masseur.

They say you analyse the past to predict the future. So, have the last 300 pages given you any clue as to what might happen next? No, me neither. The overriding conclusion is that cricket is a remarkably resilient game. In the last 400 years it has been championed and ridiculed and used and abused and battered and bruised and stretched and squashed and even shot at in the streets of Lahore. Still it thrives, alternately captivating and infuriating almost two billion people.

The parameters of cricket may have changed a thousand times, but the essentials – the bat, the ball, the stumps and the pitch – have remained basically the same throughout. Batsmen constantly find new ways to make runs, and bowlers constantly invent new deliveries to take wickets – the latest the 'Carom' ball, squeezed out between thumb and forefinger by Sri Lanka's new discovery, Ajantha Mendis. The beauty of the game, as the American philanthropist and cricket nut John Paul Getty once said, is 'its 360-degree possibility'.

It is still a game where there is decency and respect for your opponent and a general camaraderie that no other sport can match. It is fascinating and bewildering and fast and slow and regular and unpredictable and apparently static but always evolving. And, in the end, cricket is the prime subscriber to the most famous sporting line ever written:

'It's not who won or lost that matters, but how you placed the blame.'

ACKNOWLEDGEMENTS

Most books like this have a bibliography, but you're not interested in a boring list of references, are you? Instead I'd like to make special mention of a number of particularly helpful books:

A Social History of English Cricket by Derek Birley
Beyond a Boundary by C.L.R. James
A Corner of a Foreign Field by Ramachandra Guha
Anyone But England by Mike Marqusee
World Cricketers by Christopher Martin-Jenkins
Stiff Upper Lips and Baggy Green Caps by Simon Briggs
Cricket's Greatest Characters by Geoff Tibballs
Pommies by William Buckland
Sport by Tim Harris

Many thanks also to the eternally helpful librarians at the MCC, Ken Daldry and Neil Robinson, and to my trusty editors Giles Elliott and Fiona Adams. Thanks, most importantly, to my ever-tolerant wife, Tanya, for putting up with constant badgering and late nights. And finally to you for bothering to read this far . . .

ACKNOWLEDGEMENTS

INDEX

Miller, Keith 161, 207, 222
Mobbs, Edgar 162
Modi, Lalit 411
Mohammad, Hanif 169, 229, 230–1, 244
Mohammad, Mushtaq 244
Moores, Peter 384, 429
Muralitharan, Muttiah (Murali) 357–8, 387–8, 423–4
Murphy, Florence 96–7
Mushtaq, Saqlain 376
Mynn, Alfred 56, 61–3

Napoleonic wars 51
National League 243–4
'Nelson' 51–2
Nelson, Admiral Lord 51
New York 53
New Zealand 190, 210, 314, 334, 379–80
Newbolt, Sir Henry: 'Vitaï Lampada' 100–1
Newland, Richard 15, 22
Newman, Jack 190
Newton, Sir Isaac 21
Non-Smokers v Smokers (1887) 109
Normans 11
North v South game 64, 65, 67
Northamptonshire 142
'notched up' phrase 14
Nottingham Club 67
Nottinghamshire 142
Nyren, John 28, 49, 58; *Young Cricketer's Tutor* 58–9
Nyren, Richard 22, 58

Oborne, Peter 253
Old, Chris 301
Oldfield, Bert 181
Olonga, Henry 379
Olympic Games (Paris, 1900) 114
one-day cricket 201, 216, 238–9, 316, 353, 364
one-day international cricket 243, 257, 364, 368–70, 378
O'Reilly, Bill 355

Ormond, Jimmy 375
Orwell, George 200
Oval, The 75, 93, 107, 155, 193, 194
overs: extension to six balls 141, 146
overseas players: recruiting of by counties 224–5, 385–6

Packer, Sir Frank 274
Packer, Kerry 274–5, 276–7, 284
Packer's World Series Cricket 275, 276–7, 284
pads/padding 56
Pakistan 227–9, 321–2, 332, 333; and ball tampering allegations 333–4, 399–401; Gatting incident (1987) 321–3; hostilities with India 244; wins World Cup (1991) 335
Panesar, Monty 403
Papua New Guinea 196
Parkinson, Michael 104
Parr, George 74, 76
Parsi community 55
Paynter, Eddie 183
Peach, Alan 205
Peebles, Ian 216
Peel, Bobby 134
Pietersen, Kevin 270, 392–3, 393, 395, 403, 419–20, 421, 429–30
Pilch, Fuller 63, 68
Pinter, Harold 429
pitches 16, 326; better preparation of 109; nineteenth century 60–1
Pocock, Alfred 77
Pollock, Graeme 245
Ponsford, Bill 169
Ponsonby-Fane, Sir Spencer 60–1
Ponting, Ricky 392, 393
Pooley, Ted 92
press: cricket and early 66
Prideaux, Roger 252
Prior, Matt 59
Procter, Mike 121
professionals 225; and benefit